MGA ROADSTERS 1955-1962

Compiled by
R.M. Clarke

ISBN 1 870642 465

Distributed by
Brooklands Book Distribution Ltd.
'Holmerise', Seven Hills Road,
Cobham, Surrey, England
Printed in Hong Kong

BROOKLANDS BOOKS

BROOKLANDS BOOKS SERIES
AC Ace & Aceca 1953-1983
AC Cobra 1962-1969
Alfa Romeo Alfasud 1972-1984
Alfa Romeo Alfetta Coupes GT.GTV.GTV6 1974-1987
Alfa Romeo Guilias Berlinettas
Alfa Romeo Giulia Berlinas 1962-1976
Alfa Romeo Giulia Coupés 1963-1976
Alfa Romeo Spider 1966-1987
Aston Martin Gold Portfolio 1972-1985
Austin Seven 1922-1982
Austin A30 & A35 1951-1962
Austin Healey 100 1952-1959
Austin Healey 3000 1959-1967
Austin Healey 100 & 3000 Collection No. 1
Austin Healey 'Frogeye' Sprite Collection No. 1
Austin Healey Sprite 1958-1971
Avanti 1962-1983
BMW Six Cylinder Coupés 1969-1975
BMW 1600 Collection No. 1
BMW 2002 1968-1976
Bristol Cars Gold Portfolio 1946-1985
Buick Automobiles 1947-1960
Buick Riviera 1963-1978
Cadillac Automobiles 1949-1959
Cadillac Automobiles 1960-1969
Cadillac Eldorado 1967-1978
Cadillac in the Sixties No. 1
Camaro 1966-1970
Chevrolet Camaro & Z-28 1973-1981
High Performance Camaros 1982-1988
Chevrolet Camaro Collection No. 1
Chevrolet 1955-1957
Chevrolet Impala & SS 1958-1971
Chevrolet & SS 1964-1972
Chevy II Nova & SS 1962-1973
Chrysler 300 1955-1970
Citroen Traction Avant 1934-1957
Citroen DS & ID 1955-1875
Citroen 2CV 1949-1982
Cobras & Replicas 1962-1983
Cortina 1600E & GT 1967-1970
Corvair 1959-1968
Daimler Dart & V-8 250 1959-1969
Datsun 240z 1970-1973
Datsun 280Z & ZX 1975-1983
De Tomaso Collection No. 1
Dodge Charger 1966-1974
Excalibur Collection No. 1
Ferrari Cars 1946-1956
Ferrari Cars 1962-1966
Ferrari Cars 1969-1973
Ferrari Dino 1965-1974
Ferrari Dino 308 1974-1979
Ferrari 308 & Mondial 1980-1984
Ferrari Collection No. 1
Fiat-Bertone X1/9 1973-1988
Fiat Pininfarina 124+2000 Spider 1968-1985
Ford Falcon 1960-1970
Ford Mustang 1964-1967
Ford Mustang 1967-1973
High Performance Mustangs 1982-1988
Ford RS Escort 1968-1980
Honda CRX 1983-1987
High Performance Escorts MkI 1968-1974
High Performance Escorts MkII 1975-1980
Hudson & Railton Cars 1936-1940
Jaguar Cars 1957-1961
Jaguar Cars 1961-1964
Jaguar Cars 1964-1968
Jaguar MK2 1959-1969
Jaguar E-Type 1961-1966
Jaguar E-Type 1966-1971
Jaguar E-Type V12 1971-1975
Jaguar XKE Collection No. 1
Jaguar XJ6 1968-1972
Jaguar XJ6 Series II 1973-1979
Jaguar XJ6 & XJ12 Series III 1979-1985
Jaguar XJ12 1972-1980
Jaguar XJS 1975-1980
Jensen Cars 1946-1967
Jensen Cars 1967-1979
Jensen Interceptor Gold Portfolio 1966-1986
Lamborghini Cars 1964-1970
Lamborghini Cars 1970-1975
Lamborghini Countach Collection No. 1
Lamborghini Countach & Urraco 1974-1980
Lamborghini Countach & Jalpa 1980-1985
Lancia Stratos 1972-1985
Land Rover 1948-1973
Land Rover Series II & IIa 1958-1971
Land Rover Series III 1971-1985
Lotus Cortina 1963-1970
Lotus Elan 1962-1973
Lotus Elan Collection No. 1
Lotus Elan Collection No. 2
Lotus Elite 1957-1964
Lotus Elite & Eclat 1974-1981
Lotus Turbo Esprit 1980-1986
Lotus Europa 1966-1975
Lotus Europa Collection No. 1
Lotus Seven 1957-1980
Lotus Seven Collection No. 1
Maserati 1965-1970
Maserati 1970-1975
Mazda RX-7 Collection No. 1
Mercedes 190 & 300SL 1954-1963
Mercedes 230/250/280SL 1963-1971
Mercedes 350/450SL & SLC 1971-1980
Mercedes Benz Cars 1949-1954
Mercedes Benz Cars 1954-1957
Mercedes Benz Cars 1957-1961
Mercedes Benz Competition Cars 1950-1957

Metropolitan 1954-1962
MG Cars 1929-1934
MG TC 1945-1949
MG TD 1949-1953
MG TF 1953-1955
MG Cars 1957-1959
MG Cars 1959-1962
MG Midget 1961-1980
MGA Collection No. 1
MGA Roadsters 1955-1962
MGB Roadsters 1962-1980
MGB GT 1965-1980
Mini Cooper 1961-1971
Morgan Cars 1960-1970
Morgan Cars 1969-1979
Morris Minor Collection No. 1
Old's Cutlass & 4-4-2 1964-1972
Oldsmobile Toronado 1966-1978
Opel GT 1968-1973
Packard Gold Portfolio 1946-1958
Pantera 1969-1973
Pantera & Mangusta 1969-1974
Plymouth Barracuda 1964-1974
Pontiac Fiero 1984-1988
Pontiac GTO 1964-1970
Pontiac Firebird 1967-1973
Pontiac Firebird and Trans-Am 1973-1981
High Performance Firebirds 1982-1988
Pontiac Tempest & GTO 1961-1965
Porsche Cars 1960-1964
Porsche Cars 1964-1968
Porsche Cars 1968-1972
Porsche Cars in the Sixties
Porsche Cars 1972-1975
Porsche 356 1952-1965
Porsche 911 Collection No. 1
Porsche 911 Collection No. 2
Porsche 911 1965-1969
Porsche 911 1970-1972
Porsche 911 1973-1977
Porsche 911 Carrera 1973-1977
Porsche 911 SC 1978-1983
Porsche 911 Turbo 1975-1984
Porsche 914 1969-1975
Porsche 914 Collection No. 1
Porsche 924 1975-1981
Porsche 928 Collection No. 1
Porsche 944 1981-1985
Porsche Turbo Collection No. 1
Reliant Scimitar 1964-1986
Rolls Royce Silver Cloud 1955-1965
Rolls Royce Silver Shadow 1965-1980
Range Rover 1970-1981
Rover 3 & 3.5 Litre 1958-1973
Rover P4 1949-1959
Rover P4 1955-1964
Rover 2000 + 2200 1963-1977
Rover 3500 1968-1977
Rover 3500 & Vitesse 1976-1986
Saab Sonett Collection No. 1
Saab Turbo 1976-1983
Singer Sports Cars 1933-1934
Studebaker Hawks & Larks 1956-1963
Sunbeam Alpine & Tiger 1959-1967
Thunderbird 1955-1957
Thunderbird 1958-1963
Thunderbird 1964-1976
Toyota MR2 1984-1988
Triumph 2000-2.5-2500 1963-1977
Triumph Spitfire 1962-1980
Triumph Spitfire Collection No. 1
Triumph Stag 1970-1980
Triumph Stag Collection No. 1
Triumph TR2 & TR3 1952-1960
Triumph TR4.TR5.TR250 1961-1968
Triumph TR6 1969-1976
Triumph TR6 Collection No. 1
Triumph TR7 & TR8 1975-1982
Triumph GT6 1966-1974
Triumph Vitesse & Herald 1959-1971
TVR Gold Portfolio 1959-1988
Volkswagen Cars 1936-1956
VW Beetle 1956-1977
VW Beetle Collection No. 1
VW Golf GTi 1976-1986
VW Karmann Ghia 1955-1982
VW Scirocco 1974-1981
VW Bus-Camper-Van 1954-1967
VW Bus-Camper-Van 1968-1979
Volvo 1800 1960-1973
Volvo 120 Series 1956-1970

BROOKLANDS MUSCLE CARS SERIES
American Motors Muscle Cars 1966-1970
Buick Muscle Cars 1965-1970
Camaro Muscle Cars 1966-1972
Capri Muscle Cars 1969-1983
Chevrolet Muscle Cars 1966-1972
Dodge Muscle Cars 1967-1970
Mercury Muscle Cars 1966-1971
Mini Muscle Cars 1961-1979
Mopar Muscle Cars 1964-1967
Mopar Muscle Cars 1968-1971
Mustang Muscle Cars 1967-1971
Shelby Mustang Muscle Cars 1965-1970
Oldsmobile Muscle Cars 1964-1970
Plymouth Muscle Cars 1966-1971
Pontiac Muscle Cars 1966-1972
Muscle Cars Compared 1966-1971
Muscle Cars Compared Book 2 1965-1971

BROOKLANDS ROAD & TRACK SERIES
Road & Track on Alfa Romeo 1949-1963

Road & Track on Alfa Romeo 1964-1970
Road & Track on Alfa Romeo 1971-1976
Road & Track on Alfa Romeo 1977-1984
Road & Track on Aston Martin 1962-1984
Road & Track on Auburn Cord & Duesenberg 1952-1984
Road & Track on Audi 1952-1980
Road & Track on Audi 1980-1986
Road & Track on Austin Healey 1953-1970
Road & Track on BMW Cars 1966-1974
Road & Track on BMW Cars 1975-1978
Road & Track on BMW Cars 1979-1983
Road & Track on Cobra, Shelby & Ford GT40 1962-1983
Road & Track on Corvette 1953-1967
Road & Track on Corvette 1968-1982
Road & Track on Corvette 1982-1986
Road & Track on Datsun Z 1970-1983
Road & Track on Ferrari 1950-1968
Road & Track on Ferrari 1968-1974
Road & Track on Ferrari 1975-1981
Road & Track on Ferrari 1981-1984
Road & Track on Fiat Sports Cars 1968-1987
Road & Track on Jaguar 1950-1960
Road & Track on Jaguar 1961-1968
Road & Track on Jaguar 1968-1974
Road & Track on Jaguar 1974-1982
Road & Track on Lamborghini 1964-1985
Road & Track on Lotus 1972-1981
Road & Track on Maserati 1952-1974
Road & Track on Maserati 1975-1983
Road & Track on Mazda RX7 1978-1986
Road & Track on Mercedes 1952-1962
Road & Track on Mercedes 1963-1970
Road & Track on Mercedes 1971-1979
Road & Track on Mercedes 1980-1987
Road & Track on MG Sports Cars 1949-1961
Road & Track on MG Sports Cars 1962-1980
Road & Track on Mustang 1964-1977
Road & Track on Peugeot 1955-1986
Road & Track on Pontiac 1960-1983
Road & Track on Porsche 1951-1967
Road & Track on Porsche 1968-1971
Road & Track on Porsche 1972-1975
Road & Track on Porsche 1975-1978
Road & Track on Porsche 1979-1982
Road & Track on Porsche 1982-1985
Road & Track on Rolls Royce & Bentley 1950-1965
Road & Track on Rolls Royce & Bentley 1966-1984
Road & Track on Saab 1955-1985
Road & Track on Toyota Sports & G T Cars 1966-1986
Road & Track on Triumph Sports Cars 1953-1967
Road & Track on Triumph Sports Cars 1967-1974
Road & Track on Triumph Sports Cars 1974-1982
Road & Track on Volkswagen 1951-1968
Road & Track on Volkswagen 1968-1978
Road & Track on Volkswagen 1978-1985
Road & Track on Volvo 1957-1974
Road & Track on Volvo 1975-1985

BROOKLANDS CAR AND DRIVER SERIES
Car and Driver on BMW 1955-1977
Car and Driver on BMW 1977-1985
Car and Driver on Cobra, Shelby & Ford GT40 1963-1984
Car and Driver on Datsun Z 1600 & 2000 1966-1984
Car and Driver on Corvette 1956-1967
Car and Driver on Corvette 1968-1977
Car and Driver on Corvette 1978-1982
Car and Driver on Ferrari 1955-1962
Car and Driver on Ferrari 1963-1975
Car and Driver on Ferrari 1976-1983
Car and Driver on Mopar 1956-1967
Car and Driver on Mopar 1968-1975
Car and Driver on Pontiac 1961-1975
Car and Driver on Porsche 1955-1962
Car and Driver on Porsche 1963-1970
Car and Driver on Porsche 1970-1976
Car and Driver on Porsche 1977-1981
Car and Driver on Porsche 1982-1986
Car and Driver on Saab 1956-1985
Car and Driver on Volvo 1955-1986

BROOKLANDS MOTOR & THOROUGHBRED & CLASSIC CAR SERIES
Motor & T & CC on Ferrari 1966-1976
Motor & T & CC on Ferrari 1976-1984
Motor & T & CC on Lotus 1979-1983
Motor & T & CC on Morris Minor 1948-1983

BROOKLANDS PRACTICAL CLASSICS SERIES
Practical Classics on Austin A 40 Restoration
Practical Classics on Henry Manney At Large & Abroad
Practical Classics on Land Rover Restoration
Practical Classics on Metalworking in Restoration
Practical Classics on Midget/Sprite Restoration
Practical Classics on Mini Cooper Restoration
Practical Classics on MGB Restoration
Practical Classics on Morris Minor Restoration
Practical Classics on Triumph Herald/Vitesse
Practical Classics on Triumph Spitfire Restoration
Practical Classics on VW Beetle Restoration
Practical Classics on 1930S Car Restoration

BROOKLANDS MILITARY VEHICLES SERIES
Allied Military Vehicles Collection No. 1
Allied Military Vehicles Collection No. 2
Dodge Military Vehicles Collection No. 1
Military Jeeps 1941-1945
Off Road Jeeps 1944-1971
V W Kubelwagen 1940-1975

CONTENTS

5	MG — The Breed Improved	*Autocar*	Sept. 23 1955
8	The New MGA. Road Test	*Autocar*	Sept. 23 1955
11	MGA	*Car Life*	Sept. 1956
12	MG Type Ex.182	*Motor*	June 1 1955
16	Driving The New MG	*Motor Life*	Dec. 1955
18	Technical Report On The New MG	*Motor Life*	Dec. 1955
22	Sleek Fast MGA. Road Test	*Wheels*	Aug. 1956
26	MG. Ex.179	*Sports Cars Illustrated*	Jan. 1957
33	Target: 4 Miles A Minute	*Motor*	April 24 1957
34	Ex.181 — The MG Record Car	*Autosport*	Aug. 30 1957
36	Ex.181	*Autocar*	Aug. 30 1957
40	MGA Coupé. Road Test	*Motor Trend*	Sept. 1957
42	Safety Faster	*Sports Cars Illustrated*	Mar. 1958
47	Safer, Faster	*Sports Car & Lotus Owner*	April 1958
48	MGA Road Test	*Sports Cars Illustrated*	June 1958
52	Exciting New MGA	*Motor Racing*	Aug. 1958
53	MGA Plus H.R.G.	*Motor*	Nov. 12 1958
54	Manageable MGA. Road Test	*Sports Car World*	June 1959
59	The MGA 1600	*Top Gear*	Aug. 1959
60	MGA Twin Cam	*Sports Car World*	Aug. 1959
62	Two Cams Turning. Road Test	*Modern Motor*	Aug. 1959
66	How Does The Twin Cam Exist At All?	*Sports Car World*	Sept. 1959
70	MGA Speed Test	*Road & Track*	Jan. 1960
72	TR or TC — Which Is For Me?	*Sports Car World*	Oct. 1959
76	MG Under Pressure	*Motor*	May 1959
77	The Twin-Cam MG	*Motor Sport*	June 1959
79	The MGA Mark II	*Worlds Fastest Sports Cars*	1961
82	MGA 1600 Mark II Road Test	*Motor Trend*	Oct. 1961
85	Driving The MGA Again	*Motor Sport*	Oct. 1960
86	MGA 1600 Mark II Road Test	*Sydney Herald*	1962
88	30,000 Miles With An MGA 1600 Mk. II	*Motor*	Jan. 1 1964
92	The MGA. Spotcheck	*Motor*	June 18 1966
94	MGA — Classic Choice	*Thoroughbred & Classic Cars*	Mar. 1976
97	Against All Odds — MGA Rebuild	*Practical Classics*	Oct. 1987
100	MGA 1955-1962 Used Car Classic	*Road & Track*	Jan. 1984

BROOKLANDS BOOKS

ACKNOWLEDGEMENTS

We were first encouraged to devote a book to the MGA by Alan Moss, the founder of Moss Motors, when we visited his MG spares mecca in Goleta CA. in early 1980. He gave us good advice on what to include and also produced a beautiful colour slide that we used on the original cover and have unashamedly used again on this one.

Such was the thirst for MGA information that in 1983 we were asked to collate a further set of different road tests and stories on the model and we published later that year — MGA Collection No. 1 — details of which can be found at the back of this book.

In November 1988 we had reason to call Adrian Wood of Moss Spares in the UK about locating original MG literature. He solved our problem and then courteously took us to task for allowing our main MGA title to go out of print. We assured him it was an oversight and hastily contacted our printers. We have made a few editorial changes the most important of which is to put in Peter Bohrs excellent Used Car Classic on the MGA from Road & Track. It can be found on Page 100 and we would suggest you treat it as an introduction both to the MGA and this book.

The Brooklands series are works of reference for enthusiasts. They endeavour to present an international picture of a model by collecting together road tests and other stories relating to a particular marque. We are fortunate that the management of the worlds leading motoring journals are sympathetic to our motives and generously allow us to include their copyright articles in our anthologies. We are indebted in this instance to the publishers of Autocar, Autosport, Car and Driver (previously Sports Cars Illustrated), Car Life, Modern Motor, Motor, Motor Life, Motor Racing, Motor Sport, Motor Trend, Practical Classics, Road & Track, Sports Car & Lotus Owner, Sports Car World, The Sydney Herald, Top Gear and Wheels for their ongoing support.

R.M. Clarke

Strong bumpers follow the contours of the new M.G.'s front and rear wings and radiator. The curved windscreen can be replaced by a shallow screen for competitions

M.G.—*The Breed Improved*

NEW MODEL A PROFITS BY RACING EXPERIENCE

WHEN the M.G. Car Company announced its participation in the Le Mans 24-hour race, after a lapse of 20 years, the three cars entered were acknowledged to be prototypes for a possible new production car. Two cars out of three finished (one crashed), and came 12th and 17th in the classification on distance covered; the totals during the 24 hours were 2,084 and 1,961 miles respectively. Nobody will deny that this performance of the model, after the company's long absence from racing, was impressive.

From these Le Mans cars, known as the type EX 182 (a full description of which was given in *The Autocar* of June 3), has been developed the production series M.G. A. It is apparent that the experiment of Le Mans was considered successful, as the car shows no basic changes from those cars which took part in the race, but detail modifications have been made for normal road use.

Equipped with the 4.3 to 1 axle ratio, the car is capable of nearly 100 m.p.h. in touring trim with hood and sidescreens erected. At the moderate price of £884 0s 10d, including purchase tax, it becomes a serious challenger in the 1½-litre sports car class. Its appearance, with its wind-cheating body, is a complete departure from the shape of previous models from the Abingdon factory.

The four-cylinder engine is basically the B.M.C. B-Series unit, as used in the Magnette saloon. It is equipped with two semi-downdraught 1½in S.U. carburettors and the compression ratio has been raised to 8.3 to 1, with a peak output of 68 b.h.p. at 5,500 r.p.m. Maximum torque is produced at 3,500 r.p.m., at which speed the b.m.e.p. is 128.8 lb per square inch.

Siamesed inlet ports are used and the short induction manifold for the two carburettors is bolted direct to the face where these merge into a common bore; a balance pipe connects these two short induction stubs. This is different from the Le Mans cars, wherein the induction ports were connected through to the opposite side of the head and an external balance pipe was used on the other side from the manifold. Presumably this extra complication did not give a worthwhile improvement in power output on the production version.

The overhead-valve engine, with a bore of 73.025 mm and stroke of 89 mm (1,489 c.c.), has a sturdy three-bearing crankshaft which runs in white metal thin wall bearings, this type also being used for the big-ends. A heart-shaped combustion chamber is used in conjunction with in-line vertical valves operated by rockers and push rods from the side-mounted camshaft. This is driven from the front end of the crankshaft by a duplex roller chain. Lubricant is supplied by an eccentric rotor pump driven by the camshaft and this feeds the oil through a full-flow filter to the main oil gallery, from which the drillings to the main bearings are taken.

Each carburettor is fitted with a wetted gauze-type circular air filter and cool air is ducted to these from a large-bore flexible pipe with its entry placed to the left-hand side of the front grille. A high-pressure S.U. electric fuel pump is mounted on a chassis cross-member behind the driving seat and draws fuel from the 10-gallon tank. The tank, which has an external filler, is placed below the floor of the luggage locker between the chassis frame members.

From the engine the drive is taken through an 8in Borg and Beck single dry plate clutch with six pressure springs and hydraulic withdrawal mechanism.

SPECIFICATION

Engine.—Capacity: 1,489 c.c. (90.88 cu in). Number of cylinders: 4. Bore and stroke: 73.025 × 89 mm (2.875 × 3.5in). Valve gear: overhead, push rods and rockers. Compression ratio: 8.3 to 1. B.H.P.: 68 at 5,500 r.p.m. Torque: 77.4 lb ft at 3,500 r.p.m. Max. b.m.e.p.: 128.8 lb per sq in at 3,500 r.p.m. Speed on top gear at 1,000 r.p.m. with 4.3 rear axle ratio, 17.0 m.p.h.

Clutch.—Borg and Beck, 8in single dry plate.

Transmission.—Overall ratios, top 4.3, third 5.908, second 9.520, first 15.652, reverse 20.468 to 1. Synchromesh on second, third and top.

Rear Axle.—Three-quarter floating with hypoid drive. Standard ratio 4.3 to 1 (4.55 to 1 ratio available if required).

Brakes.—Lockheed hydraulic. Front, two-leading shoe; rear, leading and trailing. Drum dimensions: F, 10in dia., 1¾in wide. R, 10in dia., 1¾in wide.

Tyre Size.—5.60-15in on disc wheels. Pressures, front, 17 lb per sq in; rear, 20 lb per sq in.

Steering Gear.—Cam Gears. Rack and pinion. Turning circle L and R, 28ft.

Electrical System.—12-volt by two 6-volt batteries. 51-ampère-hour capacity.

Tank Capacity.—10 Imperial gallons. Oil sump, 6½ pints. Cooling system, 10 pints.

Dimensions.—Wheelbase: 7ft 10in. Track: F, 3ft 11⅜in; R, 4ft 0⅜in. Length (overall): 13ft. Height: 4ft 2in with hood raised. Width: 4ft 10in. Ground clearance: 6in. Frontal area (hood raised): 13.77 sq ft (approx). Weight, depending upon extras fitted, 1,900 to 2,000 lb.

Price (Basic).—With two-seater body, £595. U.K. purchase tax: £249 0s 10d. Total price in U.K.: £844 0s 10d.

Optional Extras.—Provision has been made for fitting H.M.V. car radio. Wire wheels are available as an extra if specified with order. Other optional extras are heater, white wall tyres, 4.55 to 1 axle gears, twin horns, external luggage carrier, fog lamp, overall tonneau cover, radiator blind, chromium-plated wheel rim embellishers and telescopic steering column.

M.G.—The Breed Improved...

A standard B.M.C. B-type gear box and combined clutch housing is mounted on the cylinder block at the rear engine plate. It is a four-speed unit with synchromesh on second, third and top. The ratios are: top direct, third 1.373, second 2.21 and first 3.64 to 1. From the top of the gear box casing above the selector forks, a separate casting extends rearwards and contains the mechanism of the central remote control. A short vertical lever rises from this extension and is well placed in relation to the steering wheel. The travel of the change speed lever knob is short, a desirable feature for rapid changes. An oil filler cap, with dipstick, is placed on the left-hand side of the gear box casing and is reached through a hole in the tunnel which surrounds it.

The gear box casing is extended to reduce the length of the Hardy Spicer propeller-shaft which connects the drive to the three-quarter floating hypoid spiral bevel rear axle. The standard crown wheel and pinion give a ratio of 4.3 to 1, but an alternative ratio of 4.55 to 1 is offered. An orthodox bevel gear differential with two pinions is used.

The front suspension is identical with that of the previous TD and TF models, and was also used on the Le Mans cars. It is conventional in layout, using coil springs in conjunction with unequal length wishbones. No anti-roll bar has been found necessary, and this is undoubtedly because of the low centre of gravity of the car and its mean track of 4ft, which is wide for its size.

The top wishbone consists of two forgings attached at their inner ends to the cross-shaft of the Armstrong piston-type spring dampers and bolted at their outer ends to the king-pin post. The lower wishbone is a steel pressing consisting of two identical arms bridged by a centre section which forms the seat for the helical coil spring. The upper end of the coil spring fits into a housing formed by an extension of the main front cross-member, to which is also bolted the conical rubber bump stop.

In common with other M.G. models, rack and pinion steering gear is used, mounted ahead of the suspension unit and connected to the steering arms by a short track rod at each side. A single universal joint is incorporated in the shaft between the steering wheel and the rack and pinion. Like several cars nowadays, the M.G. has, strictly speaking, no steering column, the shaft rotating where a column remains stationary. It is customary to shroud the top end of such a shaft with an extension pressing from the facia.

Half-elliptic springs are used at the rear, mounted directly beneath the frame side members. They are shackled at their rear ends and controlled by vertical piston-type Armstrong dampers bolted to the inside of the frame members. Check straps control rebound and rubber bump stops are mounted on the underside of the frame where it sweeps up over the rear axle.

Disc wheels with ventilation holes and four-stud attachment are supplied as standard, but wire-spoked centre-lock wheels can be obtained as an optional extra. Dunlop 5.60—15in tyres fitted on 4.00—15in well-base rims are used with both types of wheel.

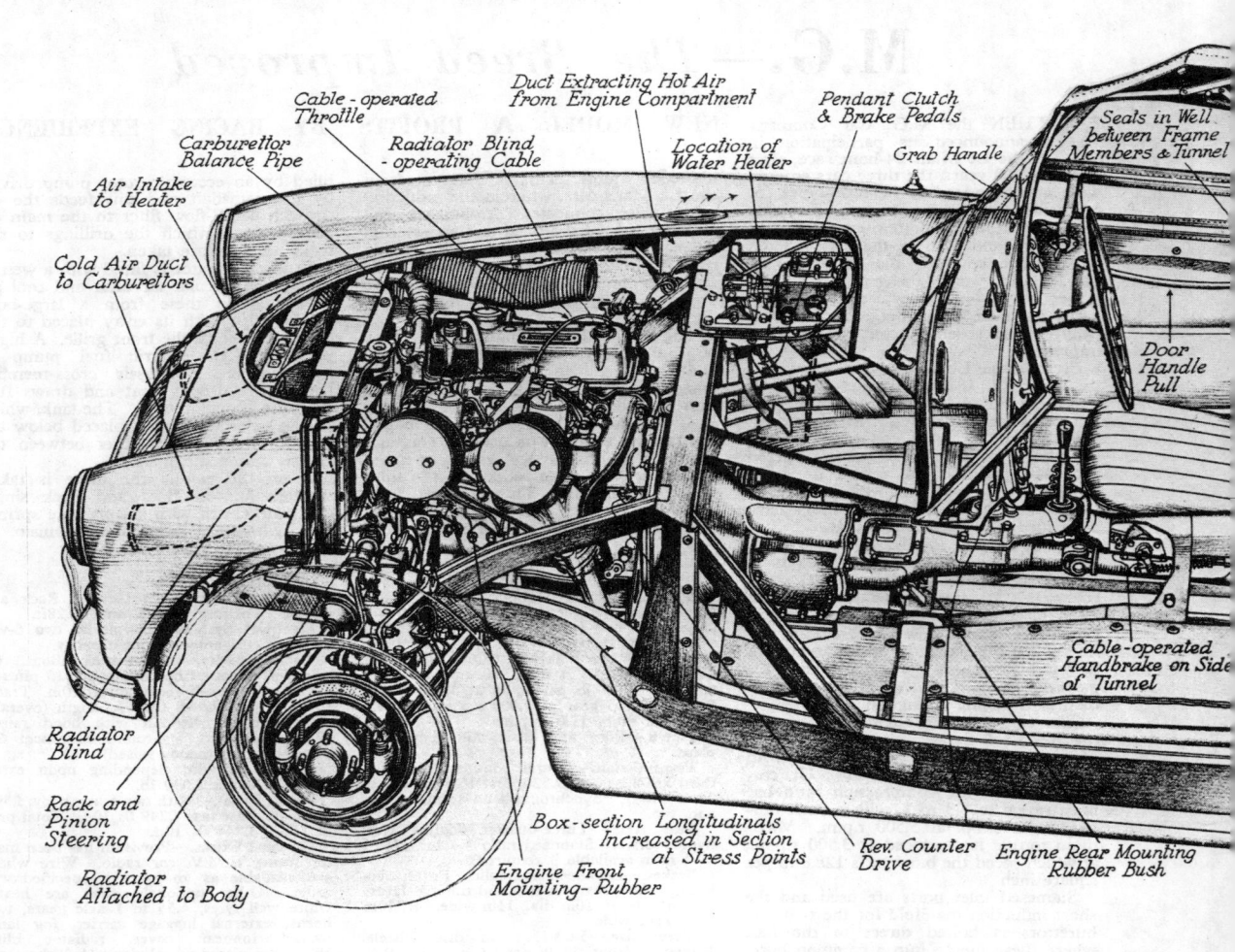

The balance pipe on the M.G. A is on the carburettor side of the head. On the Le Mans engine the ports went across the head to a balance pipe on the other side

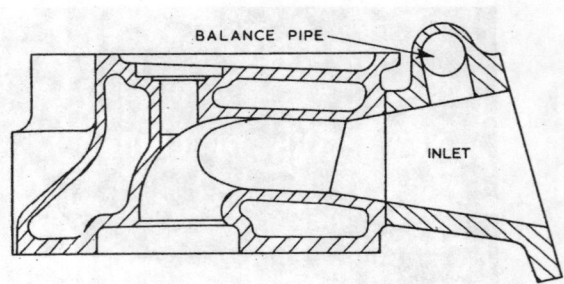

Lockheed hydraulic brakes with 10in-diameter drums and 1¾in-wide shoes are fitted. Two-leading shoe operation is used in the front drums and leading and trailing shoes at the rear. Actuation is by a pendant pedal mounted on the scuttle and connected to the master cylinder by a short operating rod. The master cylinder is a duplex unit with a similar pedal for clutch actuation. Mounted in this position, the two master cylinders are accessible for topping up with fluid. The fly-off type hand-brake lever is located between the seats close to the propeller-shaft tunnel and is connected to the rear brakes by cable.

The chassis frame is based on two side members boxed throughout their length and spaced to the full width of the body, which gives a low seating position because the floor is flush with the underside. At the front end they sweep in to give the necessary wheel clearance for the good turning circle of 28ft, which the designers have provided for easy manoeuvrability. The frame is given extra rigidity by extensive bracing at the scuttle structure over the clutch and gear box; stiffening of this section is further increased by a tubular cross-member placed under the transmission at the same point. Although it is rather heavy, the frame possesses very good torsional rigidity, which is reflected in the outstanding road-holding qualities of the car.

The body is panelled in steel and the doors in aluminium. Much research work has gone into the design of the body to reduce the wind resistance, and because of this it is a complete breakaway from the traditional lines which have been associated with this make for so many years. At the same time, the traditional M.G. character has somehow been retained, and the front grille is so styled that its classical origin is at once apparent.

Lucas double-dipping head lamps with pre-focused bulbs and blocked lenses have been blended into the contours of the front wings so that they rise above the falling bonnet line. Separate side lamps are placed immediately below the head lamps, just above the swept-round bumpers, which also carry overriders.

Separate bucket-type seats are placed low down between the widely spaced chassis side members and the propeller-shaft tunnel, to the top of which is fixed a permanent armrest. Good access is achieved by the use of forward-hinged wide doors at each side. They are hung on concealed hinges with no exterior handles, the opening being controlled by pull cables in the spacious door pockets. The hood folds away out of sight behind the rear seat, which area is also used for side screen stowage. The seat back-rests are hinged forward to allow easy access to this compartment. An overall tonneau cover can be supplied at extra charge.

Luggage space is provided above the petrol tank and access is from the outside of the car. The hinged lid to this compartment is released from inside the body by a catch behind the passenger seat. The spare wheel is placed horizontally on the luggage compartment floor, and is canvas covered.

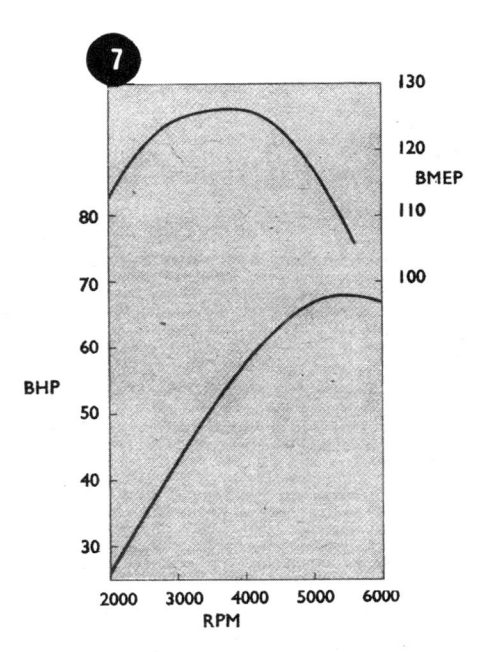

Twin six-volt batteries of 51 ampère-hour capacity are located beneath the locker floor, one on each side of the propeller-shaft.

A single-piece bonnet, hinged at its rear end and supported in the open position by a stay, gives access to the engine compartment.

The curved, one-piece, sloping windscreen is provided with grab handles at each corner which add considerably to the stiffness of this fitting and make it completely free from any vibration or other movement. The four sprung spokes of the steering wheel are arranged to give a clear view of the vital instruments in front of the driver. These consist of a 4in speedometer with dead-beat reading and incorporating a head lamp high beam warning lamp. To the left of the speedometer is a matching 4in revolution counter with ignition warning light. A combined oil pressure and water temperature gauge completes the range of essential instruments

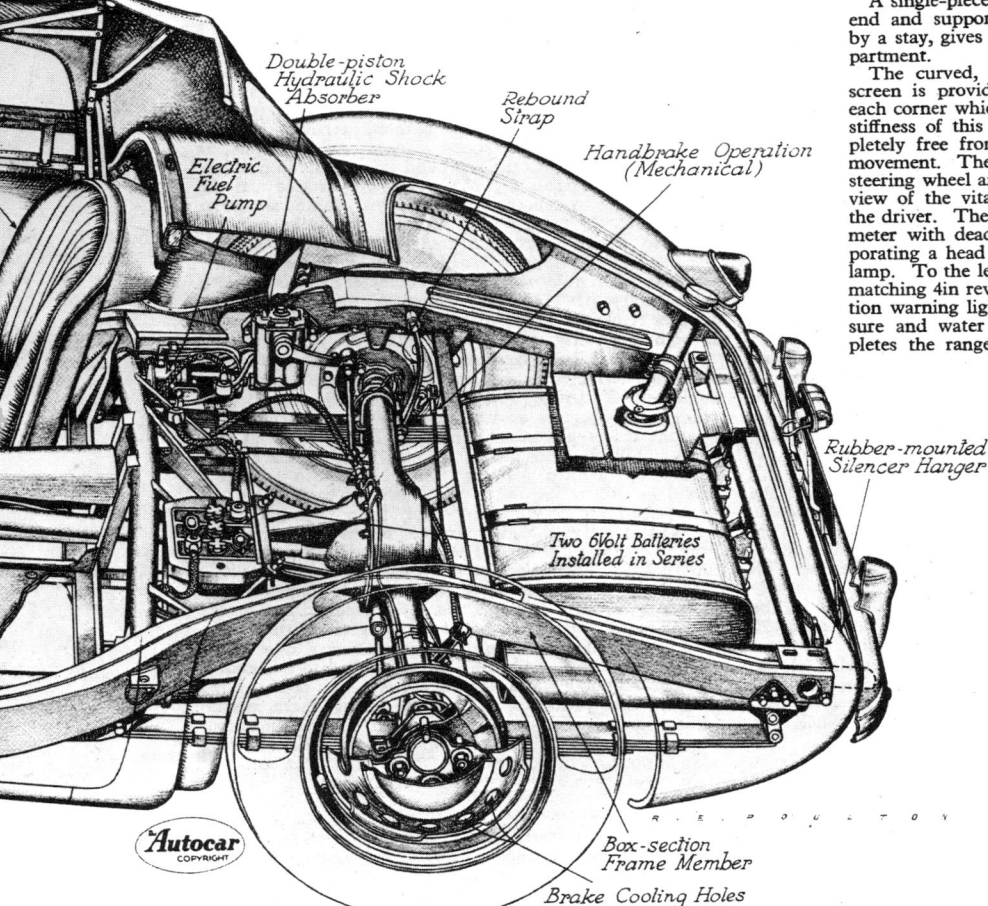

B.M.E.P. and B.H.P. curves for the engine fitted in the M.G. A

LATEST of an illustrious line: Salient features of the M.G. Model A are annotated in this special cut-away drawing

M.G.—The Breed Improved . . .

immediately in front of the driver and a rheostat-controlled panel light, map-reading light and fuel indicator gauge, make up, with the normal range of switches, the functional yet attractive facia panel.

There is a wide range of optional extras if required. Provision has been made for the fitting of H.M.V. car radio, and others include white wall tyres, twin horns, an external luggage carrier, fog lamp and tonneau cover. In the same category are a radiator blind, wire wheels, telescopic steering wheel and the axle ratio of 4.55 to 1.

This new car appears to be a worthy successor to the famous and well-loved T-types, incorporating many lessons learned in racing. At its price it is a desirable car for normal road use, yet is still suitable for competition in the 1,500 c.c. class. In view of the increasing popularity of sports car racing, there is available from the factory both the information and the necessary parts for those owners who wish to increase further the performance of the A model, in the same way as they could its predecessors.

Frontal structure, rack and pinion steering and independent suspension of the new M.G.

The Autocar ROAD TESTS

THE NEW M.G. ON THE ROAD

TO confound the critics who say that racing teaches no useful lessons comes the brand-new M.G. sports two-seater. Designated the model A—thus starting afresh after the long line of M, J, Q and R racing cars, and TA, TD and TF Midgets that rolled out of the Abingdon works—the new car is a very close development of the M.G.s that did so well in the 24-hours race at Le Mans this year.

There are naturally some differences between the racing car and the production model, but the road holding, braking and steering are unaffected and in these respects the M.G. A recalls very intimately the Le Mans car, road impressions of which were published in *The Autocar* of July 29, 1955.

The immediate impression on sitting in the driving seat was that the car had been tailored to fit, of which more later. Starting the 1½-litre B.M.C. engine presented no problems. A radiator blind, as fitted to the test car, is available as optional extra equipment and is easily operated by a control below the right-hand corner of the facia. This blind facilitates the warming-up in which any right-thinking enthusiast will indulge, although even without its use operating temperature was reached very quickly.

On opening the cable-operated throttle there came the familiar M.G. exhaust note. At no time did this become objectionable to others, and there was no annoying boom to be heard with the hood up. The car will drift along through residential areas on a whiff of throttle and with no unwelcome attention attracted.

There is immediate response to sudden pressure on the accelerator and the getaway from rest is very good, 70 m.p.h. being reached in just over 21 seconds. On wet roads, which were experienced during the taking of the acceleration figures, wheelspin was very apparent, and black lines can be left on a dry surface if the start is abrupt. At the end of the standing quarter mile the M.G. was travelling at very nearly 70 m.p.h., and this was very creditable with the load carried. Performance figures were taken with hood and sidescreens erected, except for some runs to determine maximum speed, when a small racing-type screen was fitted.

With this small screen and a tonneau cover over the passenger seat, the best speed reached was 96 m.p.h., as against 99 m.p.h. with the hood and sidescreens in position. At such high speeds the M.G. A is very stable and the driver is able to concentrate on the rev counter needle as it climbs to the orange 5,500 r.p.m. mark on the dial, and the road shooting past him and away under the nose of the car. On Continental roads it was possible to cruise for mile after mile with the speedometer needle between 90 and 100 m.p.h. The oil pressure and temperature gauge needles remained steady in spite of a considerable amount of high-speed driving.

The M.G. A is, in fact, one of those cars whose cruising speed is determined by road conditions, and this became very evident after driving fast over the French and Belgian roads. But there is no feeling at the end of a hard day that the driver has been doing most of the work. Long, winding hillside roads are a joy to traverse; the car rockets to the top in third gear, and this gear is also extremely useful for overtaking other traffic and for town use. Yet it is possible to accelerate smoothly from 12 m.p.h. using the 4.3 to 1 top gear, and the car can be very pleasant when used in a gentle fashion. The engine is no temperamental unit, liable to behave only when it thinks it will.

Fuel consumption benefits from the body shape; driving at 50 m.p.h., with short periods at 70, resulted in a figure of 30.8 m.p.g., which was achieved on a give-and-take main road in Great Britain where to maintain the predetermined average speed the available acceleration had to be used.

The road holding and steering are of a high order. Even with the tyre pressures set for fast driving, there was no feeling of discomfort or pattering when on *pavé* and other poor surfaces. Fast cornering was a joy, the driver being able to position the car exactly where he wanted, and exit from a corner is also very satisfactory. On roads just wet

23 SEPTEMBER 1955

after a sudden rainfall, the tail of the car would swing out slightly, but correction brought an immediate response and there was no lack of control. Suspension and damping is such that the whole car feels in one piece and the front end does not hop about.

The rack and pinion steering, with one of the æsthetically better types of present-day steering wheel, has a good, easy action with very little lost motion. There are two and three-quarter turns from lock to lock and the car proves to be guided by a slight motion of the hands rather than turning the wheel through a number of degrees.

Control is helped at all speeds by the excellent driving position previously mentioned. The seat is low down, below the level of the frame, and the driver's legs stretch comfortably to the pedals. The steering wheel (non-adjustable column) is at a good angle and there is plenty of room for the driver's elbows. The sight line of a tall driver is well below the top of the windscreen, and there is space for large feet in the neighbourhood of the pedals. The short remote control gear lever comes immediately to hand and the movements are precise and extremely satisfactory, the results being equally so! Occasional difficulty was encountered in engaging first gear from rest. The reverse stop spring on the car tested was also rather stiff, but experience of a similar gear box has shown that this stiffness wears off. The clutch is hydraulically operated and has a nice feel. It is capable of enabling very quick gear changes to be made without slip.

Racing experience shows in the M.G. A braking, which is all that could be required for very fast road work. Two-leading shoes in the front brakes, with leading and trailing shoes working in the rear, give the driver all the retarding power he is likely to need in normal circumstances. No fade was experienced during the test, and only when the brake performance figures were being obtained did any unevenness set in. The fitting of centre-lock wire wheels, an optional extra, would assist in cooling the drums as well as improving the already attractive appearance of the car. The hand-brake lever lies horizontally by the side of the propeller-shaft tunnel and has a fly-off action. It is easily reached and does not get in the way of the driver's leg.

Fast night driving is quite safe with the beam of the head lights, but the foot-operated dip-switch is placed rather high and is difficult to reach. It would be considerably better if it could be adjacent to the clutch pedal. There is a rheostat for the instrument lighting, and at one position of the switch the speedometer alone is illuminated. The only reflection in the windscreen comes from the tonneau cover studs immediately in front of the steering wheel. With the hood up and head lamp beams reaching away in front, the M.G. A is as comforting to drive at night as it is exhilarating by day.

Both seats have adequate adjustment and the back rest is at a comfortable angle. Some drivers would prefer more support for the thighs. The passenger has a grab handle and this also forms the windscreen frame support. As is to be expected, it is easier for two persons to erect the hood from its stowed position behind the seats, but the driver alone can manage it. The sidescreens, which have a spring-loaded flap, are simple to put into position and remove; they are each locked by one turnbuckle. Some

A new slant on the familiar M.G. front, successfully adapted

wet came in between the windscreen and front edge of the sidescreens when travelling fast, and in extremely heavy rain water dripped on to the driver's right leg from a point under the scuttle. There is a very reasonable amount of head room with the hood erect, and there was no instance of the driver's head hitting the hoop sticks when going over a bump. At speeds between 70 and 80 m.p.h. the hood

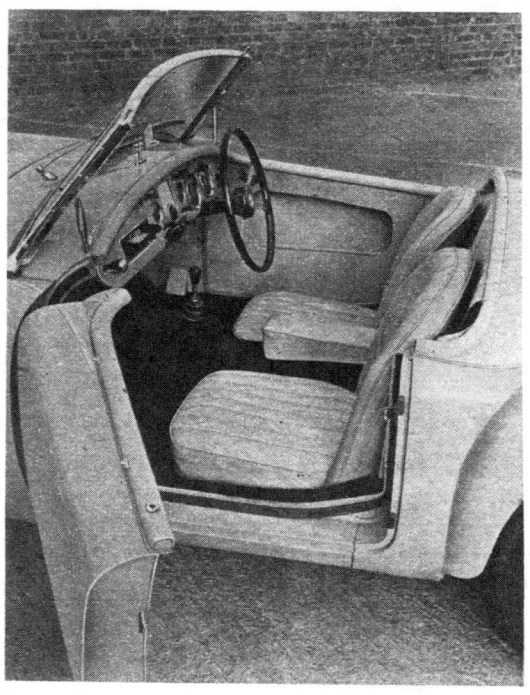

Seats tip forward if required. Instruments confront the driver but the horn is in the centre of the facia

For a sports car, luggage space is reasonable. Hood up, the new model loses nothing in smartness; the rear window is flexible

material vibrated on the frame but this noise was not experienced at lower speeds.

There is no cubby-hole in the facia; the space occupied by the radio fitted on the test car is blanked by a plate with an M.G. motif when there is no radio. A large pocket in each door is sufficient for maps, torch and the usual odds and ends crews require for a few days away from home. The pockets remain dry in rain when sidescreens are not fitted. The door handle cord is slung across the inside top of the pocket and can be reached by inserting a hand underneath the flap of the sidescreen. There are fitted envelopes behind the seats for the side curtains and these envelopes neatly conceal the hood when it is folded away.

The release handle for the luggage locker lid can be reached behind the passenger seat; there is room in the locker for a suitcase and small articles. Strapped on the rear bulkhead is the tool roll, containing the lifting jack and wheelbrace. The jack, surprisingly enough, is of the old-fashioned screw type. A starting handle is supplied and is clipped to the back of the locker. Nine points require attention with a grease gun every 1,000 miles and the twin six-volt batteries are housed beneath the luggage locker. They can be reached by removing the spare wheel.

A heating and demisting unit, available as an optional extra, was fitted to the test car. It worked well, and draws in fresh air via a long duct through the engine compartment. On the left side of the radiator, fresh air is ducted to the intakes of the twin S.U. carburettors. Hot air and fumes from the engine compartment are cleared by a vent on each side of the bonnet. As is usual with these B.M.C. engines, the oil filler is accessible, though it is difficult to see why the oil level dipstick could not be two inches longer, raising it clear of the sparking plug leads. Dynamo belt adjustment is not particularly easy with the standard tool kit.

M.G. TWO-SEATER (SERIES A)

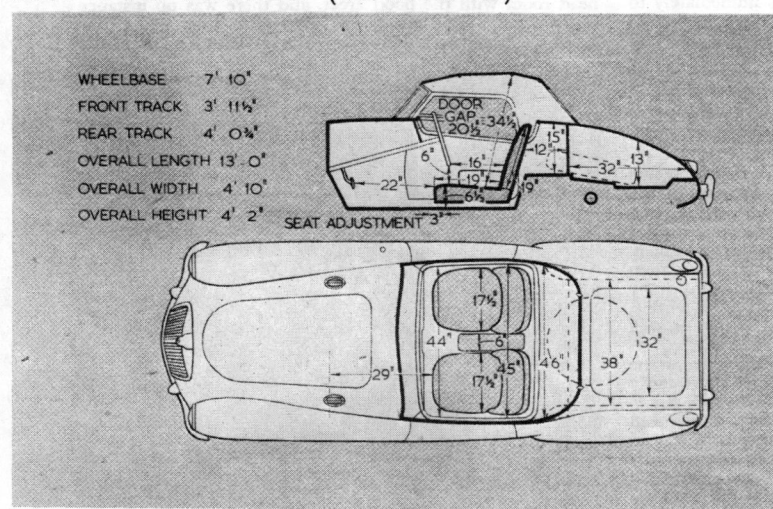

Measurements in these ⅟₁₀in to 1ft scale body diagrams are taken with the driving seat in the central position of fore and aft adjustment and with the seat cushions uncompressed

PERFORMANCE

ACCELERATION: from constant speeds.
Speed Range, Gear Ratios and Time in sec.

M.P.H.	4.3 to 1	5.908 to 1	9.520 to 1	15.652 to 1
10–30	—	8.2	5.0	—
20–40	12.2	8.0	4.8	—
30–50	12.3	8.4	—	—
40–60	13.1	9.1	—	—
50–70	15.0	10.7	—	—
60–80	18.1	—	—	—

From rest through gears to:

M.P.H.	sec.
30	4.9
50	11.0
60	15.6
70	21.4
80	32.1
90	50.1

Standing quarter mile, 20.2 sec.

SPEEDS ON GEARS:

Gear	M.P.H. (normal and max.)	K.P.H. (normal and max.)
Top (mean)	98.0	157.7
(best)	99.0	159.3
3rd	58–70	93–113
2nd	38–44	61–71
1st	20–26	32–42

SPEEDOMETER CORRECTION: M.P.H.

Car speedometer	10	20	30	40	50	60	70	80	90	100
True speed:	11	20	29	38	48	58	68	77	86	96

TRACTIVE RESISTANCE: 20 lb per ton at 10 M.P.H.

TRACTIVE EFFORT:

	Pull (lb per ton)	Equivalent Gradient
Top	203	1 in 11.0
Third	303	1 in 7.3
Second	455	1 in 4.9

BRAKES:

Efficiency	Pedal Pressure (lb)
85 per cent	100
77 per cent	50
58 per cent	25

FUEL CONSUMPTION:
27 m.p.g. overall for 672 miles (10.46 litres per 100 km).
Approximate normal range 25–38 m.p.g. (11.3–7.4 litres per 100 km).
Fuel, First grade.

WEATHER: Overcast, wet surface.
Air temperature 68 deg F.
Acceleration figures are the means of several runs in opposite directions.
Tractive effort and resistance obtained by Tapley meter.
Model described in *The Autocar* of September 23, 1955.

DATA

PRICE (basic), with two-seater body, £595.
British purchase tax, £249 0s 10d.
Total (in Great Britain), £844 0s 10d.

ENGINE: Capacity: 1,489 c.c. (90.88 cu in).
Number of cylinders: 4.
Bore and stroke: 73.025 × 89 mm. (2.875 × 3.5in).
Valve gear: o.h.v., push rods.
Compression ratio: 8.3 to 1.
B.H.P.: 68 at 5,500 r.p.m. (B.H.P. per ton laden 70.6).
Torque: 77.4 lb ft at 3,500 r.p.m.
M.P.H. per 1,000 r.p.m. on top gear, 17.0.

WEIGHT: (with 5 gals fuel), 17¼ cwt (1,904 lb).
Weight distribution (per cent): F, 51.5; R, 48.5.
Laden as tested: 21 cwt (2,254 lb).
Lb per c.c. (laden): 1.51.

BRAKES: Type: F, two-leading shoe; R, leading and trailing.
Method of operation: F, hydraulic; R, hydraulic.
Drum dimensions: F, 10in diameter; 1¾in wide. R, 10in diameter; 1¾in wide.
Lining area: F, 67.2 sq in. R, 67.2 sq in (112.6 sq in per ton laden).

TYRES: 5.60—15in.
Pressures (lb per sq in): F, 17; R, 20 (normal). F, 18; R, 23 (for fast driving).

TANK CAPACITY: 10 Imperial gallons.
Oil sump, 6½ pints.
Cooling system, 10 pints (plus 0.65 pints if heater is fitted).

TURNING CIRCLE: 28ft 0in (L and R).
Steering wheel turns (lock to lock): 2¾.

DIMENSIONS: Wheelbase: 7ft 10in.
Track: F, 3ft 11½in; R, 4ft 0¾in.
Length (overall): 13ft.
Height: 4ft 2in.
Width: 4ft 10in.
Ground clearance: 6in.
Frontal area: 13.77 sq ft (approximately) (with hood up).

ELECTRICAL SYSTEM: 12-volt; 51 ampère-hour battery.
Head lights: Double dip; 42–36 watt bulbs.

SUSPENSION: Front, independent, coil springs. Rear, half-elliptic leaf springs.

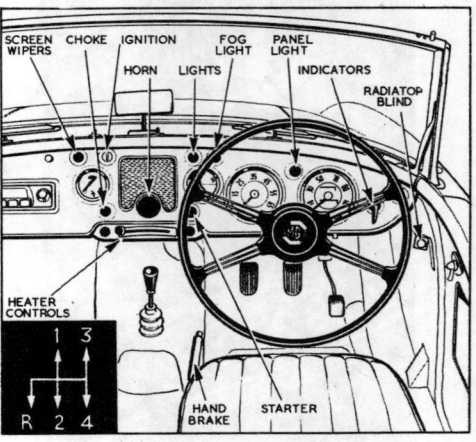

MG-A	☑☑☑☑ MEANS TOP RATING
Considering the car's price and displacement class, its top speed of 90 to 95 mph and acceleration of 10.5 seconds from 0 to 50 mph is excellent.	☑☑☑☐ PERFORMANCE
Generally a very fine rendition of the modern tradition of envelope-type, two-seat body which is also aerodynamically efficient. Only the bulging tail lamps and the efficient but impractical grille could provoke criticism.	☑☑☑☐ STYLING
Of the cars surveyed only the Porsche and Jaguar are more comfortable. Although sharper riding on rough surfaces the car is actually more comfortable than a conventional car on smooth pavement due to lack of pitching and side sway.	☑☑☑☐ RIDING COMFORT
Very good. Vision is excellent forward over the sloping hood and to the rear through the large plastic window. Comfortable, fully adjustable leather-over-foam rubber seats, and optional adjustable steering column accommodate all drivers comfortably.	☑☑☑☐ INTERIOR DESIGN
Fully up to the car's performance standard. Will delight the pleasure driver and not disappoint those who intend to use the car for serious competition.	☑☑☑☐ ROADABILITY
With its smooth clutch and brakes, easy-operating "stick" shift and precise rack-and-pinion type steering gear, the MG-A is equal to the best in all-around handling ease.	☑☑☑☑ EASE OF CONTROL
In combined traffic and open road driving the MG-A will deliver from 25 to 30 miles per gallon depending on the driver's degree of urgency.	☑☑☑☐ ECONOMY
Engine accessibility is average and there are no special problems with any of the units. Brakes are easy to adjust, as is the clutch.	☑☑☑☐ SERVICEABILITY
Engine is sturdily designed to stand up under greater stresses than will ever be placed on it. Major units such as brakes, rear axle, clutch are exceptionally trouble-free.	☑☑☑☐ DURABILITY
Above average in the important areas such as paint, fit of body panels and all operating parts. Minor details such as flimsy instrument panel mounting are below par.	☑☑☑☐ WORKMANSHIP
A real honest-to-goodness sports car at a down-to-earth price. MGs depreciate sharply the first year then level off; overall depreciation averages out better than most U.S. family cars.	☑☑☑☑ VALUE PER DOLLAR

MG-A

$2200 PORT-OF-ENTRY

AT $2200 the new MG-A represents the lowest-priced full-fledged sports car available in this country today. For many automakers, manufacturing a car at a bargain price means that the product of necessity is a good deal less than perfect. This is definitely not the case with the MG-A which in most respects is equal to sports cars costing $1000 more.

The car's frame, suspension and drive parts are ruggedly built and will take all the punishment that severe competition can offer. This means that for the ordinary driver the car will last almost indefinitely. The 1500cc displacement, 68-bhp-engine is equally reliable and trouble-free.

In the recent 12-hour endurance race at Sebring, Florida, three MG-As won the team prize as the only marque which had all starters finish. The slowest MG averaged 60 mph for the 12 hours including pit stops.

The MG-A is a pleasant and docile car to operate in city traffic or on the open road. The 4-cylinder engine idles smoothly and quietly and will not overheat whether crawling in city traffic or cruising at sustained high speeds. The hydraulically-operated clutch provides a happy combination of low pedal pressure and very positive engagement. The four-forward-speed transmission can be snap-shifted for fast acceleration, although there is a slight hitch in crossing through the "H" between 2nd and 3rd speeds. Synchromesh on the top three speeds is traditionally efficient on MGs and the A is no exception. With a little practice, smooth, fast downshifting becomes easy and polished.

The MG-A's brakes are as smooth, powerful and free from fade as on previous models. The larger pendulum type pedal is a definite improvement, however, lowering pedal pressure, and making the brakes easier to apply.

Roadability and handling are excellent as in earlier models. When the car is pushed into curves at speeds which pass the limits of tire adhesion, it goes into an easily-controlled drift. At no time is there much roll or any juddering of the rear wheels. With the recommended tire pressures the rear end will tend to drift out farther. By increasing the tire pressure by five or six pounds you can eliminate oversteer tendency at some expense to riding comfort.

The car's riding qualities are similar to earlier models: firm, well-controlled but never close to the harsh, tooth-rattling gait of some sports cars.

The new, fully-streamlined "envelope" body has improved comfort particularly in the increase of legroom. At long last there is space for the driver's left foot alongside the clutch pedal. The enclosed trunk resulting from the new body design is disappointing to those who hoped for increased luggage space. Spare tire and gas tank leave room for little else. Stowage of the folding top and side screens is neatly accomplished behind the tilting backs of the adjustable bucket seats.

Summing up; The MG-A is a beautifully handling, handsome and ruggedly made little car which will serve as inexpensive and highly practical transportation within the obvious limitations of size and riding comfort. ●

CAR LIFE ●

THE MOTOR

EX 182

NEW M.G. SPORTS CAR PROTOTYPES TO RACE AT LE MANS

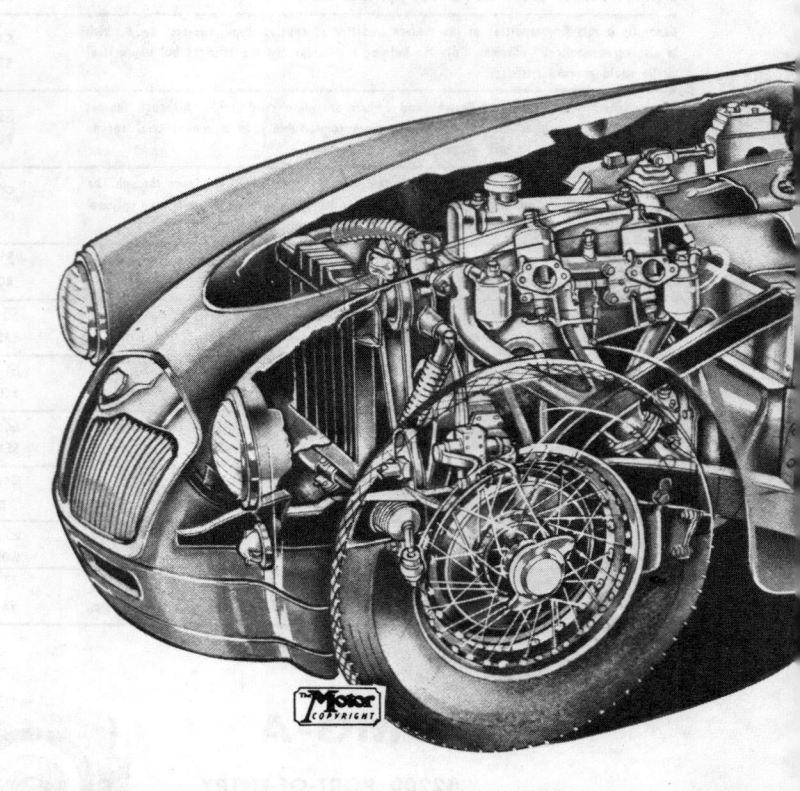

BOLDLY, the M.G. Car Company are making their re-appearance on the racing circuits (after a 20-year absence) with a team of sports cars which, although classed as prototypes, are by no means merely disguised racing cars. The green two-seaters which will start in the Le Mans 24-hour race at 4 p.m. on June 11 are the result of planning which has gone on ever since a TD-series M.G. with streamlined bodywork ran in the 1951 Le Mans 24-hours' race. Although prepared for racing, they are not models built regardless of cost simply to win races, but are prototypes from which it is hoped that an attractive production sports car can be evolved for sale at a highly competitive price in the not too distant future.

Already, the components of the four prototype cars which carry the works designation "Ex. 182" have been tested with some thoroughness. The suspension and steering are closely related to designs used on the TD- and TF-series M.G. two-seaters. The engine and brakes have been developed from those of the M.G. Magnette model introduced in October 1953. The new chassis was used as the basis of the streamlined single-seater in which records were broken at over 150 m.p.h. on the Utah salt lake in August 1954. These ingredients have been put together in cars which are intended to be good looking, strong, safe, and yet fast enough to complete the Le Mans 24 hours at 80 m.p.h. or so.

Fundamental to the new cars is the chassis, which, as indicated, has already been tried out at speeds of over 2½ miles a minute. It is not the fashionable "space frame" of ultra-light weight such as appears on many "sports" cars designed almost solely for racing, but a box section chassis, designed to combine strength with the ability to carry a comfortable body fitted with proper doors. It is anticipated that, after the race at Le Mans is over, the same cars will go on to be tested further in the very different circumstances of the Alpine Rally.

M.G. TYPE EX. 182

Engine dimensions	
Cylinders	4
Bore	73.025 mm.
Stroke	89 mm.
Cubic capacity	1,489 c.c.
Piston area	25.97 sq. in.
Valves	Pushrod o.h.v.
Compression ratio	9.4 to 1

Engine performance	
Max. power at	Approx. 82 b.h.p.
	5,500 r.p.m.
B.H.P. per sq. in. piston area	3.16
Peak piston speed ft. per min.	3,210

Engine details	
Carburetter	2 S.U. (1¾ in.)
Ignition	12-volt coil
Fuel pump	Twin S.U. electrical
Fuel capacity	20 gallons
Oil filter	Replaced by oil cooler
Electrical system	12-volt
Battery capacity	37 amp.-hr.

Transmission	
Clutch	8 in. s.d.p., hydraulically operated
Gear ratios: Top	3.7 (subject to tests)
3rd	4.69
2nd	6.00
1st	9.06
Prop. shaft	Open
Final drive	Hypoid bevel

Chassis details	
Brakes	Lockheed hydraulic (2 l.s. front)
Brake drum dimensions	10 in. by 1¾ in.
Friction lining area	134.4 sq. in.
Suspension: Front	Coil and wishbone i.f.s.
Rear	Semi-elliptic
Shock absorbers	Armstrong piston-type
Wheel type	Centre-lock wire.
Tyre sizes: Front	5.50—15
Rear	6.00—15
Steering gear	Rack and pinion
Steering wheel	Flexible, X-spoked

Dimensions	
Wheelbase	7 ft. 10 in.
Track: Front	3 ft. 11⅞ in.
Rear	4 ft. 0¾ in.
Overall length	12 ft. 6 in.
Overall width	4 ft. 10 in.
Overall height	3 ft. 5 in.
Ground clearance	6 in.
Dry weight	Approx. 14¼ cwt.

Performance data	
Piston area, sq. in. per ton	36.4
Brake lining area, sq. per ton	189
Top gear m.p.h. per 1,000 r.p.m.	21.0
Top gear m.p.h. at 5,500 r.p.m.	115
Top gear m.p.h. at 2,500 ft./min. piston speed	90
Litres per ton-mile, dry	2,980

BASED on a very strong chassis frame of box-section side-members, rigid scuttle "bridge" and tubular and box-section cross-members, the new M.G. has the fundamental ingredients for good road-holding. Setting the side members well apart allows the floor to be placed low between them. The smooth bodywork is of aluminium.

As on TD- and TF-series cars, the new chassis is based on two box-section steel side members, but is of much increased width so that the floor can be set low down between the side members instead of resting on top of them. As the drawing indicates, the side members sweep sharply outwards behind the narrow forward section which is necessary to provide a good turning circle, run straight for a distance, and sweep inwards again to pass between the rear wheels: at the rear the side members are also swept upwards, to pass over the conventional axle, the frame members being of increased width to maintain rigidity at the points where they are curved in plan.

At the front especially, very extensive bracing is provided for the box-section frame. Incorporated in the scuttle structure is a box-section "bridge" over the clutch and gearbox, formed into a complete "ring" by a tubular cross-member which dips under the transmission at substantially the same point. From the top of the bridge, box-section members extend forwards and downwards to the front cross-member, and backwards and down to the widest part of the frame, on each side of the car. Ahead of this massive bulkhead structure there is a box-section cross-member (drilled for weight reduction) to carry the I.F.S. assembly, whilst behind it there are a box-section cross-member and three tubular cross-members.

Conventional modern suspension is stated to be giving extremely good results on these cars. At the front, there are unequal-length wishbones and coil springs, with Armstrong hydraulic shock absorbers of the horizontal-piston type forming the top suspension arm pivots. At the rear, semi-elliptic leaf springs located directly below the frame kick-up are shackled at their rear ends, control being by vertical-piston shock absorbers supplemented by rebound check straps. As on other recent M.G. models, a rack and

AT SPEED on Silverstone circuit, one of the "Ex. 182" M.G. prototypes is seen in the hands of Ken Wharton.

THE MOTOR   June 1, 1955

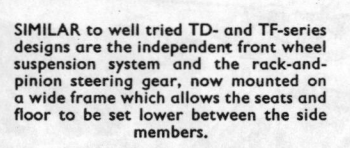

Ex. 182 - - - - - - - - - -

SIMILAR to well tried TD- and TF-series designs are the independent front wheel suspension system and the rack-and-pinion steering gear, now mounted on a wide frame which allows the seats and floor to be set lower between the side members.

form for the M.G. Magnette it produces 60 b.h.p. at 4,600 r.p.m. At Le Mans, an ingenious new version of the Weslake cylinder head will be used, early tests showing 82 b.h.p. at 5,500 r.p.m. with a compression ratio of 9.4/1, although still more power may be available after pre-race development work has progressed further.

In-line overhead valves operated by push-rods and rockers continue to be used, in combustion chambers shaped to prevent in-coming mixture escaping directly through the exhaust valve during the overlap period. Siamesed inlet ports continue to serve the front and rear pairs of cylinders respectively, but these ports have been carried straight across to the opposite side of the cast-iron head, the port extensions being linked by an external balance pipe of quite large section on the opposite side of the engine to the main inlet and exhaust ports.

Deeper Breathing

In an orthodox engine, with the common siamesed ports and with a 1-3-4-2 firing order, there are unsymmetrical flow conditions in the manifold. Suction by No. 3 cylinder has not ended when suction through the same inlet port by No. 4 cylinder commences, but these two successive suction periods of half an engine revolution each are then followed by a period during which that port is inoperative, while Nos. 2 and 1 cylinders are inducing mixture. By running the ports through the cylinder head to a balance pipe on the opposite side of the engine, flow can be maintained more steadily from both of the two S.U. carburetters, and during the "dead" interval the rear carburetter feeds via the opposite side of the engine to the front pair of cylinders, or vice versa. With this quite original arrangement, the inlet valve which is open is being fed by gas streams from both sides, and its whole periphery is effective, whereas with flow from one side only there is often less effective use of the available area of opening.

Retaining the in-line valves of a quantity-production engine, but with valve diameters increased to give extra power, the space between individual cylinders is somewhat limited. For the racing engines, cylinder heads and blocks

pinion steering gear is mounted ahead of the I.F.S. assembly, and the steering column incorporates a Hardy Spicer universal joint.

Wire wheels of the knock-on type are being used for Le Mans, with light-alloy rims to save weight. On the 15-in. rims, 5.50-in. front and 6.00-in. rear tyres are fitted. Apart from speedier wheel changes, the wire wheels provide improved air flow over the two-leading-shoe brakes, and also allow easy access to the brake adjusters.

Rather than race cars with entirely special engines, the M.G. Car Company have decided to run at Le Mans with a developed version of the British Motor Corporation "B Series" engine which, in slightly differing forms, is used in the M.G. Magnette and in various Austin and Morris models. In the touring cars this engine delivers 50 b.h.p. at 4,200-4,400 r.p.m., and in twin-carburetter

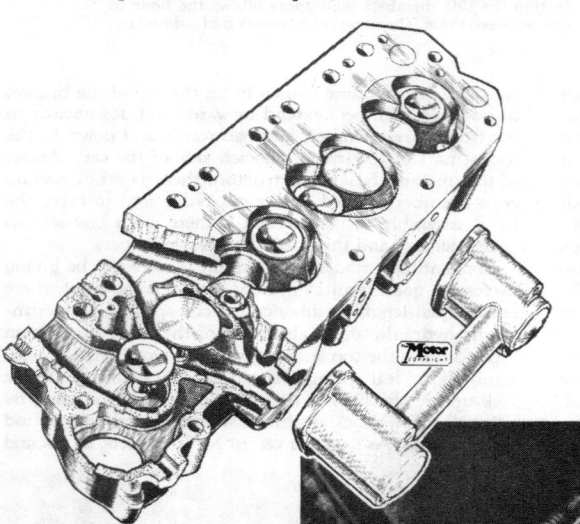

NOVEL feature of the engine is the use of straight-through inlet ports joined by a balance pipe on the far side of the block from the carburetters, to provide steady mixture flow to both sides of the inlet valves located in the siamesed ports. The drawing also shows the unusual shape of the combustion chambers, viewed from the underside. The accompanying under-bonnet photograph shows the neat layout of induction balance pipe on the opposite side of the B-series B.M.C. 1½-litre engine to the two S.U. carburetters and the exhaust system.

CONFERENCE between test runs at Silverstone, with driver Ken Wharton reporting to M.G. development engineer Sydney Enever and Abingdon General Manager John Thornley.

COVER over the passenger seat streamlines the M.G. body for use in races where the driver alone need be carried. Prominently placed, the tachometer is seen through the unusually-spoked steering wheel, and a central remote-control gear lever is also visible in this picture.

are being lapped together, and no cylinder-head gaskets will be used. As the fitting of an under-tray will prevent the free circulation of air around the sump, an oil cooler is being incorporated in the lubrication system, which is likely to contain a castor-base oil. The two S.U. carburetters will be supplied with cool air through a flexible pipe passing beside the radiator. The detail care which is being put into these engines is typified by the use of lock-wired bolts to secure cylinder block core plugs which normally are merely sprung into place.

Behind the engine, a single-plate clutch of 8-in. size and a four-speed synchro-mesh gearbox are mounted in unit with it. Hydraulic operation is used for the clutch as well as for the brakes, from pedals of the hanging type. Adapted from the type used on the Magnette, the gearbox is controlled by the central short gear-lever expected on a sports car, and has more closely spaced ratios—the layshaft actually rotates at more than engine speed. Subject to the results of tests on the actual circuit, a ratio of 3.7/1 will be used in the conventional hypoid-geared 3/4-floating rear axle, in which case 5,500 r.p.m. will correspond to 47, 71, 91 and 115 m.p.h. in 1st, 2nd, 3rd and top gears respectively.

Full-width Bodywork

Panelled in aluminium and easily removable from the chassis, the new M.G. open bodies are genuine two-seaters, although they will be raced with metal covers over half of the cockpit. The design of bodywork is planned to give a large reduction in wind resistance over previous M.G. production models, but it is hoped that it will have some of the enduring aesthetic appeal which allowed the J2-series M.G. design of 1932 to remain identifiably related to the TF-series M.G. of 1954, although it ultimately proved to set a limit of around 85 m.p.h. on maximum speed. The low and wide radiator air intake carries a chromium-plated M.G. grille which anyone can instantly recognize, although for racing some of the vertical slats will be cut away to allow a "flamethrower" long-range lamp to be recessed into the air intake. Lucas headlamps of Le Mans pattern are blended into the smooth contours of the front wings, which rise well above the low bonnet line. Cooling air escapes through holes in the top of the bonnet.

Two bucket-type seats easily reached through a pair of large doors are set comfortably between the side members of the wide chassis frame, and the four sprung spokes of the steering wheel are arranged in the manner of an "X" set on its side to allow a clear view of the vital instruments. Supplementing the rev-counter there are an oil pressure gauge, radiator thermometer, ammeter and fuel contents gauge. Low down in the frame ahead of the rear axle, a light 12-volt battery of 37 amp.-hour capacity is mounted, and also the dual S.U. electrical fuel pump. A petrol tank of 20 gallons capacity, and above it a single spare wheel and tyre, are carried inside the sloping tail of the body. A full-length undertray gives the car a smooth underside, in the interests of low-wind resistance, the exhaust system running beneath the body on the near side with a silencer (hung on metal strips incorporating bonded-rubber flexible units) at the extreme rear end. The observant will notice provision for the neat incorporation of touring-car bumpers in the body design.

As will have been gathered already, these new M.G. prototypes do not represent an effort by the British Motor Corporation to win the 1,500 c.c. class at Le Mans. The objective in this race is to test a straightforward new sports car design far more thoroughly than is possible in conditions of privacy, a design which it is believed has the characteristics of extreme sturdiness, reasonable simplicity, comfort and good looks which must go with quite high performance in any future M.G. production model. In this case, the lessons of racing may be applied with more than normal directness and speed to cars which will be sold to the public.

UNCRAMPED in dimensions, the body shape of the M.G. two-seaters which will race at Le Mans could be adapted without fundamental change to a popular-priced production sports model.

Hillclimb course used for motorcycle events gave new MG-A a tough workout. Handling is improved over T series.

DRIVING THE NEW MG

BY ALFRED COMSTOCK

Completely new, better than the T series and entirely different— that's a tall order but the MG-A from Abingdon-on-Thames fills the bill

THE 1956 MG-A is a new car from bonnet to boot. In styling, engineering and performance, it differs completely from the preceding TC, TD and TF series of the MG. Only on rare occasions has a motor car builder, of either sports or passenger types, abandoned a popular design so suddenly to undertake such an absolute and fundamental change.

How complete the changeover is mechanically is examined in detail in the technical report that appears on the following pages. Here we shall concentrate upon the effects of these changes and offer some facts and impressions obtained while driving various MG-A's made available by Gough Industries in Los Angeles.

What probably was the first U.S. action by MG-A on gymkhana-time trials type of course is shown in the four-photo series at right. The occasion actually was a dealer-and-press demonstration, with more than a dozen of the new cars available for clocked runs through the two small circuits, staged by Gough Industries on a vast parking lot of the Santa Anita horse track. This was first behind-the-wheel experience with the new car, supplemented later by more extensive hillclimb and road impressions of the long-awaited car imported from Britain.

MOTOR LIFE, December, 1955

Our first reaction, upon viewing the MG-A, was a mixture of approval which the streamlined bodywork inspired and a feeling of regret at knowing that yet another classic design has been laid to rest.

Progress probably compelled the adoption of the contemporary sports car form for the new MG, but much of the prestige the T series enjoyed unquestionably developed from its distinctive style. There is no argument, however, that the new shell is not a more practical—and even functional—arrangement.

Speed and acceleration, for instance, are improved all along the line. Naturally, much of the credit belongs to the new power train. Nevertheless, the sleeker shape, unhampered by boxy angles, slips along with greater ease and far less wind noise than the earlier models. Sturdier construction also has reduced vibration so that at 70 mph, and more, there is a feeling of smooth cruising rather than strain.

Performance of the MG-A was checked by use of a road test electric fifth wheel to insure accuracy. Indicated speedometer readings of 30, 45 and 60 mph were actually 29.5, 42 and 55 mph, respectively. Times clocked from zero to 30, 45 and 60 mph were 5.1, 9.3 and 14.9 seconds, respectively. It was interesting to find, incidentally, that the MG-A really burned rubber on a few of the starts.

Top speed was 92.5 mph, with the tachometer reading 5500 rpm. The run was made with a load of approximately 475 lbs., including driver, passenger and test equipment. With less weight, a racing screen and tonneau cover, this mark probably would have gone three or four mph better.

Some experiments with speed in the lower gears were conducted. It was found that at 6000 rpm, the MG-A would reach 72 mph in third, 43 mph in second and 26 mph in first. The steady, easy-to-read tach is orange colored from 5500 to 6000 rpm, redlined from 6000 to 6500, and has a top of 7000 rpm (a useful feature when running with a modified engine). Valve

(Continued on page 21)

Fifth wheel adjustment prior to top speed runs. New tail light design makes illumination visible from many angles, a good feature for small car on the road at night.

Cockpit now has center arm rest for greater comfort. The steering wheel has an optional telescopic adjustment.

Doors now have no outside handles, are opened by using cord barely visible here inside new large package compartment.

Trunk lid has no handle to open, is released by catch from inside. Space seems to be enough for week end luggage.

Nothing here to resemble the T series of the MG. Two ports just forward of the cowl are functional, exhaust engine heat.

MOTOR LIFE, December, 1955

TECHNICAL REPORT on the New MG

BY JOHN CHRISTY

The change is a big one and most of it is good—and here's a bolt-by-bolt evaluation that reveals what makes the machinery tick

BUILDERS of the MG scorn half measures toward any project. Though they make a small car, they do it in a great big way. When they set out to take records, they smash them by the gross. Thus, when they set out to make a model change they make a major one.

With the new 1956 type A, the change is as complete as any the company has ever made. About the only familiar items are the front suspension and the hexagonal insignia; everything else is totally different. Body, chassis, engine, gearbox, brakes and rear end are complete departures from past practice. As a result performance and "feel" are new and different. Speed is up by some 10 mph, advertised horsepower is up by five bhp over the '55 TF 1500 model and weight is down approximately 104 pounds, partially due to lighter engine weight and the totally different chassis design.

THE NEW CHASSIS

The chassis design is derived from that of the latest EX-179 MG streamliner in which Capt. George Eyston and Ken Miles set eight international and 29 new American records at Bonneville in 1954. The chassis sidemembers are steel pressings welded in the shape of an oval box section and swept out to provide a seating position between rather than above the rails. Two light channel members run longitudinally from the rear engine mount along each side of the driveline to the crossmember nearest the rear axle. There are a total of six tubular crossmembers in all, giving extreme chassis rigidity.

Front suspension is similar to that of the TD and TF series, independent, with double A-arms and coil springs. No stabilizer (anti-sway) bar is used. At the rear, extremely high kick-ups lead over the rear axle. Suspension is by comparatively soft semi-elliptic leaf springs. Airplane type hydraulic shocks are used on the rear, Armstrong piston type units are on the front. The brakes are another big change, having been increased from nine to 10 inches in diameter and one-fourth of an inch in width. Although they are of normal construction and not vented they are practically fade proof. Total braking area is 134.4 square inches.

The rear axle is a complete break with the past. The new unit looks strong enough to drive a truck. A typical BMC design, it is a three-quarter floating type with hypoid gears and a final ratio of 4.3-to-1, slightly higher than the earlier 4.55-and 5.12-to-1 ratios. It is also inter-

MG-A engine is different. Note connecting rod cap is set at an angle (not horizontal) for easier rod removal and reduced operational strain. Also new are concave piston, vertical valves, big ports.

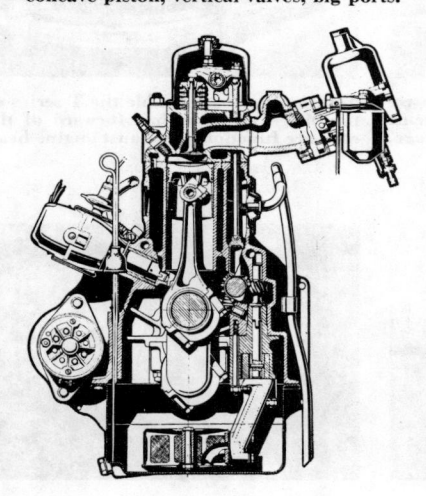

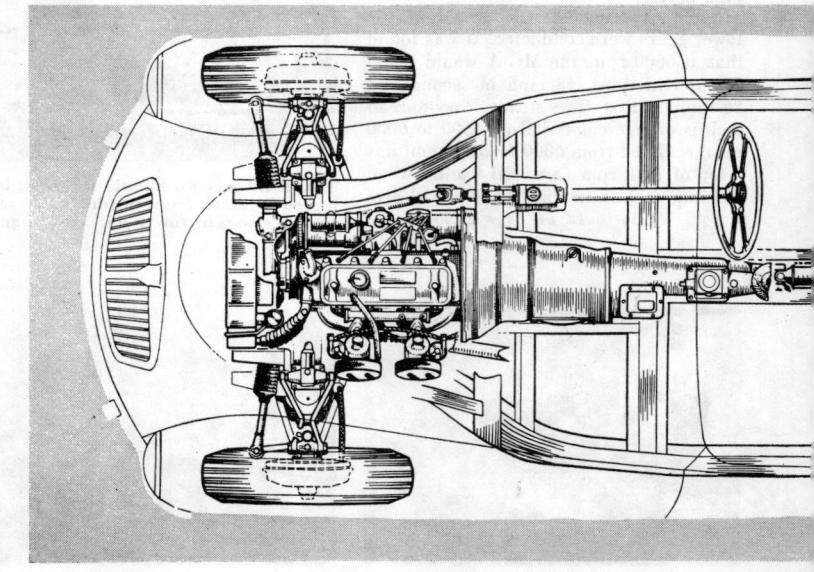

MOTOR LIFE, December, 1955

changeable with the 4.875-to-1 rear end used in the Magnette sedans. The axle shafts are considerably heavier than in earlier models and have splines with an outside diameter larger than that of the shaft itself. For the competition minded, it is interesting to note that the entire gear assembly, including differential, ring and pinion gears and differential carrier can be removed as a unit without removing the axle housing. By having two of theses carrier assemblies reasonably quick changes of final drive ratios can be made at a competition course.

A LOOK AT THE ENGINE

Gone is the old familiar XPAG and XPEG engine design and not without a small sigh of regret at the passing of the mighty mite. The new engine is a modified version of the B-type BMC engine originally used in the Morris Oxford and is both lighter and slightly more powerful than the 90 cubic inch XPEG used in the '55 models.

Basically the B-type engine is a four cylinder plant with a bore of 2.875 inches and a stroke of 3.5 inches for a total displacement of 90.88 cubic inches or 1489 cc. This represents a bore increase of .040 of an inch and a stroke reduction of the same amount in comparison with the XPEG engine. The factory claims 68 bhp at 5500 rpm as opposed to 63 bhp at 5000 for the earlier plant. Carburetors used are the familiar 1½-inch SU's.

The lower end is a rugged piece of equipment although slightly lighter than the earlier block. Crank-pin diameter is .200 larger than in the earlier engine and the main journals are, at two inches diameter, .040 smaller, a not-too-significant decrease. The three-main-bearing crank sits high in the block casting as in the late American inline engines and there is a fairly large overlap between crankpins and main journals, creating a stiff, rigid crankshaft unit and making up for the .040-inch smaller diameter of the mains. Lubrication is full-pressure with a full-flow filter and a sump capacity of a shade over four quarts.

The pistons are aluminum alloy with four rings and concave crowns. In this they are similar to those of the MG Magnette sedan but with a more shallow concavity for higher compression. From the standpoint of service the rod assembly is of considerable interest. In earlier engines, the journal ends of the connecting rods were divided horizontally. The width of the shoulder of the rod big end was such that the piston and rod assembly could not be drawn upward through the bore. This necessitated the disassembly of the piston and rod with the rod hanging inside the engine and the removal of the piston and rod from opposite ends of the cylinder. The new rods are divided diagonally at the journal end, allowing removal of the whole assembly through the upper end of the bore. Further, it is believed that the diagonal sectioning will help to prevent the rod cap studs from stretching during

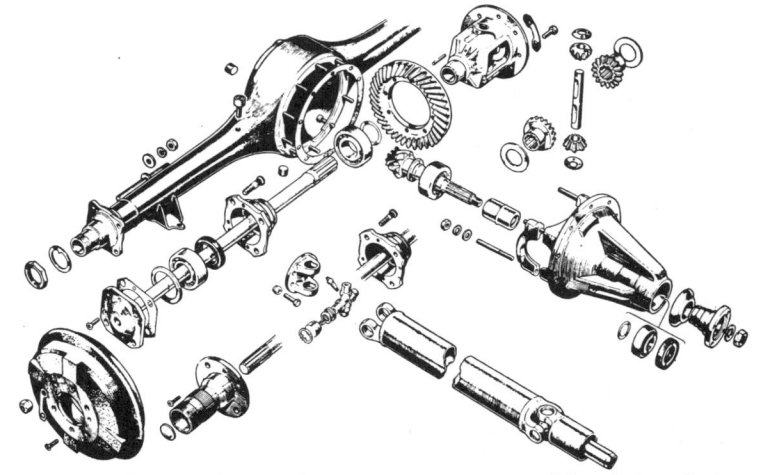

Exploded rear axle view shows two options governed by choice of wire or disc wheels. The easily removable differential carrier allows quick changes.

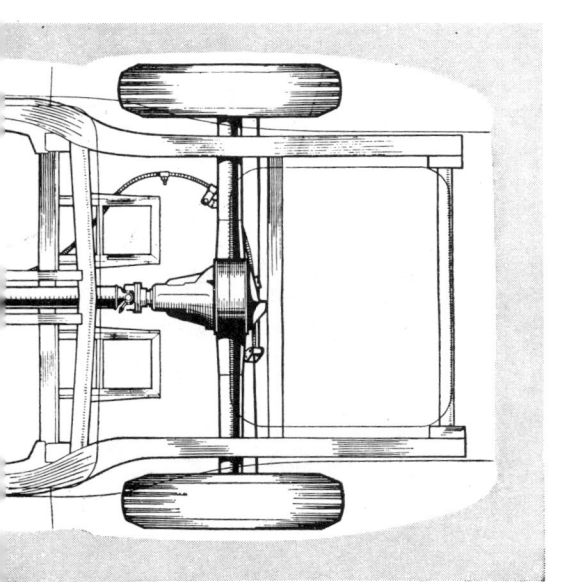

LEFT—Frame members are outswept, actually are box sections welded together. Use of six crossmembers makes for more rigid chassis. Note that this British drawing has righthand steering.

Entirely different BMC design transmission is on MG-A. The layout is longer and roomier, gears are very wide and the tail shaft is well supported at the rear. The action is superior to earlier MG gear boxes.

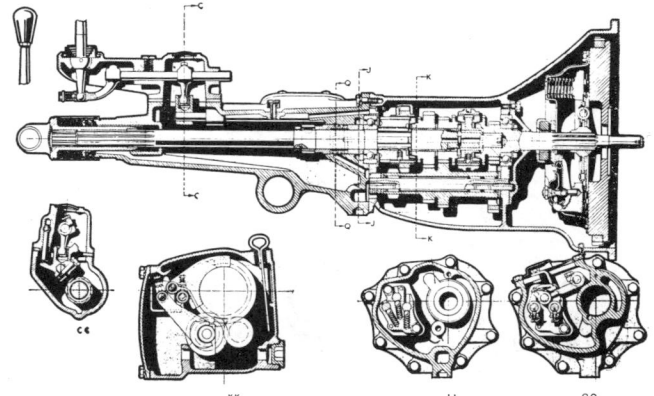

MOTOR LIFE, December, 1955

Although new MG-A valve spring is shorter, its width helps make up in effectiveness. New valves also are stronger.

Brake drum of new MG is a full inch larger in diameter, is a full quarter inch wider. This increases the braking area.

Overhead view of engine. Note two-port intake, with a small balance tube between the two carb risers behind block.

high engine speeds and rapid deceleration as in quick down-shifts. All in all, a very satisfactory layout.

The head layout is a horse of another breed, however. We don't like to second-guess professional engineers who design engines for a living but this particular design has been kicking around the engineering lofts for more years than we can remember. For the average motorist who is satisfied with a car as the factory builds it, the design and its faults will be little or no problem. For those who may wish to modify the engine or use it in competition, however, the design has considerable significance.

To begin with, the porting arrangement leaves much to be desired from the standpoint of breathing and carburetor buffeting. Intake ports are siamesed and the outer sections of the ports are little larger than the diameter of only one of the two valves served. This is common enough in utility type four-barrel engines but seldom used in high performance machinery, especially in recent years since it causes the robbing of one cylinder's charge of fuel by the next one to it in the firing order at higher rpm. The result is a definite limitation on power and engine speed increases. The earlier type TF XPEG and XPAG engines also had siamesed intake ports but of a larger area and with a divider in the center which could be removed entirely or cleaned up for better blow. The two center exhaust valves also share a single port, a fact which might make exhaust tuning extremely difficult.

Another feature with possible limitations from the standpoint of competition tuning is the valve arrangement. Unlike the earlier engines which had inclined valves and a semi-wedge combustion chamber design similar to modern ohv American engines, the BMC-designed engine has inline, vertical valves and flat chamber. This could limit compression ratio raises to around 9- or 9.5-to-for use with gasoline.

Valves in the BMC engine are considerably heavier than in the earlier engines, possibly too much so. Approximately an eighth of an inch larger than those in the '55 engine, the intake valves measure $1^{17}/_{32}$ of an inch across the head. Exhaust valves are slightly smaller than in earlier engines, being 1.320 inches in diameter as opposed to the 1.338 inches of the XPEG exhaust valve. I will probably be only a matter of time until someone chucks these BMC valves in a lathe and, with diligent application of a carbaloy tool, pares down the weight by undercutting the very thick heads in the accepted manner.

In regard to the valve springs we are not alone in holding an adverse opinion. This is the one element of the design which might rise to plague even the average driver in time. The spring length is quite short in comparison to the XPEG and XPAG springs as can be seen in the accompanying illustration. Further, it consists of a single helix rather than the double, counterwound springs used in the earlier engine. The short length, according to many British car experts, has a tendency to cause early spring fatigue and consequent valve bounce with the distinct possibility of the need for a valve refacing and seating if allowed to go untended. Spring pressures are only 77 lbs., shut, and 130 lbs., open. The pressures in the earlier engine were 114 lbs., shut, and 150., open; this with a lighter valve. Undercutting the spring seats and the use of a slightly longer spring undoubtedly would help and

(Continued on page 64)

Larger new cylinder head has heart-shaped combustion chamber for increased turbulence, with point of heart dividing intake and exhaust. T's had squish-type of chambers.

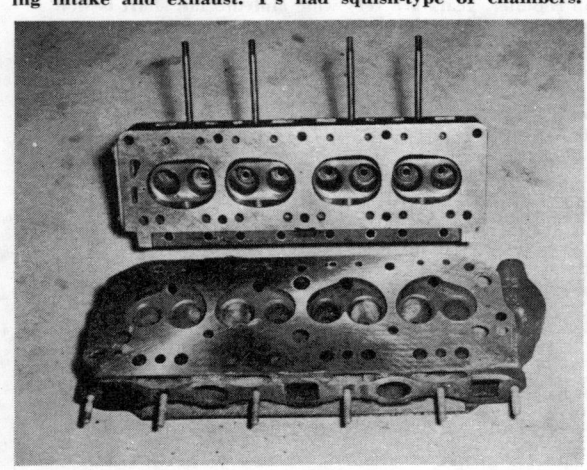

Port side of heads compared. New layout (bottom) has three exhaust ports, compared with four on earlier design. Also note Siamesed ports, in contrast to prior semi-Siamesed.

MOTOR LIFE, December, 1955

MG TECHNICAL REPORT

would be a definite necessity in any modification procedure. However, the point of valve bounce *in the stock engine* has been raised to about 6000 rpm from the 5500 rpm point in the 1250 cc XPAG engine.

By looking at the head used on the LeMans car, it is apparent that the MG people themselves realized these faults and went to considerable trouble to alleviate them. The LeMans head is a Weslake design somewhat similar to that on the Austin-Healey 100 S competition model, the engine of which is also a BMC design. This head is equipped with three large exhaust ports and a severe modification on the intake arrangement. The intake ports are bored through to the spark plug side of the head and a balance tube placed on that side. The result is that of a greater charge of mixture is carried in the ports and better breathing results. These changes, together with a slightly more radical valve timing and a compression ratio of a little over 9-to-1 gave a total of 82 bhp or 14 hp over the stock rating at a peaking speed of 6000 rpm. In a way it is unfortunate that the earlier head design could not have been incorporated in the new power plant. However, the move toward standardization within the BMC line undoubtedly prevented it. As we said, it will make no difference to the average MG owner who will have a livelier car than before and who can drive blissfully unaware of and unaffected by flow rates. It's just that we couldn't let the old engine go without some sort of salute. There are credits and debits and from the standpoint of longevity (except for those valve springs!) the credit side overbalances the debits.

INSIDE THE GEARBOX

Here is a component of the car that will be a joy to the driver who prides himself on "box work." Outwardly, when mounted in the car, the stump-levered transmission looks pretty familiar to anyone who has ever driven the MG except for one small item; reverse is to the left and back instead of to the right and back. From this point on virtually all resemblance ceases. If the older gearbox felt smooth, this one feels like a broomstick in a bucket of warm butter. Each movement is easy, sure and positive. There is no resistance except for a strong spring preventing an unintentional shift into reverse when attempting to drop back into second. Further applause may be found in the preceding driver's report.

Basically the box is a new design first used with the same ratios in the Magnette. At the introduction of that sedan it was the subject of much speculation. A glance at the diagram will show several basic differences between this and earlier transmissions, foremost being a roomier box and a longer, sturdier tail-shaft housing. As in earlier units, low and reverse are sliding spur gears while second, third and high are all synchromesh. To add to the smoothness of shifting, the clutch is hydraulically operated by a swing-down pedal in the most modern manner. The clutch and brake master cylinders are neatly paired on the firewall and easily accessible for servicing. The most noteworthy aspect of all are the evenly spaced speed ratios. For comparison (though the boxes are not interchangeable between XPEG and A-type) here are the ratios of the earlier models together with the ratios of the production A-type and LeMans models.

BOX RATIOS

	TF & TD	A-type	LeMans
1st	3.5:1	3.63:1	2.45:1
2nd	2.07	2.26	1.62
3rd	1.385	1.37	1.268
4th	direct	direct	direct

FINAL DRIVE RATIOS

	TD	TF-1500	A-type	LeMans
1st	17.06	15.94	15.652	9.065
2nd	10.09	9.429	9.520	4.99
3rd	6.752	6.309	5.908	4.69
4th	4.875	4.55	4.3	3.7

Speaking once more for the competition minded, the LeMans gearbox is obviously a piece of racing equipment, the splits being a shade close for normal street use and undoubtedly more than somewhat maddening in any kind of traffic. However, assuming one can get the gears for the switch, it would make an almost unbeatable combination in production class racing although slightly on the unethical side. Just for excitement, here are the final ratios using the A-type rear end (the LeMans final ratio is just a shade high) with the LeMans transmission gears:

1st —10.535:1
2nd— 6.966:1
3rd— 5.452:1
4th — 4.3 :1

Top speed would be the same but with proper handling, elapsed time from corner to corner could be appreciably cut. As we said, it might be considered a bit unethical but . . .

Regardless of whether one is interested in competition or just pleasurable driving, the new MG-A is one of the most intriguing cars to hit this side of the Atlantic in many a year, both from the engineering standpoint and from the point of just plain fun. From what we've been able to discover, the car is a do-it-yourself dream, every part being easily accessible and readily demountable. Best of all, virtually every nut and bolt is standardized with "Unified" or American National Fine threads and bolt heads are made to standard American hexagon wrench sizes. This, need it be said, is a welcome change from earlier days in which a set of Whitworth wrenches was a prerequisite for ownership of a sports car. •

DRIVING THE MG
(Continued from page 17)

clash was not encountered until 6000 rpm, whereas the prior stock MG's developed this condition at 5500. A worthwhile improvement.

Movement of the gear lever, with short, close throws, is easier than previously. The box, of course, is new, but the only change apparent from the driver's seat is the location of reverse; it's now to the left and down, instead of to the right.

From behind the wheel, the difference in the MG is even more pronounced. As a matter of fact, it is like a car from some other manufacturer. The MG enthusiast, however, will find that all the characteristics have been improved, nothing has been sacrificed in moving from the old to the new. Handling is better than ever and the car goes into a hard corner and comes out tight and secure. This security is further increased since the inside rear tire does not have the tendency to lift—providing a flatter ride through the most severe bends. Steering, with 2¾ turns from lock-to-lock, is quick and sharp.

Seating in the MG-A is lower and more comfortable. Legroom is ample and brake, clutch and throttle are now suspended pedals. A center armrest also has been provided and both seats are adjustable fore and aft. Clever designing of the windshield brace makes it a handy grip for entering or leaving the car. The windshield wipers now operate from the bottom, instead of the top, on the curved glass.

Experienced MG owners also will appreciate the fact that a fuel level indicator has replaced the light that formerly blinked at empty. On the other hand, the ammeter has been eliminated in favor of a blinker system. So the score is even here.

Another case of a gain for a loss is the presence of a trunk, of reasonable capacity, while the space behind the seats found in earlier models (handy for dogs and small children) has been designed out of the MG-A. Since much of the brightwork has been eliminated from the new car, it will be easier to maintain; chrome strips, headlights, areas behind the spare tire, etc., have been cleaned up considerably.

At this stage, not much information is available on the availability of normal accessories and equipment for the MG-A. Special engine kits, and perhaps the Le-Mans-type cylinder head, should be offered soon. Meanwhile, price lists at ports of entry only carry the radio at $59.95, wire wheels at $135 and whitewall tires at $35 extra.

Port of entry price of the standard MG-A is $2195, with slight increases at inland retail outlets. For a car of so many good qualities, it is worth the money. The new MG has a lot to live up to but it's off to a good start. •

Wheels road test and analysis of the—

Sleek, fast M.G. A

High performance, good handling and economy from M.G.'s all-new 1½-litre sports.

THE first M.G. — a hopped-up Morris — went on the road in 1923. It was light, had a four-cylinder engine, and could run at 80 m.p.h. It set a pattern for cheapness, exhilaration and reliability that has been kept until today.

It set a style pattern, too; the stark up-and-down shape and external slab-tank that was typical of the between-wars sports cars.

But, although its arrival is not without nostalgic regrets for some, the new M.G./A brings new virtues in place of old. The trappings that were kept right up to last year in the 1,466 c.c. M.G./TF are gone; in their place is a smoothly streamlined, two-seat body. Along with more power it has pushed the Midget's top speed from 80/84 m.p.h. to a whisker under 100 m.p.h.

The one drawback with the new A-type, the increased new-model, is that the new price, plus an increase in sales tax has pushed up its price to a whopping £1256—a long jump from the under-£1,000 Midgets that were sold here a year or so ago.

Along with the new body has come a brand new chassis. It is basically as the EX-179 that ran at Bonneville (U.S.A.) in 1954 and clocked 153.69 m.p.h. for 10 miles, and 120.75 m.p.h. for 12 hours.

This chassis has a sturdy box-section. There is an integral, triangulated bulkhead at the scuttle that stiffens the front of the car. The chassis side rails are spaced wide apart at the cockpit allowing a very low floor with seats between them. It is cranked steeply over the rear axle and protrudes to the car's tail. It is very robust in the style set by the previous TD and TF/M.G.s, but carries the penalty

WHEELS, August, 1956

of the A-type's fairly high 18¼ cwt. curb weight.

There is a new engine, too, not a further improved version of the pre-war XPAG-series that powered the previous car. It is a modified B.M.C. Series-B, similar to the units in the Austin A-50, Morris Oxford, and M.G./Magnette saloon. Twin 1½" S.U. carburettors, 8.3 to 1 compression, and a special cam have raised its output to 68 b.h.p. at 5,500 r.p.m. The capacity is 1,489 c.c.

The factory states that 70 b.h.p. will push the A-type's wind-cheating shape along at 100 m.p.h. and several overseas magazines have reported around 98 m.p.h. from the 68 b.h.p. available. Our best was 94.7 m.p.h., but we'd expect more and perhaps 100 m.p.h. bettered with slightly higher tuning. The factory has issued a book listing details up to firecracker hot for those wanting to go faster.

The A-type has had a thorough testing by the factory, who ran it at Le Mans and at the Ulster T.T. races in 1955. Both runs were sound performances for a stock car, intended primarily for road use.

The factory is currently playing with a twin o.h.c. head, but it is not available on production cars; however, it may be a sign of the future. Those with long memories will recall the famous line of o.h.c. Midgets of the early 1930's.

As it stands at present, the new A-types 95 m.p.h. top speed and 20.0 sec. standing ¼-mile give it a very satisfying performance and allow it to hold or do most of today's cars.

The gearbox must be used to get the most from the car. The well-chosen ratios and the good amount of power over a wide engine range assure a driver of keeping up with the best, particularly between 50-and-80 m.p.h.

We liked using the A-type's gearbox and thought shifting easier than on the older cars. The familiar snick was missing on fast changes, and the reverse notch is sanely placed on the 1st/2nd side of the gate and avoids the old blind alley when rushing from 2nd-to-3rd.

The box is tight, has a feel similar to slamming a door with a hydraulic snubber. We'd expect the cushioned take-up to free when the car had gone about 10,000 miles. Clutch take-up is smooth, with a touch of softness. It is ideal for city and main-road driving, but hesitates fractionally on full-throttle shifts.

The new engine is extremely smooth and appears to thrive on high revs. We thought it better than those in the older cars which tended to become a little ragged or hammery when running flat.

Engine compartment gives more accessibility than on previous cars. Familiar twin-S.U.s are retained.

Snug-fitting hood (below) has neat look, excellent weatherproof roofing.

The rev. counter has a yellow caution wedge between 5,500-and-6,000 r.p.m. and a red warning wedge between 6,000 and 6,500 r.p.m. There appears no reason to take the engine over the manufacturer's 5,500 r.p.m. peaking speed, but it will go to 6,000 r.p.m. without fuss. Valve bounce appears to be well above 6,500 r.p.m.

Although the compression ratio is rather high at 8.3 to 1, the engine is remarkably docile on premium grade fuel. There is no pinking, it pulls down to 15 m.p.h. in top gear without snatch, and doesn't get hot when run flat out for long periods. Its only fault is a tendency to run on when switched off immediately after a hard burst. However, this can be stopped if the throttle is pushed wide open immediately after the ignition was turned off. (The dying revs. pull in enough mixture to quench hot spots.)

The A-type's top-gear allows a road speed of 72.7 m.p.h. at a piston speed of 2,500 ft./min., the accepted top for continuous reliable operation. This speed is high enough in the A-type to allow interesting highway cruising over long distances without over-stressing the engine.

The A-type's ride is not downright hard, but it is not soft either. It is firm, gives the car a quick motion on highway surfaces, and gives the occupants a shaking on rougher stuff.

It is not a car intended for hard use on gravel or dirt roads, but performs well enough on them. It handles nicely on smooth, loose stuff but is not meant to be slammed

Instrumentation is neater and more legible than on TF. Note novel arrangement of steering wheel spokes.

through creeks or chopped sections in trials fashion!

Open road handling is good. It is a break away from the current British practice of built-in understeer. The A-type has gone the other way with a slight, but noticeable oversteer.

This is not pronounced and at most only amounts to slight tail drag on fast corners. It permits drifting on fast, wet, highway corners; and gives the car remarkable agility on a right-angle corner or on a very twisting stretch of road.

The A-type is more sensitive than the earlier cars that responded best when driven with some force. It is light and sensitive and handles best with a steady, guiding hand.

This expressly forbids hamfisted cornering or cross-arm correction of a slide. Both are as out of place as steering a motor-cycle through a corner.

Steering pressure only will get the nose through most corners and a quarter turn is sufficient for a right-angle. And at all times the steering must be through relaxed arms and wrists otherwise body motion is transmitted to the front wheels and causes wander.

This responsive handling is a break away from the older MG's. The A-type is swift and touchy and definitely meant for good drivers. Personally, we'd have preferred the steering's sensitiveness cut to 3¼ turns from lock-to-lock instead of the present 2¾ turns.

The driving position, although low, allows good vision all around the car. As is sports-car practice, the seat cushion is only 6" off the floor causing a driver's legs to run straight out to the pedals. We liked the back support from the seat squab but would have liked more thigh support from the cushion. The seats have a good lateral grip for both driver and passenger in a fast corner.

The steering wheel, which is adjustable for length, sits low near the top of the thighs and could get in the way of a tall driver's leg movements. However, unlike the earlier MG's, there is plenty of room around the pedals for the feet and a restful position for the clutch foot.

The instruments are a great improvement over the TF's. A reasonably sized rev. counter and speedometer sit immediately in front of the X-braced steering wheel and a combined water temperature/oil-pressure gauge sits on the facia to the left of the steering wheel. These are fairly legible and quick to read. A petrol tank gauge is fitted on the passenger's side of the facia, the first on MG's since the war. However, it is disappointingly calibrated "E-½-F".

The supplementary knobs and buttons are scattered about the facia within easy hand distance from the steering wheel. The facia horn button can be tapped by a finger without the left hand leaving the steering wheel. Extras that can be fitted to the facia are a radio (with provision for a speaker) and heater.

Erecting the hood is a slowish job for one man, but it is sturdy and weather-proof when in position. The weather seal is completed by shaped side-curtains which have spring-loaded hand flaps.

Opening pulls for the doors, bonnet, and boot are located inside the car and are a mixed blessing. Personally, we'd have preferred proper door catches and a boot handle.

The engine is very assessible under the bonnet and is straightforward enough to keep maintainence bills to a minimum.

The rear locker is mostly taken up with the spare wheel and tool kit, but there is still enough room left for two grips. There is sufficient space in the door pockets and behind the seats for odds and ends that are needed on a trip. A handy map-reading light gives fair illumination at night.

The headlamps give adequate illumination for most of the car's performance, but some form of supplementary lighting would be needed if high speed cruising was contemplated at night. The lights dip well to the left and do not trouble on-coming traffic.

The brakes, which have been enlarged to 134.4 sq. in., cope with all the car's performance and need only a light pedal. We found no sign of fade and only a slight pedal loss under really hard driving.

We liked the new car's shape, speed, acceleration, and handling; but we missed the convenient tool box, and luggage space of the older cars.

But there's no doubt this new car is better and in these days of high prices, still gives the cheapest sporting motoring.

WHEELS, August, 1956

Technical Details

Specifications

MAKE:
MG/A, 2-door, 2-passenger open sports. Our test car from Mr. James Zammit, B.M.C. Sydney, N.S.W.

PRICE AND AVAILABILITY:
£1256/4/8 (incl. Sales Tax); indefinite.

ENGINE:
4-cyl. o.h.v., 73.025 x 89 m.m., capacity 1,489 c.c., comp. ratio 8.3 to 1, 68 b.h.p. at 5,500 r.p.m., 2.62 b.h.p./sq. in. piston area. Twin SU carburettors with dry-maze aircleaners; full-flow oil filter. Capacities: Radiator, 10 pt.; sump, 6½ pt.; petrol tank, 10 gal.

TRANSMISSION:
Single dry-plate clutch; 4-speed gearbox with s/m on top three ratios, operated by floor lever; open propellor shaft; hypoid final drive, ratio: 4.30 to 1. *Overall ratios:* 4.30; 5.908; 9.52; 15.652. *Top gear m.p.h.:* 17.0 at 1,000 r.p.m.; 72.7 at 2,500 ft./min. piston speed.

CHASSIS AND BODY:
Box-section frame with separate all-steel body. Unladen curb weight: 18¼ cwt.

SUSPENSION:
I.f.s. by coil and wishbones; rear by semi-elliptic leaf. Piston type shock absorbers.

BRAKES:
4-wheel hydraulic with 2-l.s. at front; mechanical linkage to rear wheels from fly-off floor lever. Friction lining area: 134.4 sq. in. *Ratio per laden ton:* 125 sq. in.

STEERING:
Rack-and-pinion; 2¾ turns from lock-to lock; turning circle 30¾ ft.

ELECTRICAL EQUIPMENT:
12-volt ignition; 36/42-watt headlamps (l.h.d.); dual horns; flashing light trafficators; 63 amp. hour battery.

WHEELS AND TYRES:
Pressed-steel disc with four-stud attachment (wire wheels with knock-off caps optional); 5.60-15 tyres. *Recommended pressures:* 18 p.s.i. front; 23 p.s.i. rear.

OVERALL DIMENSIONS:
Wheelbase, 7' 10"; track: front 3' 11½", rear: 4' 0¾"; length, 13' 0"; width, 4' 10"; height, 4' 2"; clearance, 6".

Performance

TOP SPEED:
Average of test runs .... 93.7 m.p.h.
Fastest one way .... 94.7 m.p.h.

MAXIMUM SPEED ON GEARS:
At 5,500 r.p.m. recommended maximum:
1st, 26 m.p.h.; 2nd, 42 m.p.h.; 3rd 68 m.p.h.; top, 93.5 m.p.h. *Recommended shift points:* 1st, 15 m.p.h.; 2nd, 25 m.p.h.; 3rd, 35 m.p.h. (normal driving).

MAXIMUM ENGINE PERFORMANCE:
68.5 b.h.p. at 5,300 r.p.m. (equivalent top-gear m.p.h., 90); 89.4 lb./ft. torque at 3,560 r.p.m. (equivalent top-gear m.p.h., 60.5 m.p.h.).

ACCELERATION:
Standing ¼ mile: Average, 20.0 sec.; fastest, 20.0 sec. *Acceleration through gears:* 0-10 m.p.h., 1.3 sec.; 0-20 m.p.h., 3.0 sec.; 0-30 m.p.h., 5.1 sec.; 0-40 m.p.h., 7.4 sec.; 0-50 m.p.h., 10.5 sec.; 0-60 m.p.h., 14.3 sec.; 0-70 m.p.h., 20.0 sec.; 0-80 m.p.h., 26.8 sec.; 0-90 m.p.h., 39.4 sec.
3rd and Top-gear acceleration: 10-30 m.p.h. 8.2 sec. & 9.0 sec.; 20-40 m.p.h., 7.8 sec. & 12.5 sec.; 30-50 m.p.h., 8.4 sec. & 11.9 sec.; 40-60 m.p.h., 8.4 sec. & 11.5 sec.; 50-70 m.p.h., 8.6 sec. & 11.6 sec.; 60-80 m.p.h., 14.5 sec.; 70-90 m.p.h., 19.4 sec.

BEST HILL CLIMBING:
Top gear: 1 in 11.4 at constant 43 m.p.h.
3rd gear: 1 in 7.2 at constant 38 m.p.h.
2nd gear: 1 in 4.1 at constant 28 m.p.h.
1st gear: In excess of 1 in 3 at constant 22 m.p.h.

BRAKING:
Footbrake at 30 m.p.h. in neutral, 33.0 ft. Handbrake at 30 m.p.h. in neutral, 97.0 ft. Fade, nil.

SPEEDO CALIBRATION:
10 m.p.h. (indicated) — 11 m.p.h. (actual); 20 m.p.h.—21.0 m.p.h.; 30 m.p.h.—29.5 m.p.h.; 40 m.p.h.—38.2 m.p.h.; 50 m.p.h.—48.0 m.p.h.; 60 m.p.h.—58.0 m.p.h.; 70 m.p.h.—67.5 m.p.h.; 80 m.p.h.—77.0 m.p.h.; 90 m.p.h.—85.5 m.p.h.

TEST WEIGHT:
Driver, assistant, full tank, and gear: 21½ cwt.
Distribution: front, 11½ cwt.; rear, 10 cwt.

PETROL CONSUMPTION:
Hard driving, 26.9 m.p.g.; fast highway cruising, 28.7 m.p.g. Premium grade fuel used.

*Out to take back their records, lost a year ago,
MG did the job in spades. Just to round things out,
Austin Healey raised their own marks too.*

Photos by Dan Rubin

EX 179 howls past the happy MG crew as the 500 mile record is racked up. Lines marked in salt guide cars around big circle.

EX 179: the MG that rewrote the record books

LAST August, in their share of what is probably the busiest season the salt has even seen, the British Motor Corporation established 88 new national and international records in classes F and D with MG and Austin-Healey cars.

In spite of the fact that the present BMC organization has more practical experience in record breaking than any other firm in the world, this session was a succession of frustrating incidents. First, the Austin-Healey straightaway streamliner shed a blower drive chain on a practice run. The first attempt by MG on the 12-hour record was halted after six hours by mechanical difficulty. Then, when the Austin-Healey distance car attempted the six-hour record, fuel troubles caused this run to be postponed also. In addition to these difficulties, conditions of the salt were far from good with the ever-present threat of rain.

Wendover's air-conditioned cafe is the chief gathering place for off-salt hours. Here, in only a few hours, you become aware of the tremendous amount of automotive know-how available to BMC—Captain George Eyston, who has devoted his life to record breaking; Alec Hounslow, with more than thirty years in the MG racing and experi-

Just the thing for your MGA. Always referred to as "experimental", the twin-cam MG head is rugged and simple. Tuned exhausts are fine for the flats.

mental department; Geoffrey Healey, Donald Healey's son, who has, of late, had more than a little to do with the experimental development of Austin-Healeys; Johnny Lockett, world-famous motorcycle rider who has driven Austin-Healeys and MG's so impressively at Le Mans, and some of the finest of America's driving talent in the persons of Ken Miles and Carroll Shelby.

On Sunday, August 12, the 1500 cc MG made its first attempt for the 12-hour Class F record with a target speed of something over 140 mph. Concern had been expressed over the condition of the salt which was never too stable at best. If the salt was wet, it meant pit stops to break loose the salt that would pack up in the fender wells—and pit stops cost time.

If the course deteriorated in one section, it meant that speed would have to be higher over the remainder of the course to maintain the necessary average. On this morning, Ken Miles took the opening session of three hours beginning at six a.m. Not yet too light at this hour, the only thing that seemed real was the sharp crackle of the exhaust as Miles moved off.

Three hours passed with the speed well above what was necessary to break Bettenhausen's 1955 record in the OSCA special. At a few moments after nine o'clock Johnny Lockett took over and not even the most tense or critical ear could pick up a sour note that would give warning that this engine wouldn't run forever.

As noon approached and Miles prepared to relieve Lockett, the unforeseen happened. A rear wheel bearing let go, allowing the axle to drift out of the housing. Lockett reported that he had just caught the first hint of burning rubber when the revs mounted due to the spline in the axle leaving the differential carrier.

The rear-wheel well skirt was all that had prevented the wheel and axle from leaving the housing entirely and this had been responsible for the smell of burning rubber. Six hard-earned hours of record speed were wasted as far as the twelve-hour goal was concerned and the engine that a few minutes before had only a little over six hours to run now had an additional twelve.

On Monday a new course was prepared (under the supervision of Captain Eyston) for the Austin-Healey Class D distance run of six hours scheduled for Tuesday. Tuesday did not dawn bright and clear. A few scattered drops of rain only a few moments before the six o'clock start seemed to promise more rain before the day was over. In fact, the grey veil of a rainstorm obscured the horizon to the east.

At six o'clock on the dot the car started its run. The

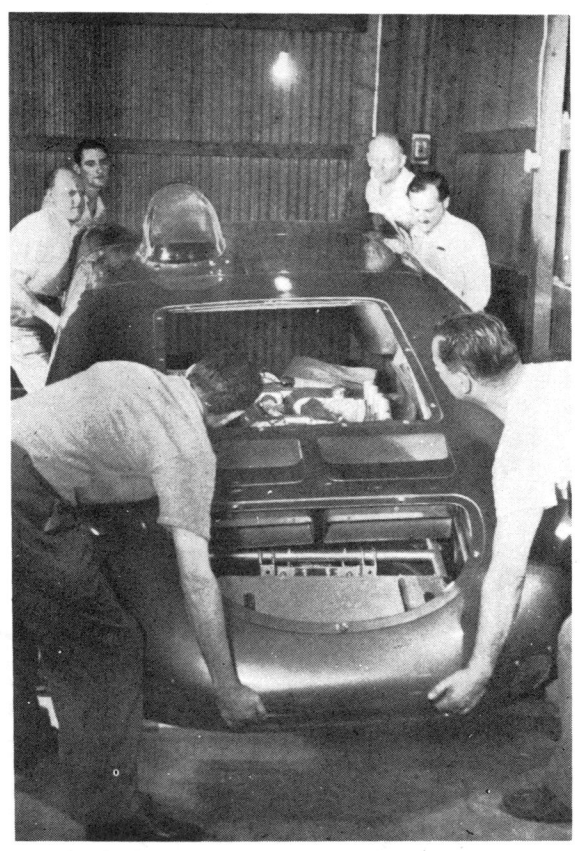

The chassis is ready and the crew lowers the self-supporting body in place. Twin ducts carry air up and away from the oil and water radiators.

Oil cooler connections are potential trouble sources, and get last-minute checking here. Low front radiators require reservoirs at cowl.

EX 179

75 NEW RECORDS FOR MG

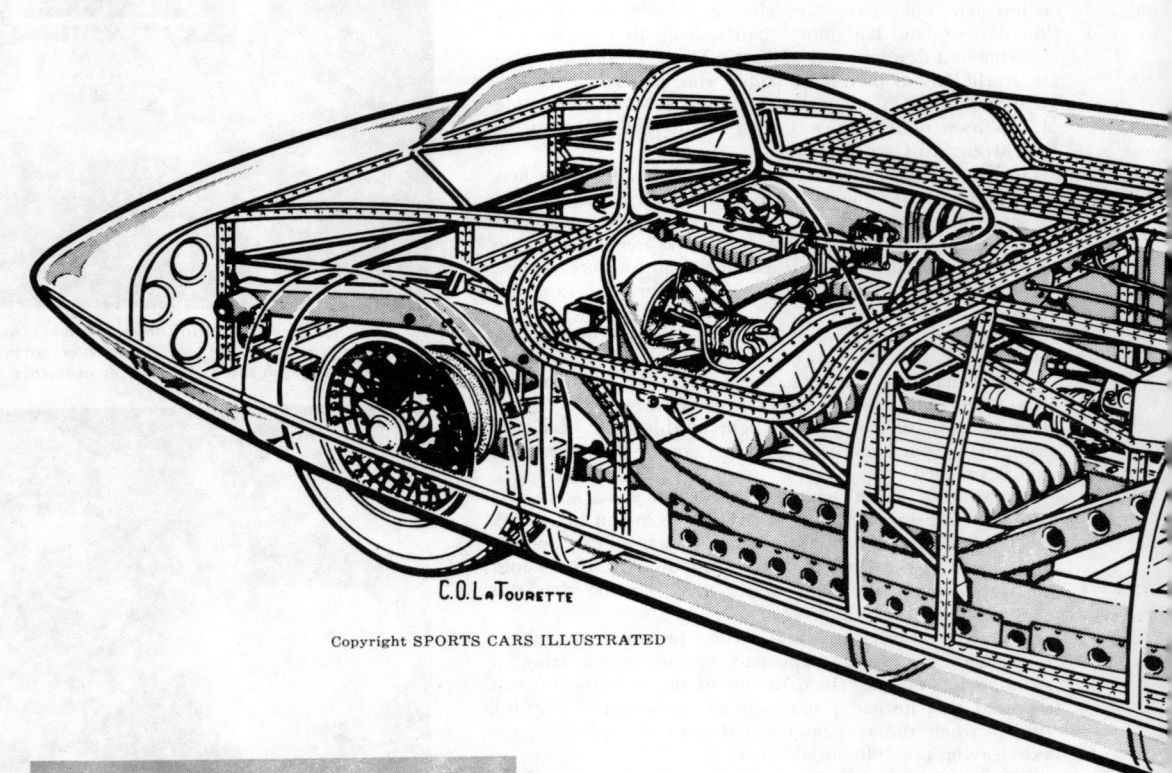

Copyright SPORTS CARS ILLUSTRATED

MG RECORD CAR SPECIFICATIONS

BODY: Overall length .... 188 7/8 inches
  Overall height to top of
    driver's cowl .... 40 5/8 inches
  Overall height to top of scuttle .. 31 5/16 inches
  Overall width .... 63 1/2 inches

WHEELBASE: 95 inches
  Front tread .... 47 3/8 inches
  Rear tread .... 48 1/2 inches

FUEL TANK: 30 1/2 gallons

FUEL RESERVE WARNING: 4 1/2 gallons

TAP RESERVE: 2 1/2 gallons

DRY WEIGHT:
  no oil, water or fuel .... Total: 1538 pounds
                            Front: 893 pounds
                            Rear: 648 pounds
  with driver, oil, water
  and fuel (30 gallons) .... Total: 1964 pounds
                            Front: 1077 pounds
                            Rear: 887 pounds

*MG CLASS F SPEED RECORDS
August 18, 1956

DISTANCE	INTERNATIONAL STANDING	NATIONAL STANDING	NATIONAL FLYING
25 K	*	142.38	155.04
25 M	*	146.90	155.02
50 K	148.39	148.39	155.05
50 M	150.89	150.89	155.13
75 K	*	150.39	155.11
75 M	*	152.39	155.24
100 K	151.75	151.75	155.24
100 M	153.12	153.12	155.34
200 K	153.66	153.66	155.43
200 M	154.30	154.30	*
250 K	*	153.99	155.38
250 M	*	*	*
300 K	*	154.22	155.39
300 M	*	142.96	143.46
400 K	*	*	*
400 M	*	143.12	143.51
500 K	142.97	142.97	143.45
500 M	141.17	141.17	141.47
1000 K	141.66	141.66	141.91
1000 M	141.46	141.46	141.61
2000 K	141.86	141.86	141.97

INTERNATIONAL

Time	Distance	MPH
1 hr.	153.98	153.98
3 hr.	429.2614	143.09
6 hr.	853.6681	142.28
12 hr.	1700.5653	141.71

AMERICAN STANDING

Time	Distance	MPH
1 hr.	153.98	153.98
3 hr.	429.2614	143.09
6 hr.	853.6681	142.28
12 hr.	1700.5653	141.71

AMERICAN FLYING

Time	Distance	MPH
1 hr.	155.38	155.38
3 hr.	425.9703	141.99
6 hr.	855.5774	142.60
12 hr.	1700.5653	141.81

*All records subject to confirmation by FIA and United States Auto Club. August 18, 1956: Ten-mile flying start International Class F — average two-way straight course driven by Johnny Lockett at 170.15 mph.

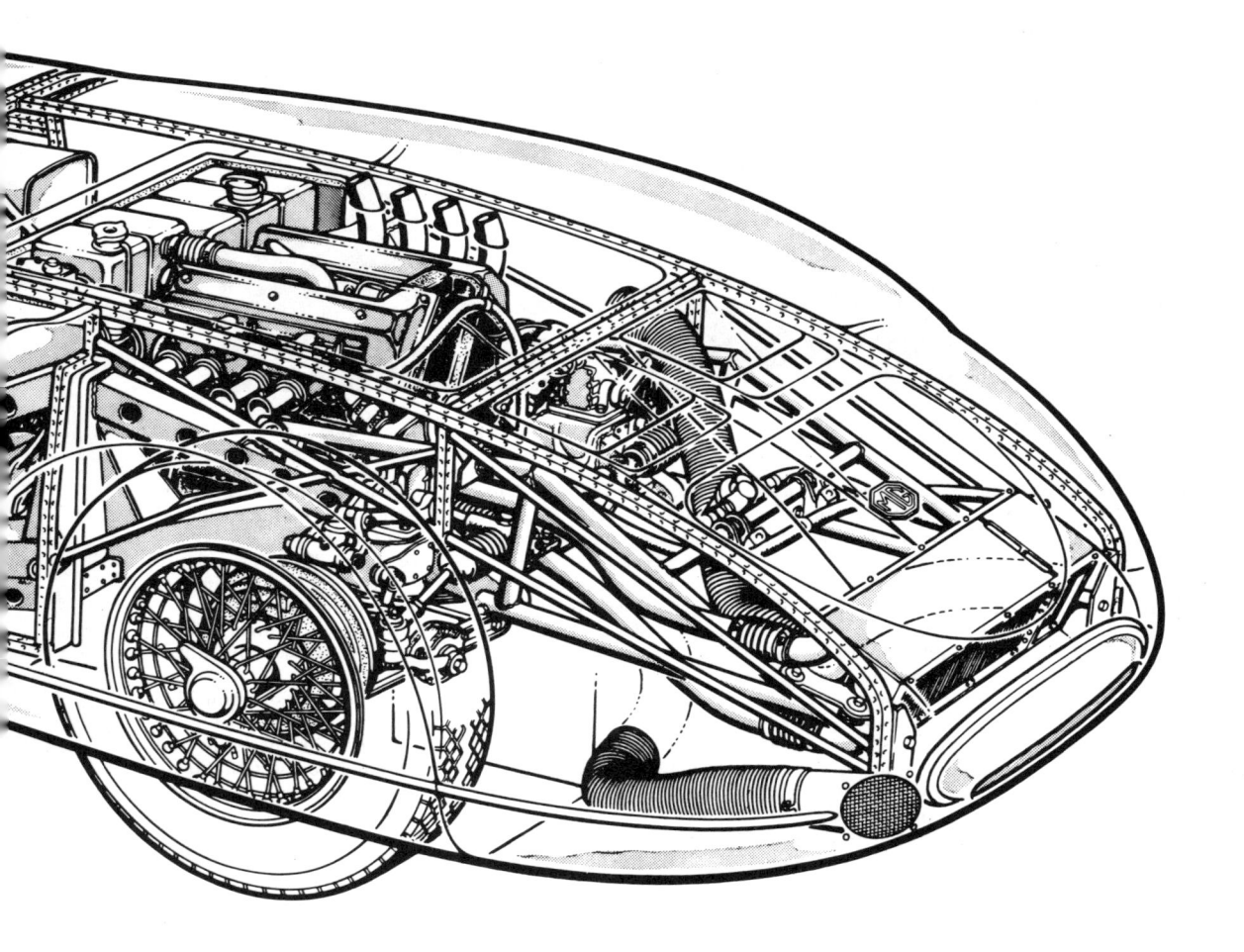

Cam drive is two-stage, by gear and chain. Large-capacity water pump has engine-speed belt drive, and special ignition angles to right.

Shroud-type cam followers are used in the MG record engine, which also carries 40 mm Webers. Throttle linkage is simple.

Construction of cam drive is still a tool-room job. Special water circulation system has tiny block holes, keeps cylinders warm and head cool.

Adjustable Andrex shocks are added to lever types. Axle oil radiator is competition must.

exhaust note of the new six-cylindered engine was noticeably different from that of the MG four that had run two days before. Even with this difference, at the start of the second lap an untrained ear could detect that all was not well in the six-cylindered department. Another lap brought no improvement in its health and the run was called off. After a considerable amount of feverish pit acitivity, the run was started again, but for the second time was called off. Difficulties with the fuel, or fuel system were described as the cause of the trouble and the run was postponed until Friday.

Wednesday saw the 1500 cc, Class F, MG back on the salt for an early start. This time nothing untoward happened and all Class F records up to 12 hours were taken at an impressive speed, with improvement over Sunday's record.

Four days later this car, with the sprint engine, established a new ten-mile flying start record of 170.15 mph under the piloting of Johnny Lockett. This year, MG earned everything they got and a lot of credit should go to Hounslow and his crew for the preparation and to the two drivers, Miles and Lockett, who apparently never made a mistake and were so proud of the car that you'd think they had built it.

The chassis and body of the MG are not new although the engine, which will be discussed later, is of new, experimental design. Incidentally, this engine received no more than a tappet check between the end of its six-hour run and the beginning of the second run of 12 hours.

Externally, this car bears more than a little resemblance to the record car used by Goldie Gardner and it is a further development of the EX 179 that set the 12-hour Class F records in 1954. At that time, it used a well souped 1500 cc rocker-box engine. This time there was a considerable difference in the engine type.

The chassis consists of two 14-gauge box-section side members that are actually prototype MGA units. The main firewall bulkhead is built in unit with the frame and triangulated with additional perforated box sections to insure rigidity and adequate frame stiffening. A tubular extension to these main side members is used to carry the radiator and oil cooler.

The rear axle layout is a straightforward Hotchkiss drive. It is attached to conventionally shackled semi-elliptic springs by U-bolts. These springs are heavily taped and four shock absorbers are fitted. Straps are also provided to snub rebound. A small oil cooler is fitted to the rear of the differential casing. It's interesting that this is located in such a manner that air currents from up-and-down movement of the rear axle are used instead of any direct flow from the outside. Straight-cut gears are used for ring and pinion

Standard MG suspension and brake components are used in EX 179, as below. Andrex shock is mounted as in old TD-Mark II, on lower arm.

Cockpit of Austin-Healey streamliner on lower right is fitted out for both safety and comfort. Manifold pressure gauge reads to 30 psi.

The Healey saltbuster, at right, is a fearsome sight as it poises for run. Shape is clean, but flat flanks may be sensitive to side winds.

instead of the more normal spiral or hypoid types. Although noisier, straight gears do simplify bearing and lubrication problems.

Front crossmembers similar to the TF MG carry standard suspension components of coil springs and "A" frames. Steering is by MG rack and pinion. In addition to the hydraulic shock absorber incorporated in the upper "A" frame, another of the friction type is used. Standard hydraulically-operated MG brakes are fitted to all four wheels. The body framework, which is made up of small round tubes and perforated square section tubes attaches to the chasssis at 14 points.

In order to avoid complications in removing the body, all the instruments are carried on an instrument panel attached to the main chassis frame. Attached to and removable with the body are the air ducts that carry air from small intakes in the front to the cockpit and the carburetors.

The body shell is made of 18 gauge half-hard aluminum and is fully streamlined. A plastic bubble covering the driver's side of the cockpit is incorporated with the head faring. This helps insure that wind resistance and drag are near the absolute minimum. The driver's position in the cockpit is on the right hand side. This is a change from the original EX 179 made necessary by the new engine installation. With the experimental engine the stubby exhaust pipes project from a hole in the left-hand side of the engine compartment and it was necessary to get the driver out of the exhaust stream. The left-hand side of the cockpit is completely taken up by the 34.5 gallon fuel tank. As would be expected with a distance record car, the driver's accommodations are comfortable. Not much space is wasted however—the steering wheel even being of a special shape to clear the driver's legs.

The bellypan that completely encloses the underside is made of 14 gauge half-hard aluminum and serves as a cockpit floor.

The four-cylindered engine, never mentioned without the addition of the word, "experimental", seems to be pretty rugged and reliable. The block and crankshaft are the production B type units; the bore and stroke being 73.025 mm x 89 mm (2.87 x 3.5 inches). The block is very short and rigid and the practice of extending the crankcase casting well below the center line of the crankshaft contributes a great deal towards bottom-half strength.

The three main bearing crankshaft is a steel forging with main bearings of two inches diameter and the crankpin journals, 1.875 inch. It has balance weights on each side of the center main bearing and one on the inner side

Record Runs —

of both the front and rear mains. The H section connecting rods are tempered steel forgings of the same quality steel as used in the crankshaft. They're of slightly thicker section than the production connecting rods. This extra thickness is probably gained by slightly blocking open the dies during forging.

Following the practice of keeping the engine as short as possible, the connecting rod journals are offset in relation to the cylinder bores. Both the end connecting rods, number one and four cylinders, are offset outwards and the two inner rods are offset towards the center of the engine. The big ends of the connecting rods are split diagonally to allow each piston and connecting rod to be removed by pushing it upwards out of its bore. Forged aluminum three ring pistons establish a compression ratio of 9.2/1.

The light alloy two-cam head carries each camshaft in three plain bearings. The intake and exhaust valves are disposed at an included angle of 80 degrees. Ferrous valve seat inserts are used. The valves are actuated directly from the camshaft through cups that are fitted over the coil springs and valve clearances are effected by means of an adjustable pad contained in the end of the cup.

The cam tower is separate from the head and bolts up to the block in the same manner as the stock timing cover. Primary cam drive is by means of gears from the crankshaft. This cuts down the secondary drive, which is by chain to the camshafts, to half-engine speed. Reducing both the length and the linear speed of the chain is an important consideration in a high revving engine.

The Lucas magneto is driven by means of a skew gear from the front of the crankshaft. Two dual throat Webers supply the carburetion and are fitted with ram tubes that pick up the air from a balance box. One hundred bhp is claimed for this engine used for the straightaway runs red-lined at 6000 rpm. The sprint engine used for the straightaway runs is identical to the distance engine, with the exception of a higher compression ratio necessary to run on an alcohol mixture.

Whereas MG used one car with different engines for their distance and straightaway records, Austin-Healey brought two complete cars. Since both these cars have basically the same engines of rumored prototype design, it would be well to discuss them here before taking a look at the cars. Of six-cylinder, pushrod-operated overhead valve layout, the block and cylinder head are cast iron.

The bore and stroke of 79.4 mm x 89 mm (3.125 inches x 3.5 inches) give a capacity of 2639 cc's (161.61 cubic inches) and a piston area of 46.2 sq. inches. The head is of Weslake design and has the now famous heart-shape combustion chamber. The intake ports are siamesed as are the exhaust ports for the inner four cylinders (two-three and four-five). The engine of the distance car uses a compression ratio of 9.3/1 and runs on premium fuel.

Carburetion is by three dual throat Webers. The exhaust system utilizes split headers that collect the exhaust gases from cylinders one, two, three and from cylinders four, five, six. This engine develops 150 bhp at 5000 rpm on gasoline.

In the streamlined straightaway engine the Godfrey K-300 supercharger is chain driven from the front of the crankshaft. A single SU carburetor is used. Three hundred bhp at 5000 rpm is claimed for this engine on a specially blended alcohol fuel.

The Austin-Healey distance car, which on Friday after its earlier difficulty, set new six-hour records at over 145 mph, is quite interesting in that it is fully road-equipped. It has a standard electrical system including headlights and tail-lights. Dunlop disc brakes operate on all four wheels. The passenger's compartment, although covered with an aluminum tonneau cover for the record runs, is actually suitable for carrying a passenger.

The car claims a basically Austin-Healey 100 chassis and body, although the body has been extensively modified at the nose and tail to improve the streamlining. The long nose is reminiscent of the Mondial Ferrari and the lengthened, streamlined tail carries a large faired headrest. Dunlop knock-off disc wheels and 6.50 x 16 Dunlop racing tires are used. The gearbox is a standard four-speed Austin-Healey unit without overdrive. A final-drive ratio of 2.7/1 representing a speed of 31.75 mph per 1000 rpm or about 160 mph at 5000 rpm was fitted.

The straightaway car uses an Austin-Healey 100 chassis with standard wheelbase, ground clearance, and track dimensions. The body follows the usual streamlining practice and the cockpit is cowled to enclose the driver. It is equipped with Dunlop disc brakes, knock-off disc wheels, and Dunlop racing tires. A David Brown four-speed gearbox, incorporating overdrive, used in conjunction with a final drive ratio of 2.466/1 gives a speed of 43.50 mph per thousand rpm in top.

On August 21st this car was driven by Donald Healey to a two-way average of 200.9 mph for the flying mile. This was not a record attempt, a certified run of substantially over 200 mph being desired by Donald Healey.

All in all this was a record session that BMC can be proud of. The MG succeeded in establishing an impressive number of records at fantastic speed for a 1500 cc engine. The Austin-Healey distance car came through very well by establishing the records needed to put the marque in possession of every record from one mile to 3000 miles.

April 24, 1957

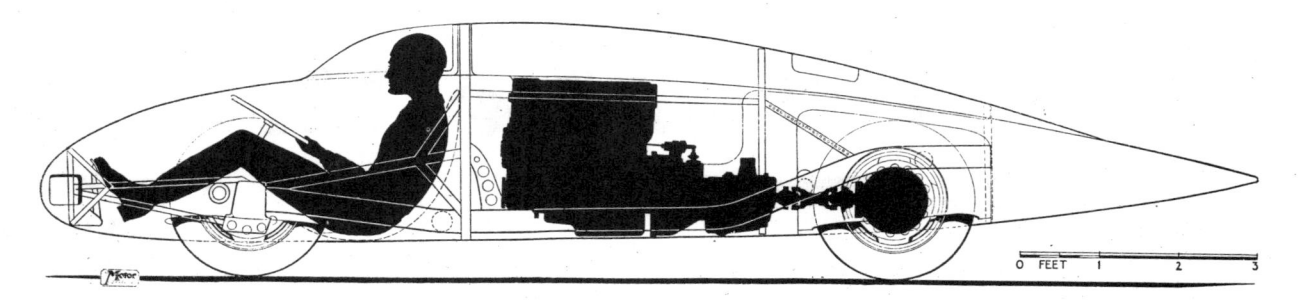

Target: 4 Miles a Minute

Exclusive Details of New 1½-litre M.G. for Record Attempts by Stirling Moss

THE exclusive scale drawing at the head of this page shows the striking layout and proportions of the entirely new M.G. record car which—as first revealed in *The Motor* last week—is being built at Abingdon for attacks on International Class F (1,500 c.c.) records on the Bonneville Salt Flats, Utah, in August with Stirling Moss at the wheel.

Compared with its very famous forerunner, the M.G. EX 135, in which Lieut.-Col. A. T. Goldie Gardner broke a whole series of International records between 1938 and 1952, the layout of the new car, EX 181, has been completely reversed. The driver now sits in a semi-reclining position in front, Napier-Railton fashion, with the engine amidships.

This has, of course, been done primarily in the interests of streamlining, which yields even bigger dividends than increases in engine power at the speeds envisaged owing to the cube law governing wind resistance and speed. Extensive experiments in a high-speed aircraft wind-tunnel have been carried out with scale models, as a result of which minor but important modifications to the initial design have been effected.

One photograph on this page is of an earlier scale model (which has been superimposed on a Utah background to give an impression of how EX 181 will appear in action) and the other shows the final full-scale wooden jig which will be used for forming the body. Comparison of the two shows how the fairing behind the driver's head has been carried through almost to the extremity of the flat tail, whilst the frontal area has been reduced slightly by allowing incipient bulges for front-wheel clearance.

In this connection, it is noteworthy that the car is severely crab tracked to enable the classical rain-drop shape to be approached as closely as possible without the disturbing effect of prominent bulges to accommodate the rear wheels.

At the moment, full technical details cannot be revealed, but it can be disclosed that the front suspension is of the M.G. A type, that the centrally-located engine is a specially-developed supercharged unit based on the B.M.C. B-type engine, from which the drive is by a very short propeller shaft to a de Dion-type rear axle layout; and that the main frame is tubular.

Target speed for EX 181 is 240 m.p.h. plus, which represents an increase over the existing fastest-ever Class F record (Goldie Gardner's 204.2 m.p.h. for the kilometre with the M.G. EX 135 at Desau in 1939) of some 40 m.p.h.

H. C. HASTINGS

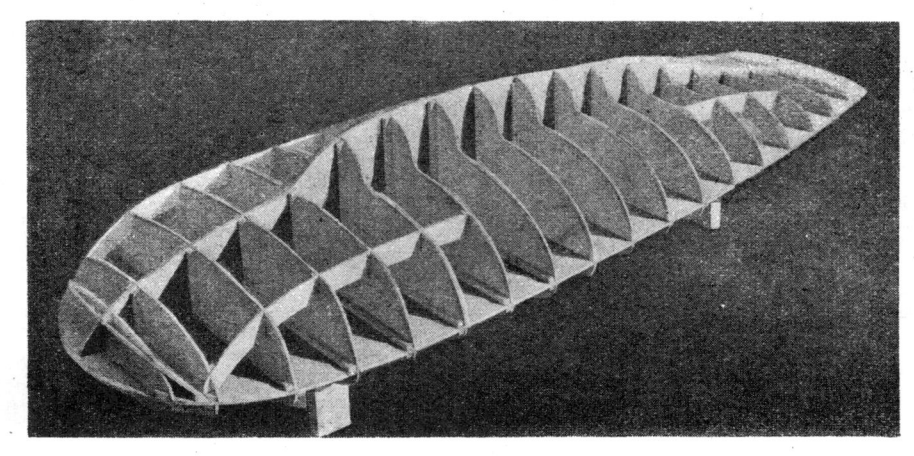

JIGGERY-POKERY.—Wind cheating has been carried to a fine art on the new M.G. record car. Above is a photograph (superimposed on a Utah background) of a scale model used for initial wind tunnel tests and (left) the full-scale wooden jig on which the final modified body will be formed (see text). Overall height is only 39 in.

AUTOSPORT, AUGUST 30, 1957

EX. 181–The M.G. Re

A Theo Page dra
charged M.G. with
last week broke
Class F records,
the flying kilo
at 245.64 m.p.h.

L AST Friday, on the Bonneville Salt Flats, Utah, Stirling Moss set up five new International Class F speed records in the 1½-litre supercharged M.G. experimental streamliner EX.181. The records taken were as follows:—
  1 kilometre: 245.64 m.p.h.
  1 mile: 245.11 m.p.h.
  5 kilometres: 243.08 m.p.h.
  5 miles: 235.69 m.p.h.
  10 kilometres: 224.70 m.p.h.

The M.G. Car Company made its first official—and successful—attempt on an International Class record in December, 1930, when the car officially designated EX.120, and popularly known as the Magic Midget, covered 50 miles at Montlhéry in the hands of Capt. G. E. T. Eyston at a speed of 86 m.p.h.

In June, 1931, in what was then popularly known as the "baby" car class (with engines up to 750 c.c.), M.G. were the first car of this size to break a record at 100 m.p.h., this over five miles, again at Montlhéry and again in the hands of Capt. Eyston. In December, 1932, 120 m.p.h. was achieved, and in October, 1946, Lt.-Col. "Goldie" Gardner drove his 750 c.c. M.G. record-breaker EX.135 at Jabbeke at 159 m.p.h.

In the next larger capacity class, International Class G (up to 1,100 c.c.), Capt. Eyston exceeded 120 m.p.h. for the first time in October, 1934, and Col. Gardner covered one mile at 187 m.p.h. in November, 1938. In January of the following year Col. Gardner's M.G. was the first car in Class G to exceed 200 m.p.h.

On this occasion too the engine was enlarged slightly, subsequent to the Class G record, so as to bring it into the next larger class, Class F (up to 1,500 c.c.), and with this the car reached 203 m.p.h. over the Flying Mile on the Autobahn at Dessau in Germany in 1939.

This last record has remained unbroken ever since, and all this time the next milestone—four miles a minute—has beckoned, with, just beyond it, the 250 m.p.h. mark. The target of this new attempt was the former objective—240 m.p.h.—and this has been substantially beaten.

The engine of the record car is basically a B.M.C. "B" series power unit—such as is currently used, in varying stages of tune, in the Austin A55. M.G. Magnette and M.G.A, Morris Oxford, Nash Metropolitan and Wolseley 1500 and 15/50. A twin overhead camshaft

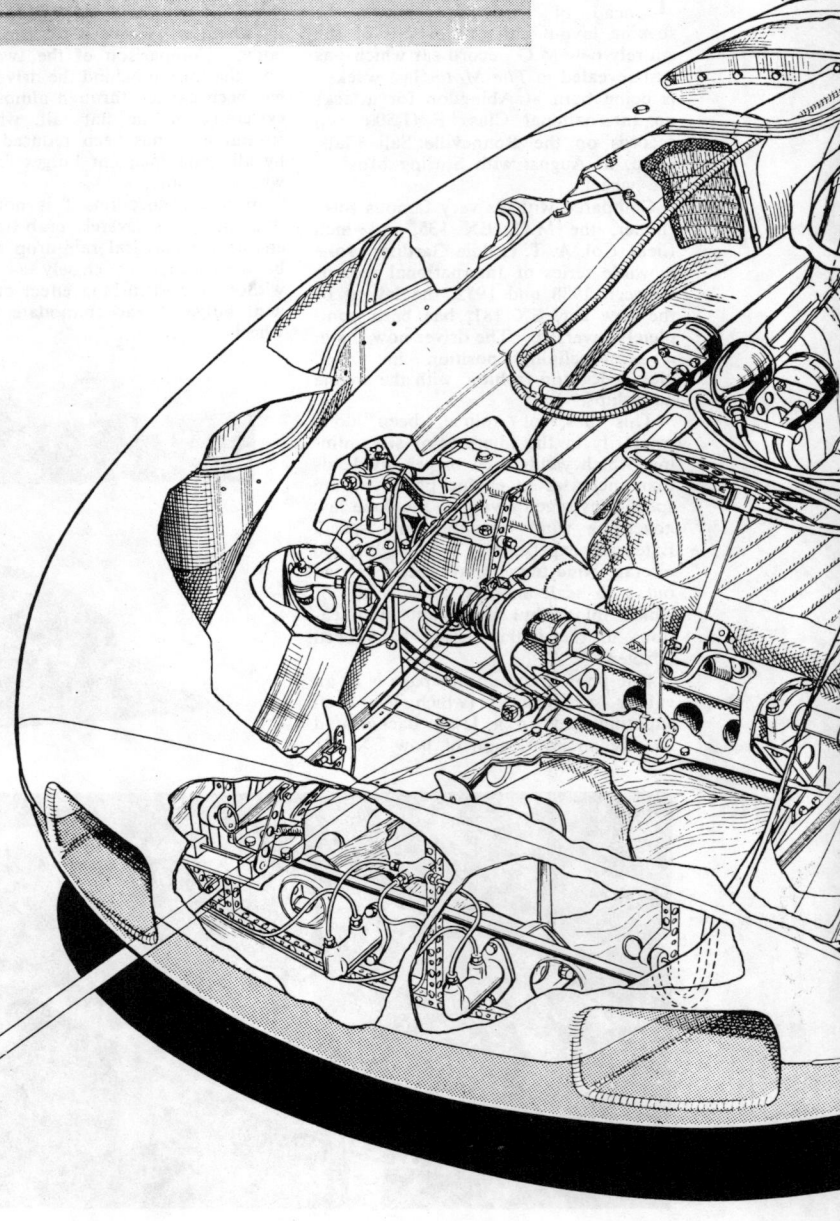

AUTOSPORT, AUGUST 30, 1957

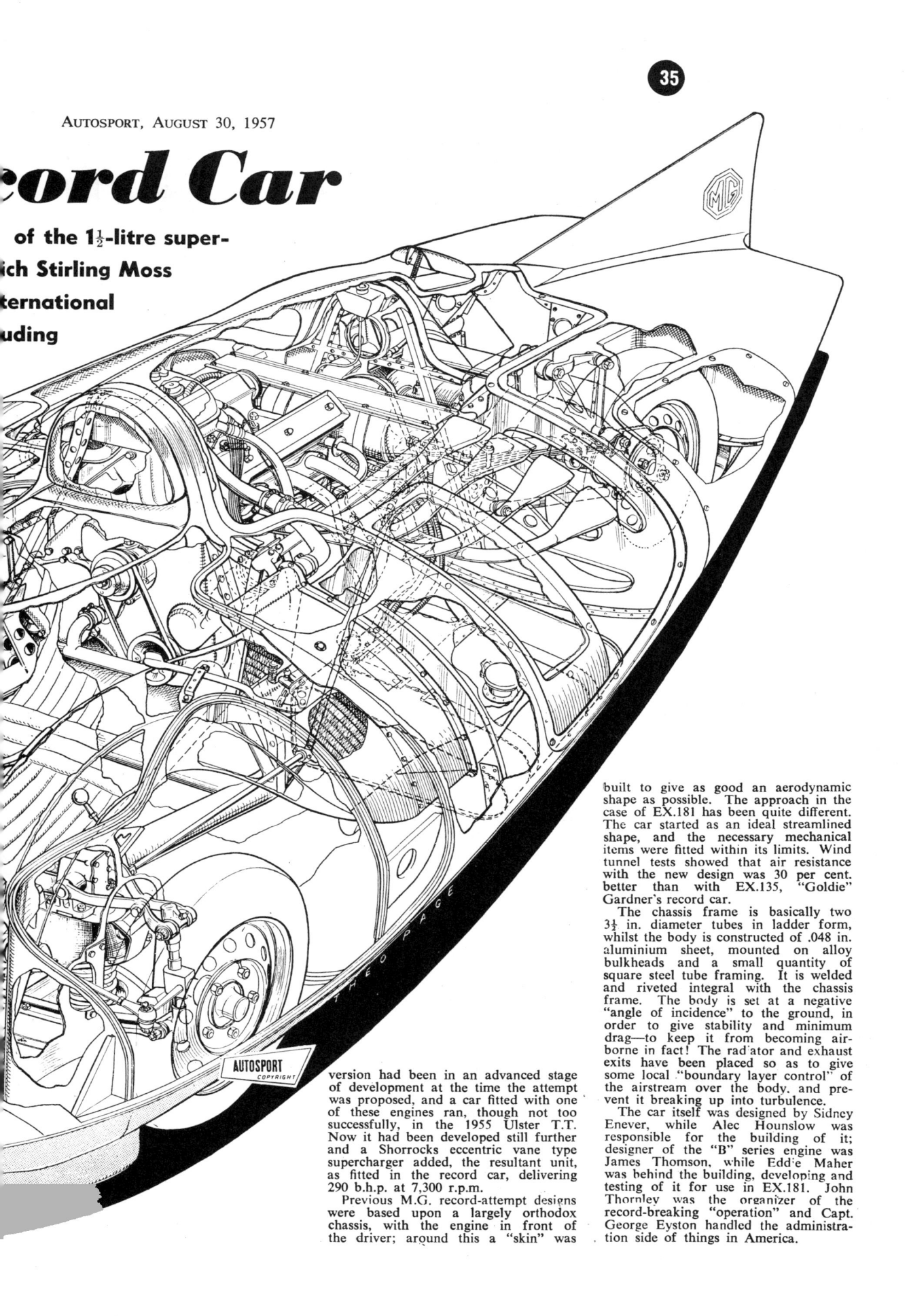

cord Car

of the 1½-litre super-
ich Stirling Moss
ternational
uding

built to give as good an aerodynamic shape as possible. The approach in the case of EX.181 has been quite different. The car started as an ideal streamlined shape, and the necessary mechanical items were fitted within its limits. Wind tunnel tests showed that air resistance with the new design was 30 per cent. better than with EX.135, "Goldie" Gardner's record car.

The chassis frame is basically two 3¼ in. diameter tubes in ladder form, whilst the body is constructed of .048 in. aluminium sheet, mounted on alloy bulkheads and a small quantity of square steel tube framing. It is welded and riveted integral with the chassis frame. The body is set at a negative "angle of incidence" to the ground, in order to give stability and minimum drag—to keep it from becoming airborne in fact! The radiator and exhaust exits have been placed so as to give some local "boundary layer control" of the airstream over the body, and prevent it breaking up into turbulence.

version had been in an advanced stage of development at the time the attempt was proposed, and a car fitted with one of these engines ran, though not too successfully, in the 1955 Ulster T.T. Now it had been developed still further and a Shorrocks eccentric vane type supercharger added, the resultant unit, as fitted in the record car, delivering 290 b.h.p. at 7,300 r.p.m.

Previous M.G. record-attempt designs were based upon a largely orthodox chassis, with the engine in front of the driver; around this a "skin" was

The car itself was designed by Sidney Enever, while Alec Hounslow was responsible for the building of it; designer of the "B" series engine was James Thomson, while Eddie Maher was behind the building, developing and testing of it for use in EX.181. John Thornley was the organizer of the record-breaking "operation" and Capt. George Eyston handled the administration side of things in America.

EX 181

EX181 undergoing proving trials at an airfield in this country. The rear fins provide stability, their dimensions having been arrived at after a series of wind tunnel tests with models

Stirling Moss Establishes Five New International Class F Records for M.G.

A VERY successful M.G. outing to Utah was concluded last Friday when Stirling Moss set up five new Flying Start International Records in Class F (1,101 c.c. to 1,500 c.c.) driving the latest of a long line of record cars from Abingdon, EX181. The new records, subject to ratification, broke the old ones by over 40 m.p.h. They already stood to the credit of M.G. and had been established by Lt.-Col. A. T. G. Gardner in the earlier car EX135; the first three had been set up on the Dessau autobahn in 1939 and the last two at Utah in 1952. The new records, with the old ones in brackets, are: 1 kilometre 245.64 m.p.h. (204.3), 1 mile 245.11 m.p.h. (203.9), 5 kilometres 243.08 m.p.h. (200.6), 5 miles 235.69 m.p.h. (189.5), 10 kilometres 224.70 m.p.h. (182.8).

There was some anxiety in the M.G. camp following the successful attempts on the Class G records which were concluded on 17 August, when heavy rain flooded the hard Utah salt flats and made them quite unusable for high speeds. As it was not possible to retain the use of the flats after Saturday, 24 August, Moss in consultation with Capt. George Eyston—who was in administrative control of the project—decided to make an attempt on Friday evening, because there was always the possibility of some further rain. Conditions were not ideal, but the main target of 4 miles per minute was achieved and it would seem to have made the records safe for some time to come, particularly with the knowledge that in better conditions the car in its present trim is capable of even higher speeds.

IN THEIR APPROACH to this latest series of record attempts M.G. had a great deal of successful background material upon which to draw, but it was obvious that if the target of raising the existing record by such a large amount was to be achieved, then a completely new approach to the layout of the car would be necessary. The previous cars had been substantially orthodox sports cars in layout, with the exception of the body. To reduce frontal area and drag the vertical height had been compressed to little more than the overall diameter of the tyres and the body was provided with an aerofoil form to cheat drag.

Wind tunnel tests, and figures recorded in previous record attempts with EX135 and EX179, proved that for such a layout their shape was very nearly the best obtainable; but to propel either of them at speeds in excess of four miles per minute would require at least 350 h.p. This was considered to be beyond the capabilities of an engine which at that time had never been supercharged. There were other engines available, but it was considered that the maximum return in prestige would be obtained with an engine of 1½ litres capacity. Such an engine existed in the form of a B.M.C. B series power unit which had been fitted with a twin overhead camshaft cylinder head and which ran in the T.T. at Dundrod in 1955, when it was installed in one of the works M.G. As. In its unsupercharged form one of these engines had been previously installed in EX179 and achieved 170 m.p.h. over ten miles in 1956.

After preliminary investigations of several theoretical layouts, one of flattened torpedo form (which is a substantial aerofoil in plan and elevation) was selected. It is set at a negative angle of incidence to the road to provide the desired balance of stability and minimum drag. This arrangement provides a slight downward pressure at the front and a negative pressure at the rear of the car. Wind tunnel tests showed that although the frontal area of EX181 was only 10 per cent less than EX179, the wind resistance was over 30 per cent less. With rolling resistance and under-body drag taken into account it was estimated that the new car required approximately 20 per cent less overall power than its predecessors for an equivalent speed.

This shape of body required some changes in the disposition of components and driver so that it is no longer an orthodox layout. The engine is amidships, partly to increase traction on the rear wheels, and the driver sits in a semi-reclining position in front of it. The front track is full width slightly forward of the broadest part of the body. At the rear the track is very narrow to place the wheels within the overall width of the body and in such a position that their height does not require panel bulges.

To achieve this layout the tyres (only 24in outside diameter, specially developed by Dunlop) are the smallest ever used for such speeds. To reduce pumping losses each runs in a separate box which has a detachable cover so that wheel changes can be made easily. Two 3½in diameter steel tubes form the main chassis side members. Front suspension is similar to the M.G. A with wishbones, coil springs and lever arm hydraulic dampers. Steering is rack and pinion.

A Riley R.M.A. gear box with special running gear is bolted directly to the engine and transmits the drive through a short shaft to the chassis-mounted final drive unit which, in effect, is the nose piece of a normal axle minus the differential. The rear axle is of the de Dion type controlled by parallel radius arms, with a quarter-elliptic leaf spring at each side. As braking is not a primary requirement there is a single disc mounted inboard on the off side of the final drive unit.

Personnel behind the creation: (left to right) J. Thompson, chief engineer, J. Goffin, and E. Maher, chief experimental engineer, of Morris Engines, Ltd., S. Enever, chief engineer, A. Hounslow in car, with John Thornley, director and general manager, talking to him, G. Iley, assistant general manager, and T. Mitchell, responsible for detail design, all of M.G.

30 AUGUST 1957

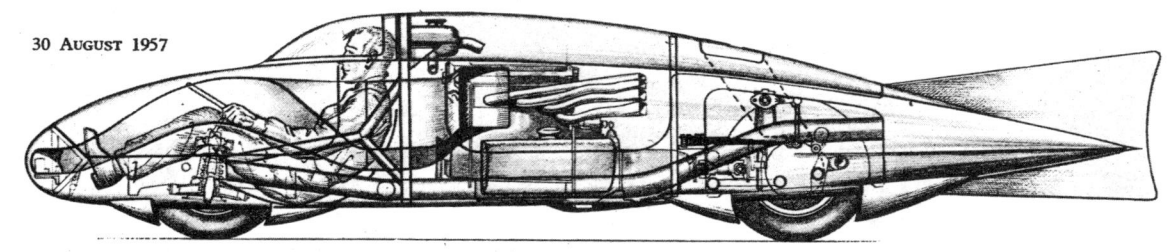

The layout of EX181 is quite different from previous M.G. record cars. In this latest of a long line of successful record breakers the driver is seated in a reclining position ahead of the engine. The rear wheels are severely crab tracked

Below: The power unit ready for installation at Abingdon after development by Morris Engines, Ltd., Coventry. The Shorrocks supercharger is fed from two S.U. carburettors and driven by spur gears from the front of the crankshaft

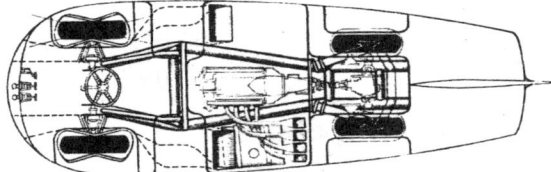

The primary gears are lubricated by jets from the main oil pressure system. A duplex roller chain with adjustable jockey sprocket and two dampers completes the camshaft drive

The car was constructed at Abingdon to the designs of Sydney Enever, chief engineer of M.G., and the engine was built at Morris Engines, Ltd., Coventry, under the direction of their chief engineer, Jimmy Thompson.

As stated, there was already in existence a twin overhead camshaft engine adapted to the B.M.C. B series power unit, which in its unsupercharged form had developed 110 b.h.p. at 7,000 r.p.m. It had a two-stage chain drive to the camshafts and the valve layout followed the design used on the Wolseley Six-Eighty and Six-Ninety engines. The tappets were screwed into the large diameter hollow valve stems and adjusted by means of special spanners.

When the decision was taken to supercharge this engine it became necessary to incorporate certain detailed modifications. These were limited because although detailed changes to the cylinder block could be made, the basic dimensions, such as bore, stroke, face heights from the crankshaft centre line, and shaft centres were to be maintained so that, should the design have future production applications, tooling changes would be small.

A target of 280 b.h.p. was set and the work of providing the supercharger was undertaken by Shorrock Superchargers, Ltd. At that time they had a new unit under development which was calculated to provide a boost pressure of 30 lb per sq in at approximately 7,000 r.p.m. In fact, as installed on the engine, it delivered 32 lb per sq in at this speed. To provide the

Left: Details of the combustion chamber and valve gear. The valves have an included angle of 80deg equally spaced on either side of the vertical centre line. Right: Covers are removed on the exhaust side to show the camshaft and valve gear. Piston type tappets operate in a sleeve formed integral with the valve guides. The exhaust valve stems are sodium cooled and plugged at the head end

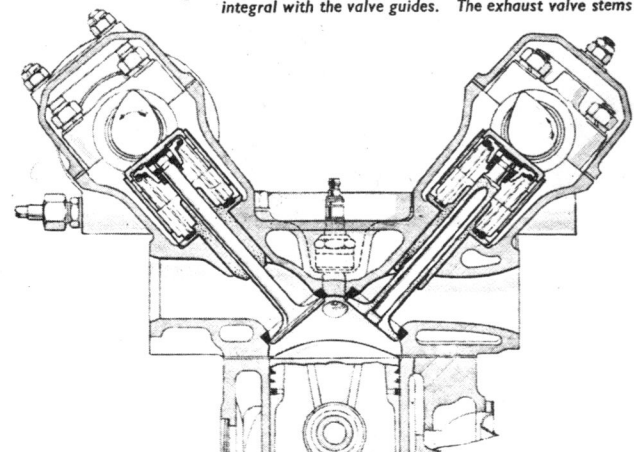

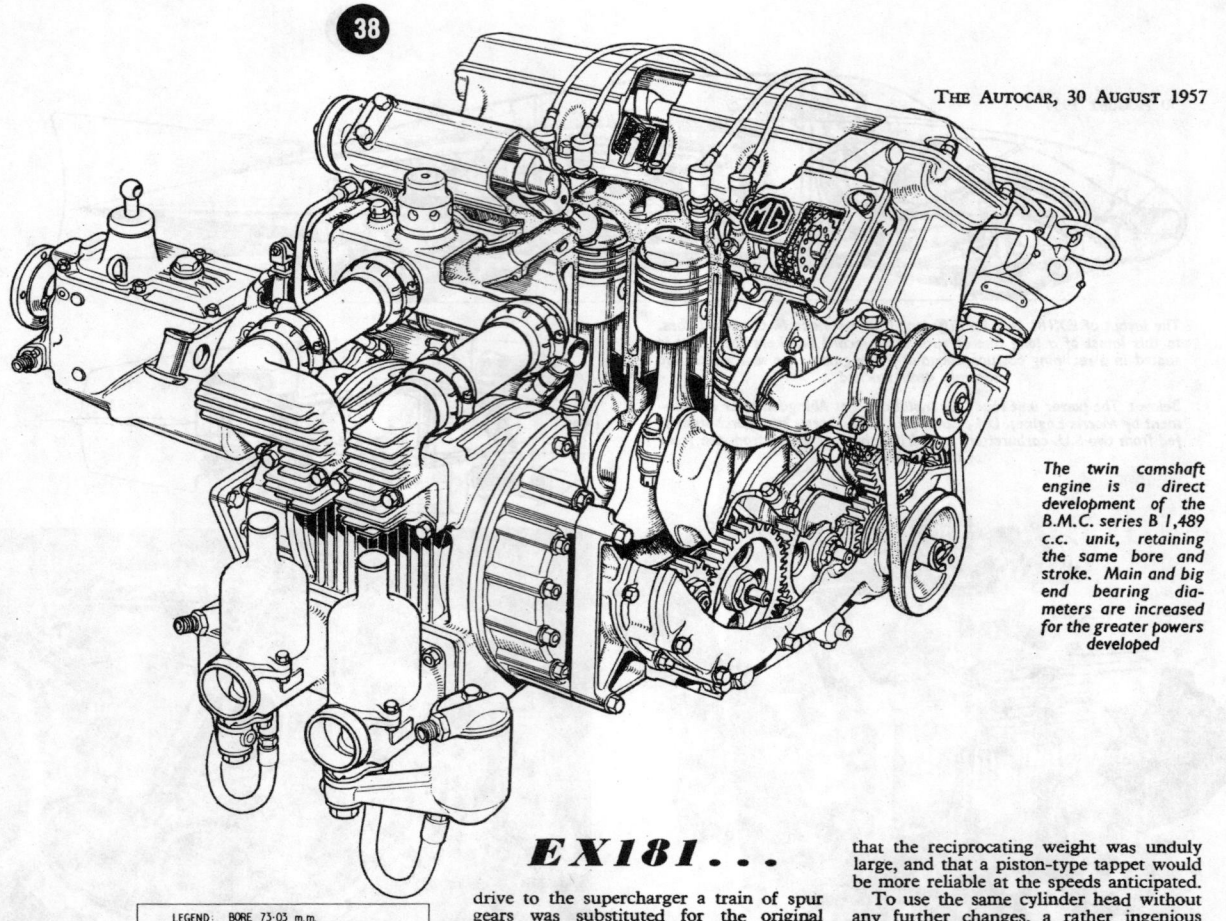

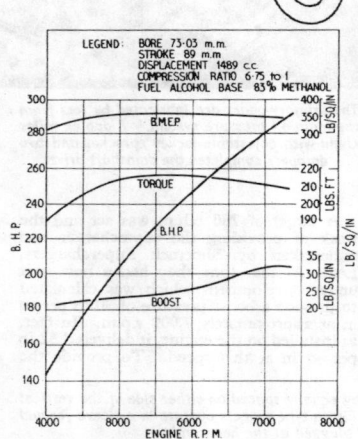

The twin camshaft engine is a direct development of the B.M.C. series B 1,489 c.c. unit, retaining the same bore and stroke. Main and big end bearing diameters are increased for the greater powers developed

EX181...

Power curves of the twin camshaft engine in its supercharged form. Peak b.m.e.p. is 352 lb per sq in running on alcohol fuel

drive to the supercharger a train of spur gears was substituted for the original primary chain in the camshaft drive. This arrangement retained the same centre for the side camshaft of the production engine, which was replaced by a jack shaft to drive the oil pump and rev counter. Alternative ratios of 0.9, 1.0 and 1.1 were provided for the supercharger. Development showed the first to be successful and the other two were not used.

Detail changes to the engine included a stiffer crank with increased bearing sizes —the mains going up from 2in to 2⅜in diameter, with steel bearing caps; and the big ends were increased from 1⅞in to 2¹⁄₁₆in; this latter change also enabled stiffer connecting rods to be used.

There is no direct water passage between the cylinder head and block, each having separate feeds. This arrangement eliminated the use of a normal gasket, and the fire joint between head and block is a sheet steel ring formed with a single pressed corrugation, which is compressed when the head is tightened.

The other major change was to the valve gear, for in the original design it was felt that the reciprocating weight was unduly large, and that a piston-type tappet would be more reliable at the speeds anticipated.

To use the same cylinder head without any further changes, a rather ingenious method was adopted. The valve guides, made in copper-bronze, were extended to surround the springs and form an individual tappet block for each valve. Clearance is adjusted by the usual varying thickness of biscuit between tappet and valve stem. The tappets are of case-hardened steel; originally the cam face was chrome plated, but the chrome was subject to considerable scuffing and was removed. This—and early trouble with piston crown burning until the shape was modified to remove local heat concentration—were the only major problems encountered during development.

As installed in the car the engine delivers 290 b.h.p. at 7,300 r.p.m. and the second unit delivers 300 b.h.p. at the same speed.

In achieving its target the car has proved the soundness of the original conception and the joint efforts of Abingdon and Coventry should enhance further the sales of B.M.C. products in America, particularly of the M.G. A, which is sold in larger numbers than any other sports car.

SPECIFICATION

ENGINE

No. of cylinders	4 in line
Bore and stroke	73.025 × 89 mm (2.875 by 3.5in)
Displacement	1,489 c.c. (90.88 cu in), supercharged
Valve position	Overhead, twin camshafts
Compression ratio	6.75 to 1
Max. b.h.p.	290 at 7,300 r.p.m.
Max. b.m.e.p.	352 lb sq in at 5,600 r.p.m.
Max. torque	216 lb ft at 5,600 r.p.m.
Carburettor	Twin S.U., 2⅛in diam.
Supercharger	Shorrock eccentric vane type
Fuel tank capacity	7.9 Imperial gallons
Cooling system	Two aluminium, aircraft-type radiators

TRANSMISSION

Clutch	Triple plate, Borg and Beck 7¼in diam.
Gear box	Four speeds, no reverse
Gear box ratios	4th: 1.0, 3rd, 1.48; 2nd, 2.29; 1st, 3.395.
final drive	Spiral bevel, ratio 1.94 to 1, or 1.825 to 1.

CHASSIS

Brakes	Girling disc; inboard mounting (one on rear wheels only)
Suspension: front	Parallel wishbones and coil springs
rear	De Dion axle with quarter-elliptic leaf springs
Dampers	Lever-arm piston type; hydraulic
Wheels	15in steel disc; bolt-on
Tyre size	15 by 4.5 (24 in O.D.) Dunlop special
Steering	Rack and pinion

DIMENSIONS

Wheelbase	8ft
Track	Front, 3ft 6in; Rear, 2ft 6¾in
Overall length	15ft 1¼in
Overall width	5ft 4¼in
Overall height	To top of driver's cowl, 3ft 2¼in. To top of body shell, 2ft 6¾in
Dry weight	14 cwt, 3 qr, 3 lb

PERFORMANCE DATA

Top gear m.p.h. at 1,000 r.p.m.	36.2 with 1.94 axle ratio
	38.6 with 1.825 axle ratio
Torque lb ft per cu in engine capacity	2.35
Weight distribution (dry)	F. 49.7 per cent
	R. 50.3 per cent

Pit Stop at Sebring

The new MGA Sports Coupe

a class of its own...

Your first mile behind the wheel of an MGA will show you why these rugged little speedsters won the Sebring 12 Hour Grand Prix Team Trophy and placed first and second in class. And one quick look tells you the MGA is tops in smartness too. The sleek, low lines of both the Sports Roadster and its new "twin", the all-weather Sports Coupe, are a mark of distinction everywhere you go.

Ask your dealer to tell you about the 12 months' warranty on parts and the surprisingly modest cost of an MGA.

Safety MG fast

Represented in the United States by

hambro AUTOMOTIVE CORPORATION • 27 West 57th Street, New York 19, New York

A product of The British Motor Corporation, Ltd. • Sold and serviced by a nationwide network of distributors and dealers.

ROAD TEST

IT IS SAFE to assume that when Morris Garages, Ltd., began experimenting and successfully competing with specially tuned versions of Morris Oxfords in 1923, the experimenters little dreamed that the end product of their labors would be the MG Car Company, currently one of the mainstays of the sprawling British Motor Corporation. For those early pioneers spawned a giant by British standards—a giant which has produced some of the finest and most exciting low and medium-priced sports cars in the world.

From the days when the MG Company was formed in 1929 to produce the now fabled "M" type midgets until the present, an enormous amount of development on the race courses and highways of the world has assured customers of quality merchandise. And now the evolvement of the envelope-bodied "A" roadster into a roll-up window coupe version seems destined to introduce MG to many more persons. These people would be sports car enthusiasts if the price were right and if the car offered American-type weather protection. MG's coupe fulfills both these requirements and more, as we shall see.

Essentially, the coupe is mechanically identical to the roadster. The only differences in the two cars are in actual body areas relating to the top, and in richer appearing, more attractive interior trim in the coupe. MG's stylists have handled the difficult task of turning a roadster into a true coupe in excellent fashion. The finished product is esthetically pleasing, as well as highly functional.

PERFORMANCE

Max. speed in gears, 1st 32 mph, 2nd 53 mph, 3rd 79 mph, top 101.2 mph. Acceleration: from standing start to 45 mph 7.4 secs., to 60 12.3 secs., ¼-mile 19.0 secs., and 73.6 mph, 30-50 mph 4.9 secs., 45-60 5.4 secs., 50-80 15.7 secs. Fuel consumption average for 815 miles 24.2 mpg.

SPECIFICATIONS

ENGINE: 4-cyl. ohv. Bore 2.875 in. Stroke 3.5 in. Stroke/bore ratio 1.22:1. Compression ratio 8.3:1. Displacement 90.88 cu. in. Advertised bhp 72 @ 5500 rpm. Bhp per cu. in. .79. Piston speed @ max. bhp 3208.3 ft. per min. Max bmep 128.4 psi. Max torque 77.4 lbs-ft. @ 3500 rpm.

TRANSMISSION: Hydraulically operated single dry plate Borg & Beck clutch, 8 ins. dia. 4 forward speeds, top 3 synchronized. Overall ratios: 15.652, 9.52, 5.908, 4.3 Rear axle ratio 4.3:1. (Optional 4.55:1.)

CHASSIS: Box section frame, tubular cross member at transmission. 5.60 x 15 tires. Lockheed hydraulic brakes, front—2 leading shoe, rear—leading and trailing shoe, 10 ins. dia. x 1.75 ins. wide. Rack and pinion steering gear, with 28-ft. turning circle, 2.75 turns lock-to-lock.

DIMENSIONS: Wheelbase 94.0 in., overall length 156.0 in., overall height 50.0 in., overall width 57.3 in., minimum clearance 6.0 in., front tread 47.9 in., rear tread 48.8 in., weight 2120 lbs. (50.5% front, 49.5% rear), weight/bhp ratio 29.5:1.

PRICES (F.O.B. port of entry): $2750.

ACCESSORIES: H.M.V. radio $65, heater and defroster $65, whitewall tires $45, adjustable steering $17.50, wire wheels $135, luggage rack $49.95, windshield washer $17.50.

ASBESTOS shields carburetors from exhaust manifold in compact engine installation. Unusual door handles resemble hold-down bracket for top.

MOTOR TREND/SEPTEMBER 1957

Unique vertical door handles, which reminded several observers of hold-down clamps for a removable hard-top, wrap-around windshield and rear windows, and the small but efficient no-draft windwings give the coupe all the essential creature comfort features of many big cars.

Open the rear-hinged bonnet and the first impression is that here is an engine compartment with no waste space where nearly everything is readily accessible. The four-cylinder, ohv engine, which cranks out a healthy 72 bhp at 5500 rpm from its just under one and one-half liters of displacement, is neatly positioned, facilitating changing of plugs, checking of oil and other essential service items. The two SU carburetors, adjacent to the exhaust manifold, are separated from it by an asbestos covered shield. The hydraulic master cylinder for brakes and clutch sits up high on the left-hand side of the firewall.

The coupe's body follows the same high quality finish as the roadster's. Bumpers offer considerable protection in comparison to most sports cars. Body panels are ripple-free and fit well. The grille is vulnerable and "A" owners are keeping several independent grille guard firms in business.

The trunk compartment is admittedly small with the flat-mounted spare tire taking up a great deal of room. Luggage stowing requires ingenuity. As usual, MG includes a complete set of tools which strap to the bulkhead above the spare. The trunk is opened by an inside handle behind the driver's seat.

Design of the coupe's chassis has been carried out with rigidity and strength in mind. What was a strong frame for the roadster becomes even stronger with the addition of a steel top. Sweeping the frame out at the mid-section allows for a low seating position between the rails rather than above them.

Surprisingly enough, front suspension is identical with previous TD and TF models, utilizing coil springs with unequal length wishbones and hydraulic shocks. At the rear, two longitudinal half-elliptic springs with double piston hydraulic shocks complete the conventional layout.

MG A COUPE

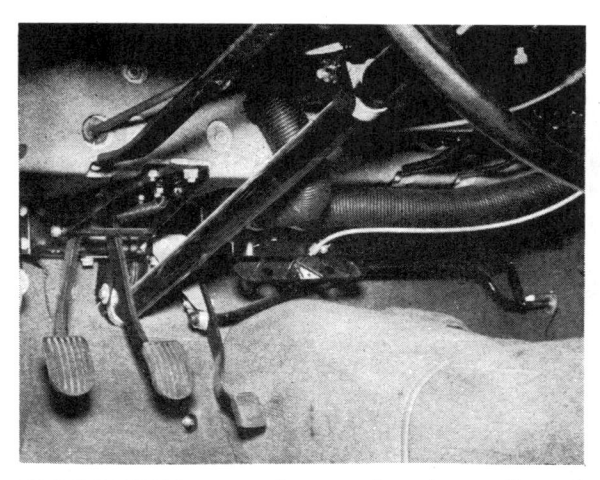

PENDANT PEDALS are too close together, do not offer sufficient room. Throttle-to-brake foot pivot is easy.

STORAGE SPACE behind leather-covered bucket seats is negligible, is reduced by spare projecting from trunk.

INTERIOR DETAIL is more luxurious than roadster, instrument layout unchanged. Short throw shift is ideal.

TRUNK CAPACITY is limited, requires ingenuity to slow luggage. External rack is available as optional extra.

PHOTOS BY BOB D'OLIVO

An MT Research Report by Allan Stockton

Roadholding, however, is anything but conventional. Feather-light rack and pinion steering responds to the slightest pressure and recovers naturally. Body roll in hard corners is very slight and the car can be powered through at speeds which should be confined to the race course. There is no tendency to swap ends, and with a little practice, a skillful driver can put the "A" into a four-wheel drift, recovering by easing up on the throttle and correcting with the wheel. A contributing factor to good handling is excellent weight distribution—very near 50-50 with a full tank of Mobilgas in the test car.

A high speed run across several miles of undulating desert highway proved conclusively that the coupe doesn't wallow coming out of dips and feels secure on most any road condition. In effect, cruising speed is limited only by traffic conditions and good sense. The car feels as solid and safe at our indicated top speed of 102 mph as it does at an easy 60. Incidentally, maximum speeds in gears as listed in the performance chart are speeds at which valve bounce was audible.

Safe high speed is a function of good brakes. The coupe's pass with flying colors. Fade *can* be induced but it takes an inordinate number of panic stops. For all practical purposes, the brakes are fade-, swerve- and grab-free. During a genuine emergency stop, I had occasion to lock all four wheels laying down two absolutely straight black strips of rubber.

Ride can be classed as comfortable sports car, firm but not rough. There is just enough road feel to let you know what sort of surface you're on. Personally, I feel that the bucket-type seats in the coupe do not offer enough support in the small of the back for long trips but this is a minor annoyance in relation to the plus factors of the car.

As with many sports cars, entry can be tricky. The doors open only about 70 degrees and from the front of the seat to the front of the door cutout is approximately ten inches—not any too much legroom. Duck your head and you're in—headroom is good once you're inside. Passenger stretch-out space is adequate and a center mounted armrest is a nice touch. An armrest on the driver's door would be appreciated, as would an ashtray.

The car starts quickly, hot or cold, and we found it unnecessary to use the choke.

A short, tunnel-mounted gear lever is within easy reach of the wheel and does its job in a precise, crisp fashion. This is one of the major joys of driving the coupe. Vision is good with no blind spots. A quick look through the wheel brings the easy-reading speedometer and tach into ready view. The oil pressure-water temperature gauge is "out in right field" and a number of drivers who race their MG's have reversed this instrument with the gas gauge, making for a simpler quick view of this vital information. A foam rubber strip at the top of the leather-covered recessed dash is an added safety feature.

The roll-up windows, which will probably sell as many coupes as any single feature, crank all the way down at a rapid one and one-half turns. At 50 mph with windows down, there is a distinct drumming, but opening the windwings stops it.

With production currently set at some 200 coupes per month, the MG Car Company should have little difficulty in selling a good portion of them in the U.S. Residents of colder climes can no longer claim that MG's are only for outdoor types. This neat little package is liable to make an enthusiast out of Grandma.

MOTOR TREND/SEPTEMBER 1957

Safety Faster

by John Christy & Dennis May

DURING THE COURSE of the production run of the T series MG Midgets the men of Abingdon faced up to the fact that wherever MGs are run there'll be those who want more. They'll want MGs, to be sure, but what they want is *more* MG than the dealer is prepared to handle as a matter of course. Something else that was realized was that such people aren't always filled to the brim with bravado when it comes to experimentation — they'd rather bite off a small piece, savor it, then — maybe — come back for more. Thus the stage-by-stage form of soup-cooking that invariably is the form followed by Abingdon's sages.

Now — and at long last — the MG racing department, largely in the person of Mr. Sidney Enever, has counterparted the instructions that came with the late lamented XPAG and XPEG engines powering the T series. These formulae for fun have been released exclusively to SCI in advance of publication date of the factory book. The directions that follow omit nothing the factory included and indeed add some touches not in the book. One section, in fact, does *not* hold benefit of official blessing but more about that later. In the following, wherever special parts are needed they are listed by number as well as description.

One other point of note is that these directions apply to any BMC B-Type engine no matter what the application. The only proviso being that these directions begin with the engine in late series MGA tune — the others must be brought to that stage first insofar as equipment goes, with exception of course of the special parts. These can be purchased directly and substituted for the original items without concern for the MGA stage of tune.

The basic material is a rugged piece of work indeed and the bare block has, in the latest record car, held together while poking out just a tad less than 290 hairy-legged horses with a supercharger boost of 30 psi. Consequently what follows is not likely to shorten the life of the engine if properly done and properly stoked when installed. However, in their always-cautious way the makers have pointed out that super-tuning of this nature is grounds to void the new-car guarantee.

The major difference between the MGA and previous models is that the entire souping process can be accomplished with parts which can be ordered directly out of the MG parts catalogue by any dealer or distributor. As with earlier models the operation can be conducted in easy stages, four in number with two sub-options for special circumstances. Each of these has been thoroughly tested by the MG racing department under the personal direction of Sidney Enever. Each option was built, run on the dynamometer, torn down and then rebuilt and re-tested. Mr. Enever is not one for half-measures where his customers are concerned.

Before getting to the actual stages, for the benefit of those who would prefer to stay within the SCCA and CSCC specifications for production racing, let's cover just what can be done legitimately to get the best out of the engine. Since this engine is a mass production item, it is to be expected that variations in output will occur in the over-the-counter item. About the only

MGA head with gasket shows why combustion chambers should not be carved. Any reshaping would affect gasket sealing. At right, diagram shows the point at which radius must be ground to avoid hot spot and to allow fitting of special pistons.

Misalignment is present in any production engine. Exhaust ports may be cut out to align with gasket. Intake ports are ground as shown in diagram (below).

thing that the racing clubs will allow is the smoothing off of these inequalities but you'll be surprised at the amount of difference such smoothing will make. The first point to tackle is the breathing. It should be, but often isn't, understood that intake and exhaust manifolds are seldom accurately matched to the ports involved. Either they are offset slightly or, due to casting tolerances, different in size between manifold and port. Competition rules specifically state that these may be matched up — just take care that the matching doesn't require a quarter-inch of "alignment" grinding. This, however, is only the first step. Tolerances in mass production also allow for variances in several other departments to points far different from those the design engineers intended.

Take valve springs for example. There are two per valve on late models. The outer spring should have an installed pressure of 50 lbs. and a compressed pressure of 105 lbs. The inner coils should have an installed rating of 30 lbs. and a compressed reading of 60. On newly run-in engines variances have been found running all the way down to compressed readings of 80 for outer units and 45 for the inner springs. Since the designed valve-bounce point is 6000 rpm with the full pressure operating it can readily be seen what such lowered pressures can do to top engine speed and valve life.

If you are competition bent and the production category is your *forte*, it would be best when having a 5000 mile valve-lap done to have the springs checked as well. If any are found wanting as to length and pressure it would be advisable to hie oneself down to the nearest MG parts emporium and check out a handful of springs, selecting carefully only those that produce top pressure. This procedure has been known to allow engine speeds higher even than the recommended 6000 rpm with no sign of valve float. Carrying this business one step further you can also grab a fistful of pushrods and find a set in which each piece is the same weight as the other seven. With the cast cams now being used variations in timing aren't as frequent as they once were but if you're really serious about this production competition it might pay to check and if necessary give the stick a touch or two to bring it dead on. Each of these little things helps — not much individually, true, but in the aggregate they can amount to the difference between also-ran and prize-taking.

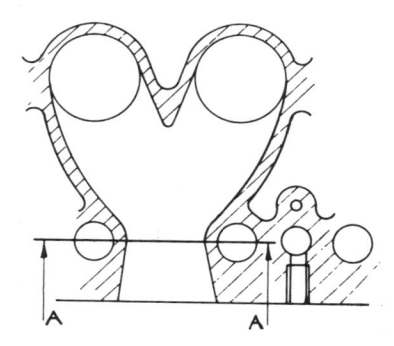

A template should be made to the above diagram to indicate proper port size.

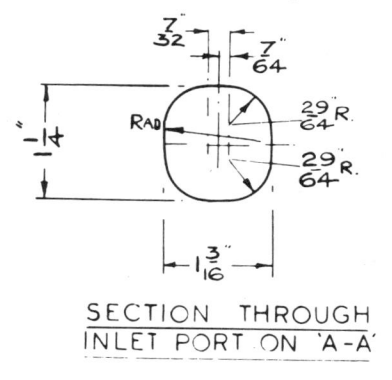

SECTION THROUGH INLET PORT ON 'A-A'

The one thing not pointed out above but vital in the foregoing and an absolute must in what is to follow if the last penny's worth is to be extracted from each operation, is static and dynamic balancing of crank, rods, pistons and the flywheel-clutch assembly. A four-barrel engine is not the smoothest mechanism in the world and anything that can be done to make it smoother will pay off both in power and in service life with a plus factor in increased useable rpm. If you cannot have this done in your area or the size of the working budget won't allow it, you can do without and the engine won't come unsoldered but the man who *has* had it done will, all other factors being equal, do you when the chips are down in competition.

Now let's get down to the business at hand — that of extracting more horses than originally intended for this particular stable.

STAGE 1

This operation is the mildest form of hop-up but is basic to all the steps that follow. Some of it has been done on late engines from #17152 at least as far as general dimensions are concerned but even these can stand a touch up with the polishing stone to take care of production tolerances. It is designed to take partial care of the prime gripe of every knowledgeable speedcrafter who has ever taken a good long look at this engine — the complaint that the intake ports are not only siamesed but that each port is smaller in area than just one of the two intake valves it serves.

Inspection of the ports of the MGA head will show that they are tapered inward for a distance of about one inch at which point they widen out into a large chamber feeding two intake valves. The point at which the port is narrowest is the point of attack. This narrow throat can be enlarged to 1-3/16 inches in width and 1¼ inches in height. You can probably increase each dimension by 1/32 if you are braver than Dick Tracy but take care! The reason for the narrowing is that two water passages run vertically alongside each intake port — you're not drilling wells, so be conservative with the grinder. Radii of the corners of this passage are also large, being 29/64 of an inch at each corner. The factory suggests that a metal template be cut to those dimensions and attached to a long bolt. In this way the port can be ground to a point just allowing this template to pass through.

The dimensions given for the template apply to the area at line AA. Care is essential here since water passages are placed very close to narrow portion.

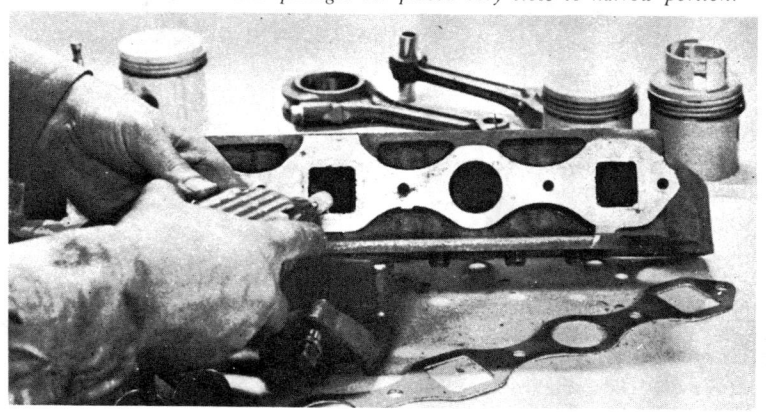

B-Type BMC head is a sturdy, solid item and quite free of tendency to warp. Valve gear is equally rugged and unbreakable although valve springs are short.

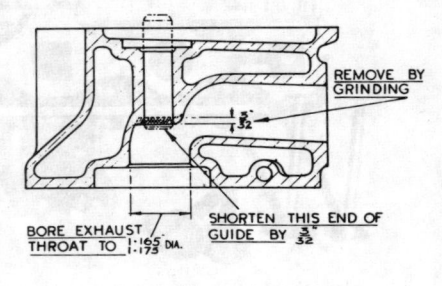

Exhaust throat and valve guide should be altered on early engines as shown.

Lightly grind and polish the entire manifold and port system or all that you can reach but be careful not to alter the shape of the passages other than described above. Do not change the shape of the valve throats except on engines prior to #4045 in which the exhaust throat should be bored to 1.175 of an inch and the valve guide shortened 3/32 of an inch. Later engines already have this modification.

The heart shaped combustion chamber is the final point of attack in this stage insofar as chopping metal goes except for a final matching of ports to manifolds. You will note that the combustion chamber peaks between the valves and in many engines this may come to a sharp point while in others it will be somewhat rounded. If this is as far as you intend to go with the engine grind this to a 1/8 of an inch radius. If you intend to go further or there is a possibility you might succumb later to power-hunger, grind it to a 3/16-inch radius — this last to make room for a piece of equipment about which we will talk later. The chambers are already pretty well finished by the factory but they can stand a careful polishing, being careful not to grind metal away since all you can do is lose compression thereby. Any enlargement around the walls might also impair the gas seal.

Finally, if you live sufficiently close to sea level you can try the slightly richer SU carburetor needles marked C.C. The net result will give 75 bhp at 5750 rpm and if all the balancing and selective fitting of valve gear described earlier is done you might just pick up a bit more. The factory says 75, though, and they own the dyno.

STAGE 2

This one is strictly for low and mid range rpm charge, and in fact does less than nothing at the top end except for cutting back peak speed. The idea is to gain two or three bhp at the middle range (around 3000 rpm) and it might be useful for dragging, gymkhanas and stump-pulling contests. The effect is achieved by a switch to a cam with some of the characteristics of a tractor layout, at least on paper, coupled with the procedures as outlined in Stage 1 and a new ignition.

The cam is listed as part #1.H. 603 (which is *not* a competition part number) and its characteristics are as follows: Intake opens 5° BTDC and closes 45° ABDC, exhaust opens 40° BBDC and closes 10° ATDC. Valve lift is .322 of an inch and tappet setting is .015 of an inch.

The ignition recommended by the factory for this dragster is part #1.H. 1036. The standard igniter can be used if finances prohibit but the replacement item has an advance curve tailored to go with the 603 cam and the valve characteristics it produces. Setting on this ignition is four degrees before top dead center.

For additional urge this stage has a sub-option guaranteed to make other MGA owners extremely envious at least until you hit about 4500 rpm. You will note that unlike the recommendations for the XPAG and XPEG engines no head milling has been mentioned. The reason is simple — it's not necessary. The stock MGA pistons come with concave heads with a depression cavity of 4.85 cc. The factory has very obligingly built a set of pistons without this cavity and installation of these will raise the compression ratio from the stock 8.3 to 1 up to a respectable 9 to 1. These are listed as part #1.H. 1078 and come complete with rings and wristpins.

This stage if carried through to the compression boost should give about the same top end as the stock product and at the same time give a healthy boot in the back at normal cruising speeds — ideal for the stop-light grand prix. It will also make things very tough for tech inspectors at production races, particularly those held on tight courses.

STAGE 3

This one is so simple that it barely needs mentioning, aiming only to produce more

MGA valves are meaty items that can take a good amount of cutting down.

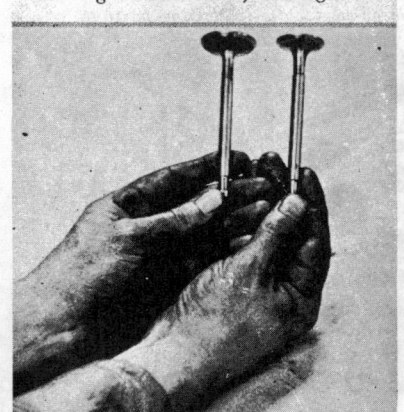

Here is where care pays off. Select all valve gear so that each component matches its counterpart in weight, using the lightest pieces as criteria.

power at the top end and make for a general improvement over the whole range. First, carry out the Stage 1 directions as described. Then install the flat-top I.H. 1078 pistons as described in the latter part of Stage 2. This requires premium fuel and a switch to Champion N-5 plugs for street use and N-3 plugs for racing or for continuous high speed driving. Use the standard igniter and keep the setting at four degrees BTDC. The C.C. carburetor needles are prescribed in place of the stock G.S. needles. According to how well the Stage 1 directions and the selective fitting have been carried out the engine should now deliver between 78 and 80 bhp at 6000 rpm with something extra in hand if the valves don't float.

STAGE 4

This with its sub-option is the big step — as close as the factory will allow to full race, at least officially.

The start is as always with the Stage 1 operation and the rest of the rites that should precede it. Then make sure your corner gas station has super-premium 100-plus octane fuel because you're going to need it if the engine isn't to sound like a handful of dry peas in a coffee can.

After solving the above, order a set of pistons, part #I.H. 1108 which will give the engine a compression ratio of 10 to 1. These have raised domes and necessitate the chamfering of the combustion space divider as described in Stage 1 to a radius of 3/16 of an inch. These pistons have floating wristpins so a special set of connecting rods will also have to be purchased. These come in matched sets, one set numbered AEH 431 for cylinders two and four and the other set numbered AEH 433 for cylinders one and three. *Do not mix them up!* The pistons are shaped to fit the combustion space and will only fit with the sloping face *toward* the spark plug. With the pistons installed, put a small roll of plasticine or putty on each piston and install the head temporarily; then turn the engine over by hand for one complete revolution. Remove the head and measure the clearance between the piston and the combustion space divider as indicated by the clay on the piston. If the clearance is 1/16 of an inch you're in good shape, otherwise grind enough more off the divider to make up the clearance.

Before installing the pistons it might be well to observe a point of caution. A compression ratio of 10 to 1 on this block is quite a squeeze and it's best to be sure things are going to hold. To really be sure, remove all the studs and smear lapping compound on the head or the block and then work the head over the block to mate-lap the surfaces to a perfect fit. Ordinary silver (aluminum) paint makes the best gasket sealer. After final assembly be sure to follow the MG company's directions for torquing down the head. This is one operation where you must beg, borrow or otherwise acquire one very necessary tool — a torque wrench. No one can guess an accurate torque setting with a power-bar and Mr. Enever and company are very specific. Their prescription is 50 lb-ft, no more and *no less.*

As of this point you should have 86 bhp on tap at 6000 rpm but if the purse can stand it, this isn't the end, although it is about as far as one would want to go if the car is to be used essentially on the public thoroughfares.

Still within the area of Stage 4 is one more shot. By this time more carburetion is indicated and here we go to 1¾ inch SU carburetors. The part number for these is AUC 780 and they demand a special manifold which for the MGA *is* in the catalogue, numbered AEH 200. This last is still a production item and needs the polishing treatment described in Stage 1. The AUC carburetors are fitted with .100

Any and all connecting rods, whether new, used or otherwise should be carefully aligned before use and after a balance job if the engine is to stay in one piece under added racing stress.

Gears can be set up as semi-quick-change units by pre-assembling the set in the carrier. This allows the gear swapping to be done in unit merely by dropping drive shaft and half-pulling the axle shafts to allow removal.

Stock pistons have concave crowns as shown at right. Flat top pistons are intermediate at 9 to 1. A second set not shown, raises compression to 10/1.

MGA

jets and K.W. needles. If richer needles are indicated use R.F. and if leaner operation is wanted K.W. 1 needles will do the job.

The big jugs should be mounted with neoprene gaskets and double-coil spring washers under the nuts, which should be safety wired. The gasket is also a catalogue issue piece bearing the designation AHH 5791. No air cleaners are supplied with these and it's unlikely they'll be wanted but if they are send the carb number to any large U.S. speed shop and they will probably be able to supply the cleaners. This final operation in the Abingdon stable is worth 88 bhp at 6000 rpm.

STAGE 5

The MG people do not list this stage but from certain catalogued parts, a bit of experience and items available from some of the better knotfarms in the U.S. it appears that there are still more horses that can be fitted under the MGA hood. This last series is only for the strong of heart and experiment-minded. It has not, repeat, NOT, been checked out on the Abingdon dyno and has no official blessings from Mr. Enever. Let's explore the possibilities anyway.

First let's take a close look at the catalogue. There we find part number 1H 1025 which is described as a hard-face Bright Ray exhaust valve. H-m-m-m. A little farther down the list are part numbers 1H 1111 and 1H 1112. These are heavy-duty valve springs, inners and outers respectively. Getting interested? There's more — an oil cooler kit listed as part number ARH 0088. Abingdon says that the special valve springs will raise the point of valve bounce to 6400 rpm but the company won't admit to more power — just sustained power. The other items are interesting chiefly from the point of view of keeping the thing together at continued high speeds.

This being the case maybe we can rifle the till just a little further. Let's look at that cam for a bit. The hottest cam available from the parts bin is the one which comes stock with the car. This has a .357-inch lift and a 252 degree duration on both intake and exhaust. While we know that not much more lift can be tolerated, we also know that American cam grinders don't consider anything under 270 degrees much in the way of duration unless valve acceleration is very rapid which it isn't in this case. Several of the better cam grinders have MGA grinds worked out and others will work out and tailor a cam to your needs. Among the former is Ed Iskenderian and among the latter are Ed Winfield and Racer Brown.

There is probably a very good series of reasons why MG didn't make a hotter cam available, most of which center around the awful exhaust layout and a time element since they've been busy with other things. We'll sympathize over the time problem and go on to the exhaust.

The problem here is that the center two exhaust valves feed into a siamesed chamber and port. However the outlet is pretty robust and we might even be able to cheat about $\frac{1}{16}$ of an inch in size. This way we can treat that port the same as we used to do with the center two on the earlier block, running that into a balance box at a point just under the fire wall. The outer two are run together and thence to the balance box. True, the results won't be quite as good as the same ideas applied under a four-port but it'll be one big improvement over the stock manifolding. Any good header system would.

Alright — the factory says 6400 rmp can be had with the special valve springs and stock valves. That fact has been tested. We also know that any lightening of the valve train will pay off in a raised float point. That too has been proven for years. As a starting point take the pushrods. When you select your balanced set use the lightest one as a standard. Next, take your valves to a *good* machine shop, preferably one that specializes in speed work and have the man undercut the valves. But *carefully* — if you remove much the service life will be shortened and the strong springs may tend to tulip them. If you are patient and dexterous, the final piece of work can be polished (not ground down) rockers. The minute amount of metal ground off in the polishing will not make too much difference but in a way such things are satisfying. In any event the lightest pushrods obtainable and the undercut valves should allow engine speeds above 6500, possibly even within an ace of 7000 rpm depending on the cam selected.

With such a range of engine speeds cam selection becomes a matter of "what do you want to use it for?" Limits of good sense should apply with an upper limit or peak speed for a full-race conversion coming in about 6500 rpm tops, leaving any extra bonus for inevitable over-revving during those times when the chips are down in the final laps of a race. With the cam and exhaust modifications listed, added to the full Stage 4 layout it would be advisable to run richer needles than the standard K.W., the R.F. pins being about the right starting point. Since there are no factory test figures available here it would be best to use a mixture analyzer to check the effects of the better scavenging afforded by cam and headers and if any error is to be made let it be on the rich side.

Regarding this last part — our own Stage 5 — the authors wish to point out that this is meant only to point a direction and individual advice should be sought from *competent* professionals in your area or among the special parts makers regarding individual problems. Further, unless you are really gone on racing, serious racing that is, it would be best to stick with the proven factory modifications since these as we've said, have been tested not once but often.

As with the full house XPEG, the all-gone MGA has a lot more urge than the stock machine and as a result there is considerable added strain on the driveline. The anonymous oracle at Abingdon has foreseen these difficulties and has as usual come up with the answer in a choice of new clutch springs or a complete new clutch assembly. The springs are standard after engine number 16225 and have a pressure range of 180/190 lbs. Their part designation is 1H 1024. For the full treatment, though, there is part number AHH 5457, a special competition clutch which is a pretty fierce item but one that will take everything you can put through it with the hopped-up B-type engine.

GEARING TIPS

At long last the factory will publicly admit that they can sell the close ratio gearboxes used in the EX182 LeMans cars. A few of these gearsets have come to this country but they seem to have been held pretty close to the vests of the distributors and dealer-sponsored cars. Now they're a catalogue item. The specs on this box read:

Third gear: 1.27 to 1, Second: 1.62 to 1, First 2.45 to 1. The following parts are needed to rebuild your gearbox to these ratios:

1H 3297   Clutch shaft
1H 3298   Countershaft drive gear
1H 3299   2nd speed mainshaft gear
1H 3300   3rd speed mainshaft gear

In addition to these, there is a range of six rear end ratios giving ratios of 5.12, 4.88, 4.55, 4.30, 4.11, and 3.9 to 1. The last two are newly available. As with all the B-type BMC rear end set-ups the rear end gears are housed with the ring, pinion and attendant bearings in unit in a readily removable housing. Assuming you have enough money to make things really easy, you can pre-assemble gear sets and have what amounts to a semi-quick change rear end. It's a pretty expensive way to do things but it works.

The foregoing operations, at least after Stage 3, add up to a bit more than their counterparts applied to the earlier engines in dollars but MG has made it easier by cataloguing a number of parts that had to be made up for the early engines. The additional cash involved is made up for by the ease of purchase and the bolt-on quality of most of the operations. Also a mite more GO is on tap for the later engines when things are carried through far enough — more power is available for a reasonably tractable street machine than was available in the full race conversion of the XPEG although the earlier engine could be twisted somewhat tighter, 7000 rpm and more being available when desired.

As the man said: "You pays you money and you takes you choice."

John Christy & Dennis May

SAFER, FASTER

Increased performance and greater comfort for the MG-A

EXACTLY a year ago we published the reactions of the Lotus Editor to his new MG-A. In the intervening twelve months the car's mileage has increased by 16,000 miles, solid contact was unfortunately made with a bus, a hardtop has been added and the engine given the Speedwell "treatment." If the former two items were at all detrimental to engine and beauty then the latter two have more than rectified matters. These interesting additions prompted us to examine 333 KMC again.

Before the winter commenced in earnest it was decided to fit a hard-top to the MG-A. At the rear—the whole unit being easily removed in a few minutes.

Sliding perspex side screens, also made by Universal Laminations, were fitted and have been found to be a great improvement over the standard screens with hinged flap. The special side-screens are the exact size of their standard counterpart and thus can also be used in conjunction with the ordinary hood. The forward half of the screen consists of a fixed perspex panel—the rear half sliding forward to give ventilation or ample room for hand signals. No more lost driving gloves through the "mouse-

The already handsome lines of the MGA are improved by the fitting of a removable hard top by Universal Laminations.

is used daily on business in London, necessitating long spells exposed to the elements, this move was definitely desirable. The addition transformed the car into a very snug little two-seater saloon and it is a pleasure to drive at high speeds without the accompanying crack of the hood against metal stays.

Glass fibre is currently being put to many different uses, and it is this substance which forms the basic shell of the top fitted to the car by Universal Laminations of Holland Park Mews. The ⅛ in. moulded shell is covered on the outside by P.V.C. hooding which gives excellent waterproofing and is resistant to all climatic conditions. Interior trim in cream plastic is very neatly executed and is thoroughly in keeping with the high standard of finish already evident in the car. The hardtop is held in place by four clamps and by two bolts at

trap " type flap of the standard side-screen!

With wrap-round, "Californian" type rear window and flowing water gutter, the hard-top certainly adds still further to the graceful lines of the MG-A. Comfort is greatly increased, for although the standard hood is good the weather, under really bad conditions, had a habit of finding its way indoors! A neat roof light is fitted to the hard-top which further increases the saloon effect and is a great asset on rallies or for reading the newspaper during rush-hour travel!

There is no doubt that the advent of the hard-top has widely increased the popularity of sports cars. With such a fitting, one can have a delightful Grand Turismo vehicle in the winter months and then, with the coming of spring, the top can be left in the garage and the joys of open-air motoring enjoyed to the full. Continued on page 65

SCI ROAD TEST: MGA

SPORTS CARS ILLUSTRATED

Coming and going, it has urbane distinction...

IN SCI's TEST report on the MGA roadster (Jan. '57) we praised the quality built into that modestly-priced car and lamented its very few but discordant sub-standard incongruities, such as inner door panels of impermanent-looking fiberboard. These economies have been eliminated from the MGA coupe, making it consistently and harmoniously a quality product. It is the best-built MG to date and by far the most luxurious and comfortable.

The coupe's base price is $300 higher than the roadster's current $2450. Why that much difference? A great deal of the extra cost is in the doors: in roll-up windows, no-draft vents, chrome window frames and distinctive, well-engineered external door handles which do not exist, along with locks, on the open car. Then there is the top itself and the high cost of the dies for stamping it. And there are the wraparound windshield and the extreme-wraparound rear window that give superb visibility and are important extra-cost items.

The MGA roadster, being very aggressively a sports car, is noisy. Because of the resonant characteristics inherent in a metal top the coupe might be expected to be even noisier. But it is quieter, due to careful sound-proofing of the cockpit, even to foam-rubber insulation of the firewall. The sounds that do reach the occupants are pleasantly appropriate to what the "A" actually is: a touring-competition vehicle. The blipped engine revs with that exhilarating whir that usually is a mark of good high-performance machinery and the gearbox growls and sings, reminding the forgetful that under this sophisticated exterior the classical MG breed has been maintained. Although perfectly audible, engine noise does not begin to become obtrusive in top gear until about 4000 or 70 mph is reached. Beyond that point it becomes loud indeed and it takes on a strongly hammering note.

We feel that the finest single feature of the MGA is its road-holding and this is linked with its worst aspect in the inexorable way that the sides of a coin are linked. The A's cornering ability is quite awe-inspiring—the sort you might expect to find in a much more costly competition car. It is a very real source of safety and a great source of gratification to the driver, whether he be a cautious novice or jaded veteran. The car is fiercely tenacious in its side-bite, even in pouring rain, and practically devoid of lean or tire noise under high centrifugal g's. *But* this laudable performance is purchased at the cost of a naggingly choppy ride, even with soft tire pressures of 20 psi. With the tires inflated to recommended high-speed pressures the ride becomes definitely abusive.

The hard springs and shock absorbers of the MGA smooth bad bumps very well, and we never felt the suspension bottom on the roughest roads. It's the small surface irregularities that are telegraphed to the car's occupants with a staccato chop, making minimum tire pressure more or less mandatory for general touring. This criticism of the MGA is one that will do the car no harm in the eyes of hardened *aficionados*. But it most definitely will limit the appeal of this otherwise extremely appealing car in the broad market that potentially is its own in this country. Equal cornering ability can be combined with a genuinely comfortable ride

Coupé

. . . and it's perfect for racing, ideal for rallies

through major change in suspension design. To date, MG is under no compulsion to take this step. But the day will come when competitive conditions will demand it and we hope that MG is planning with this in mind.

At the moment, MG's acceptance in the U. S. continues to climb. MG sales never have been higher: against approximately 1300 cars sold in the western U. S. in '56, over 3000 were sold in '57. This still is a seller's market and the reason for the increase in sales is an increase in supply. The augmented supply is due not so much to increased production or shipping facilities as it is to the practice of crating cars for shipment. This permits cars to be stacked two deep in the holds of vessels that formerly carried only a single level of cars per deck. The crating, however, is costly and it contributes to a sizeable increase in the cars' retail price. Nevertheless, MG can still argue with persuasion that its car is the lowest-priced *real* sports car on the U. S. market.

It seems correct to say that the MGA's roadholding is its best feature because it is such a vividly salient one. But the A's brakes are just as excellent and are completely above criticism, certainly as far as the hardest conceivable touring use is concerned (for racing, special hard linings are readily available). These brakes registered a virtually nil reaction to our telling ten-stop fade test. And the A's steering also belongs in the superlative category. The rack and pinion mechanism is quick, free of backlash, light but solid in its feel, with just the right touch of self-righting action and with no noticeable communication of road shock to the adjustable spring-spoke steering wheel.

The MGA's performance is thrusty enough to make it an exhilarating car to drive, as its lively acceleration times point up. The transmission gear ratios are very happily chosen and good acceleration for highway passing is available in third up to at least 70 mph. Our test coupe's gearbox contained a bug that the roadster's did not: the load spring that is intended to hold the shift lever on the right-hand (third and fourth gear) side of the H-shaped shift pattern did not function, making it a very easy matter to nick first on an upshift from second to third; easy to remedy, but a point to watch. As with the roadster, it was not difficult to land in reverse by mistake when dropping from third to second. A very comfortable arm rest runs between the two seats and, whether this is used or both hands are on the wheel, the stubby and solid shift lever is perfectly at hand.

The engine of our test coupe surprised·us with its willingness to start instantly after two days of standing in the open in cold, wet weather, and with its very quick warmup. At least as praiseworthy was its very good fuel economy, even when driven hard with liberal use of gears and throttle on the highway and in city traffic. Thus flogged it still gave a cheerful 25 mpg, plus.

We don't know what was in the fuel tank when we took delivery of the coupe, but its engine would run on for 20 seconds or so after the ignition had been switched off. This also was true of our test roadster, but less so. Running the coupe on 102-octane Shell cured this except for an occasional single kickover. In terms of vibration, there is no comparison between the power unit of the MGA and its milder sister-engine which propels the Austin A55. The A55's is very smooth and silent. The hotter-cammed, dual carb MGA version is *not* ... in exchange for which it slams out 39 per cent more horsepower!

The MGA's clutch is stiff but it has a soft, smooth takeup. The flyoff-type hand brake is located on the passenger's side of the shaft tunnel: a socially strategic feature. The instruments are excellent; with nearly the entire world's automotive industry abandoning the ammeter for a warning light we're not about to chide MG for doing the same.

Two anomalies result from the conversion of an originally laid-out right-hand drive car to left-hand drive. In the home-market model the very important combined oil pressure and water temperature gauge is located alongside the tachometer, right in front of the driver—as it should be—and the fuel gauge is in a corresponding position, in front of the passenger, where it need be referred to only occasionally. In the changeover to left-hand drive the speedometer and tach migrate as they should to the new driver's position, but the vital oil-water instrument stays in its original spot, now out of the driver's field of vision. Similarly, the windshield wipers park to the left, out of the right-hand driver's way. In the left-hand (U. S. drive version they still park to the left, just as the hand brake stays in foreign territory. Other objections: at its price the car could afford an ash tray; and, as reported of the roadster, the seat backs should be re-contoured to support the entire back instead of only the shoulders.

So much for negative comment, most of which is fairly trivial and can be corrected by the owner who cares. On the positive side there are many points in addition to those already noted. The MGA's general and detail finish is excellent, actually rich in its appearance. So is its overall look, which wins admiring attention everywhere. It's a car in which the owner can take as much pride of possession as he might in other cars that cost much, much more. It belongs, perfectly, at the swankiest spa and has an urbane, cool distinction that the cherished T-series, with its flavor of flaming youth, never could aspire to. The MGA coupe is the snuggest MG yet, the most comfortable in all kinds of weather and for all kinds of touring. Its necessarily limited luggage accommodation is no problem if you add the natty luggage-rack option. It is a perfect car for rallying and it's ideally adapted to racing. It has the broadest appeal of any MG ever made.

Griff Borgeson

Door latch is original, practical and convenient. It operates with a real "feel of quality."

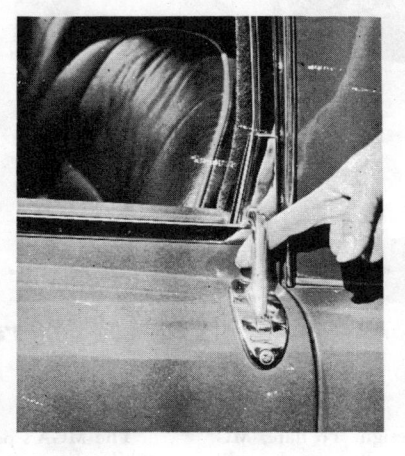

Though the engine room looks crowded, all service-demanding organs are highly accessible.

Body has a well-knit look that reflects underlying quality of the car. Wraparound windshield and wide, curved rear window give optimum visibility fore and aft. Only drawback is limited luggage capacity of trunk.

Under adhesion-limit cornering, the MGA rides flat and shows only a slight tendency to drift gently at the rear. The car is fiercely tenacious in its side-bite, giving it awe-inspiring turning characteristics. On the other hand, the ride is a hard one, with small irregularities in the road telegraphed to the driver with a staccato chop. Softer tires are indicated for a smoother ride.

MGA COUPE

PERFORMANCE

TOP SPEED:
- Two-way average .... 101 mph
- Fastest one-way run .... 103 mph

ACCELERATION:

From zero to	Seconds
30 mph	4.8
40 mph	6.9
50 mph	10.7
60 mph	15.4
70 mph	20.8
80 mph	30.3
Standing ¼ mile	19.5
Speed at end of quarter	68 mph

SPEED RANGES IN GEARS:

	MPH
I	zero to 28
II	zero to 46
III	5 to 71
IV	9 to top

SPEEDOMETER CORRECTION:

Indicated	Actual
30	30
40	39
50	48
60	58
70	67
80	75

FUEL CONSUMPTION:
- Hard driving .... 20.8 mpg on speed runs
- Average driving (under 60 mph) . 27 mpg, plus.

BRAKING EFFICIENCY 10 successive emergency stops from 60 mph, just short of locking wheels, registered ⅔g on all stops without noticeable increase in pedal pressure.

RATING FACTORS:
- Bhp per cu. in. 0.79
- Bhp per sq. in. piston area 2.78
- Torque (lb-ft) per cu. in. 0.85
- Pounds per bhp—test car 29.2
- Piston speed @ 60 mph .... 2007 fpm
- Piston speed @ max bhp .... 3210 fpm
- Brake lining area per ton ...... 129 sq in
- Mph per 1000 rpm 17.44

SPECIFICATIONS

POWER UNIT:
- Type .... In-line four
- Valve arrangement .... Pushrod operated ohv
- Bore & Stroke .... 2.87 x 3.50 in (73.025 x 89.0 mm)
- Stroke/Bore Ratio 1.22/1
- Displacement .... 90.88 cu in (1489 cc)
- Compression Ratio 8.3/1
- Carburetion by .... Dual 1.5 in inclined S.U.
- Max. Power .... 72 bhp @ 5500 rpm
- Max. Torque .... 77.4 ft-lbs @ 3500 rpm
- Idle Speed .... 750 rpm

DRIVE TRAIN:
- Transmission ratios
  - I 3.64
  - II 2.21
  - III 1.37
  - IV 1.00
- Final drive ratio (test car) 4.30
- Other available final drive ratios . 3.70, 4.10, 4.55
- Axle torque taken by .... Springs

CHASSIS:
- Wheelbase .... 94 in
- Front Tread .... 47.4 in
- Rear Tread .... 48.8 in
- Suspension, front .... Independent, by coil springs and wishbones
- Suspension, rear .... Semi-elliptic
- Shock absorbers .... Lever & piston
- Steering type .... Rack & pinion
- Steering wheel turns L to L 2.7
- Turning diameter .... 28 ft.
- Brake type .... 2 leading shoe front, 1 leading, 1 trailing rear
- Brake lining area .... 134.4 sq in
- Tire size .... 5.60 x 15

GENERAL:
- Length .... 156 in
- Width .... 58 in
- Height .... 50 in
- Weight, test car .... 2100 lbs
- Weight distribution, F/R 50.5/49.5
- Fuel capacity .... 12 U. S. gallons
- Price .... $2695 with disc wheels, $2785 with wire wheels
- Importer .... Hambro Automotive Corp. 27 West 57th St. New York 19, N. Y.

Externally unchanged, the MGA Twin Cam in chassis form looks very different from its standard counterpart. Disc brakes and centre-lock disc wheels are distinguishing features.

EXCITING NEW MGA

COMPETITION-MINDED MGA owners have for some time given voice to the opinion that their cars are a little underpowered; the new special equipment version, known as the "MGA Twin Cam," which also has the added advantage of disc brakes, should really be the answer to their prayers. To avoid any misunderstanding it must be emphasised that the standard MGA, with push-rod engine and drum brakes, will continue in production; in addition it has been stated by the manufacturers that the engineering changes necessary for the installation of the twin-cam engine and disc-brakes are so extensive that conversion of existing cars is not practicable.

Outwardly the "Twin Cam" model is virtually undistinguishable from the standard car, except for the fitting of centre-lock disc wheels, behind which lurk the Dunlop disc brakes. On the road, however, the difference should be very easily noticed, for the makers claim that acceleration from 0-100 mph occupies only 31 seconds, and 0-110 about 38 seconds; maximum speed is said to be in the region of 120 mph.

This improved performance has been obtained in two ways, by the fitting of chain-driven twin overhead camshafts, operating valves set at an angle of 80 degrees, and by an increase of capacity (bore size goes up from 73.025 mm to 75.406 mm) to 1589 cc. The latter is designed to bring the car as near as possible to the limit of its class (up to 1600 cc) in the Gran Turismo category. The crankshaft has been stiffened, new connecting rods and pistons are fitted, and the maximum power output is 108 hp at 6700 rpm, with a very creditable 97 hp at 5000 rpm. Compression ratio is 9.9 to 1, to take advantage of "Super" grade fuels. The Dunlop disc brakes are fitted to all four wheels and their performance should be well in keeping with that of the engine.

Optional extras include special seats, a wood rimmed steering wheel, an oil cooler and a full width plastic competition windscreen, which materially reduces the car's frontal area. A selection of alternative gearbox and final drive ratios is available, and development work on tuning stages for the engine is in hand. Also obtainable are such more "normal" extras as radiator blind, adjustable steering column, tonneau cover, twin high-note horns, windscreen washer, heater, fog lamps and radio.

The new power unit is directly developed from the unsupercharged twin ohc engines used in EX 179 at Utah in 1956, when 62 new International and American Class "F" records were set up. Supercharged, the same basic unit was fitted in the streamlined record car EX 181 which last August, driven by Stirling Moss, covered a flying kilometre at 245.64 mph.

The MGA Twin Cam will be available as an open two-seater form at £1265 17s. (inclusive of tax) and in coupé form at £1357 7s. The steering and roadholding of the standard car are recognised as among the best in their class, and the added performance should greatly enhance the appeal of the new model.

Conventional live rear axle is mounted on semi-elliptic springs controlled by piston-type shock absorbers

AUGUST, 1958

LUIGI MUSSO

LUIGI MUSSO, Italy's only Grade One driver at the start of this season, was fatally injured when his Ferrari left the road and overturned during the French Grand Prix at Reims on 6 July. Musso was in second place at the time, and it seems that it was his determination to keep within striking distance of Hawthorn which cost his life.

Following the loss of Alberto Ascari and Eugenio Castellotti, the death of Musso is a tragic blow to Italian motor racing—and indeed to the sport as a whole. The Roman driver was very much aware of his responsibilities as Italian champion and this, together with his great courage, sometimes made his driving brilliantly spectacular.

Musso, who was 31, had a long list of successes to his credit, especially in sports car racing, and his most recent victory was gained in this year's Targa Florio, in which he shared the driving of a Ferrari with Olivier Gendebien. In 1956 he was second (with Schell) in the Sebring 12-hours Race, and third in the Mille Miglia, on both occasions at the wheel of a Ferrari, and in 1957 he shared the driving of the Ferrari which won the Buenos Aires 1000 kms event.

In 1957 Musso was at one point the only driver in a position to challenge Fangio for the World Championship, a situation which resulted in a fantastic, but unsuccessful, drive in the Grand Prix of Pescara, for which he obtained the use of a privately-entered Formula 1 Ferrari —a tribute to his prestige with the Italian people. The same wild enthusiasm from his country folk which greeted his short-lived lead at Pescara was again evident at Monza only a week before his death, when he gained an initial lead in the first part of the 500 Miles event, performing prodigies with an unsuitable car until cockpit heat and exhaust fumes overcame him.

His greatest achievement in a Formula 1 event was probably his second place, together with a record lap in the 1957 French Grand Prix at Rouen. A week later he won the non-Championship Grand Prix of Reims for Ferrari at an average of 123.4 mph. The following Saturday he finished second in the 1957 British Grand Prix at Aintree. He was also second in this year's Argentine and Monaco Grands Prix, as a result of which he became (temporarily) leader in the World Drivers' Championship.

Fatal accidents are fortunately extremely rare in Formula 1 racing, and it seems all the more tragic that Musso should have lost his life on the type of circuit on which he was at his best. His fellow drivers, of all nationalities, mourn his passing; Italy will find it extremely difficult to replace him.

November 12, 1958

M.G. A plus H.R.G.

An Algebraic-sounding Formula for Speeding up a Sports Car

GLIMPSE beneath the bonnet of the M.G. A shows the special cylinder head, re-positioned S.U. carburetters and a swept exhaust manifold leading to the normal silencer.

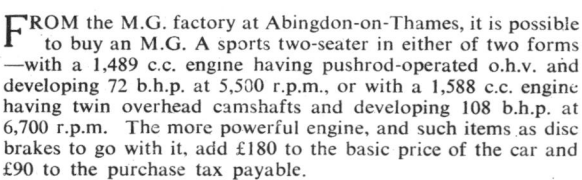

INVISIBLE to the passer by, the special cylinder head has a layout as shown below in the sectioned plan of its rear half. In place of siamesed inlet ports between the pushrods, there are individual ports on the opposite side of the engine.

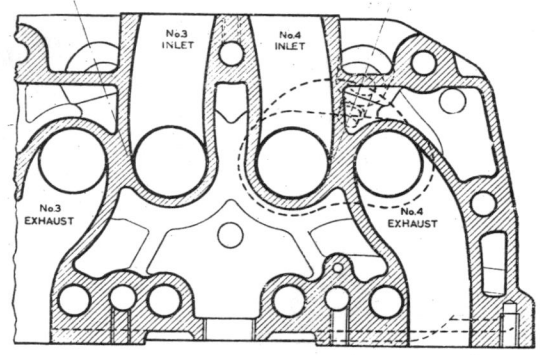

FROM the M.G. factory at Abingdon-on-Thames, it is possible to buy an M.G. A sports two-seater in either of two forms —with a 1,489 c.c. engine having pushrod-operated o.h.v. and developing 72 b.h.p. at 5,500 r.p.m., or with a 1,588 c.c. engine having twin overhead camshafts and developing 108 b.h.p. at 6,700 r.p.m. The more powerful engine, and such items as disc brakes to go with it, add £180 to the basic price of the car and £90 to the purchase tax payable.

We have recently been driving an M.G. A two-seater of the milder type, fitted with a special light-alloy H.R.G. cylinder head, a Derrington exhaust manifold, and pistons raising the compression ratio to 9.3:1, these three items involving a parts bill of £88 12s. plus fitting costs but no purchase tax. Data tabulated on this page shows that, whilst an unmodified clutch prevented the extra power being used to the full in "racing" starts from rest, the tuned car had in effect a 10 m.p.h. lead over the normal car from 60 m.p.h. onward, reaching 100 m.p.h. when the untuned car had reached 90 m.p.h. In fact, the tuned low-cost engine went about half-way towards the sheer performance of the twin-cam unit at much less cost, and went far more than half way towards the more potent engine's performance in respect of torque for top gear hill-climbing or acceleration. Maximum speed with the H.R.G.-Derrington modifications was not recorded, as the suggested rev. limit of 6,000 r.p.m. is reached at about 102 m.p.h. on the usual 4.3:1 gear, but the extra power is obtained without the mechanical noise of twin camshafts and with excellent fuel economy.

Replacement of Siamesed inlet ports on the same side of the engine as the exhaust system by individual ports on the opposite side is the main feature of this cylinder head. Also, light alloy replaces iron for the casting. An existing exhaust manifold can be retained, but the sheet-metal manifold fitted to our test model gives around 2 b.h.p. extra at medium speeds without interfering with the normal silencer's effectiveness. The normal S.U. carburetters are retained with the H.R.G. cylinder head.

Makers: H.R.G. Engineering Co., Ltd., Oakcroft Road, Kingston By-pass, Tolworth, Surrey. V. W. Derrington, Ltd., 159 London Road, Kingston-on-Thames, Surrey. **Prices:** Cylinder head and parts for fitting, £58 10s. Exhaust manifold, £17 10s. High-compression pistons, £12 12s.

	M.G. A Coupe (Test No. 30/57)	M.G. A with H.R.G. head	M.G. A Twin-cam (Test No. 22/58)
ACCELERATION TIMES from standstill			
0–30 m.p.h.	5.0 sec.	5.1 sec.	2.6 sec.
0–40 m.p.h.	7.2 sec.	6.8 sec.	4.4 sec.
0–50 m.p.h.	10.8 sec.	9.1 sec.	7.3 sec.
0–60 m.p.h.	15.7 sec.	13.0 sec.	9.1 sec.
0–70 m.p.h.	21.4 sec.	16.6 sec.	12.3 sec.
0–80 m.p.h.	32.1 sec.	23.0 sec.	16.2 sec.
Standing ¼ mile	19.8 sec.	18.6 sec.	18.1 sec.
ACCELERATION TIMES in top gear			
20–40 m.p.h.	13.6 sec.	8.9 sec.	10.7 sec.
30–50 m.p.h.	13.8 sec.	9.7 sec.	9.7 sec.
40–60 m.p.h.	12.6 sec.	10.0 sec.	8.0 sec.
50–70 m.p.h.	13.7 sec.	10.7 sec.	9.4 sec.
60–80 m.p.h.	17.6 sec.	11.9 sec.	13.9 sec.
ACCELERATION TIMES in 3rd gear			
10–30 m.p.h.	8.1 sec.	6.7 sec.	8.3 sec.
20–40 m.p.h.	7.9 sec.	6.0 sec.	6.5 sec.
30–50 m.p.h.	8.1 sec.	6.7 sec.	6.5 sec.
40–60 m.p.h.	8.7 sec.	7.0 sec.	5.5 sec.
50–70 m.p.h.	10.4 sec.	7.6 sec.	5.5 sec.
60–80 m.p.h.	—	—	8.3 sec.
MAXIMUM SPEED. (Mean of opposite runs)	101.2 m.p.h.	not timed	113.0 m.p.h.
MAXIMILE SPEED (Timed ¼ mile after 1 mile accelerating from rest)			
Mean of opposite runs	92.0 m.p.h.	102.3 m.p.h.	101.3 m.p.h.
Best time equals	94.8 m.p.h.	103.4 m.p.h.	104.2 m.p.h.
FUEL CONSUMPTION			
At steady 30 m.p.h. on level	—	51.5 m.p.g.	37.0 m.p.g.
At steady 50 m.p.h. on level	43.2 m.p.g.	44.5 m.p.g.	33.5 m.p.g.
At steady 70 m.p.h. on level	31.2 m.p.g.	34.5 m.p.g.	29.5 m.p.g.
At steady 90 m.p.h. on level	24.8 m.p.g.	25.0 m.p.g.	22.0 m.p.g.
Overall consumption	27.6 m.p.g. for 742 miles	28.0 m.p.g. for 465 miles	22.2 m.p.g. for 1,593 miles

DOUG BLAIN

FIRST OF

IT happens to the best of us.
Suddenly, for no apparent reason, we get the urge to improve on something we have for long regarded as near-perfect.

That's how it was with S.C.W.'s Road Test routine. For some time we had been itching to bring it into line with latest overseas developments. The big problem was to find time.

Then recently it really began to look as if we were getting somewhere. Photographer Sandford's MG A, which he'd been nursing carefully through its first 5,000, was nearing peak form. The new-model season was nearly over and things were a little easier around the office. The time was obviously ripe.

So one evening I sat down and got stuck into it. The object was to perfect a Road Test routine as good as, or preferably better than, that of any other magazine in the world. A pretty high aim, yes, but there was no point in trying for anything lower.

First requirements for the perfect sporting car test, I decided, were these:
- Reliable top speed figures.
- Truly comprehensive acceleration times.
- Accurate, scientific braking data (something no other Australian magazine has yet offered).
- A precise, progressive photographic record of cornering ability.
- Accurate figures for maximum speeds in gears.
- Precisely calculated technical data.

This three-shot series sets a standard for future S.C.W. new car Road Tests. Look closely at the pictures and you'll see painted on the glassy surface of our favourite S-bend three white arrows. They're a guide to photographer Barry Sandford: in future he'll point his extra eye at each arrow in turn and record the antics of every car we try. M.G. pix, incidentally, show car's wonderful controllability.

SPORTS CAR WORLD, June, 1959

DRIVES THE:

Manageable M.G.A

S.C.W.'s NEW, E-N-L-A-R-G-E-D ROAD TESTS

- Scientific accelerative force and rolling resistance figures.
- Some form of standard procedure for evaluating both acceleration and braking capabilities **together**.
- A timed hillclimb.

It all seemed possible. Gathering all that data would take time, but so what? The result would surely be worthwhile. S.C.W.'s enthusiast readers would have exactly what they wanted, we would be happy in the knowledge that we were giving our test cars the fairest possible trial, and the manufacturers and distributors would profit from the recognition that the tests must inevitably gain. They know already that we never thrash our cars, nor do we try to make them do things they were never designed to do.

Why did we choose a privately owned M.G. for this test?

We did it because we think that in many cases a private car, loved and nursed from new, will perform better than the average hard-driven demonstrator. We also know that the latest M.G. is particularly responsive to careful usage, and Sandford's car seemed an ideal machine with which to kick off this series.

The M.G. A is a handsome car by any standards. It does not have a trace of Italian or anything else in its lines, yet it is graceful and balanced without being too conspicuous.

Mechanical layout is conventional, and how. Twin 1½ in. SU's feed the four-cylinder B.M.C. engine. Drive goes through a four-speed gearbox (synchro, top three) to a live axle. Suspension is by coils at the front and cart-axle leaves at the back.

Getting in is easy. The doors are wide, and they open wide. I found myself toeing chunks out of the door trim, though, trying to edge my feet past the seats. Aluminium kick plates would fix that.

Driving position is what I call traditional. Instead of sitting right back to your work in the modern Continental manner, you find yourself with the wheel in your lap demanding to be held with bent arms. The system allows a snug cockpit, making for good streamlining. It has no disadvantages, because the M.G.'s steering is geared high enough to make big arm movements unnecessary. Even on the Elbow at Foley's, where I did the timed ascents, the close-up driving position was never an embarrassment.

Instrument layout is among the best yet on a modern, low-priced sports car. Speedometer and tach, properly calibrated, live right in front of the master of ceremonies. To their left are oil pressure and water temperature gauges, on a single dial, and the fuel gauge—which proved to have some pretty strange habits.

The A-type has tick-tick turn signals and a penetrating horn. Controls for both are on the dash, an arrangement w h i c h takes some getting used to if you're uninitiated.

The gear lever is right where it ought to be. It has a luscious movement, nice and short between gears, but on Sandford's car it was very stiff across the neutral gate. Snatch changes produce lusty clicking noises from the box —not a real fault, but with a little wear it could become a heck of a nuisance.

The hand brake flies off when you lift it momentarily.

The passenger has a map-reading light. Another good thing.

There's no glovebox, but that doesn't matter much because the door pockets hold all the riff-raff that most people like to cart around with them anyway. I was a little disgusted at the standard of the trim, especially around those pockets. Surely B.M.C. could spare something a little better than plastic-covered cardboard? Think how nicely trimmed the old TF was, then look at the A.

No. On second thoughts, you'd better not . . .

But you can't have everything, and this car's roadholding really is marvellous. Crammed fiercely into the downhill S-bend we'd selected for our photographs, the little black demon just couldn't do a thing wrong. The faster I took it down through the top right-hander, across the gap and then hell-for-leather through the bottom sweep, the better it behaved. With the power hard on in third gear, the tail would break at the entrance to the second bend, which is taken from the extreme right of the road. Then, held gently in check with one hand while my left paw caressed the gearstick ready for anything naughty, it would swing sweetly out until the nose was headed just right. A touch on the throttle, and we were away.

Just like that. No noise, no fuss, no salted peanuts.

Mild oversteer — just what you want.

Pedal placement on the A, incidentally, doesn't allow heel and toe changing in the true sense. Instead, you brake with your toe and punch the loud lever with the side of your shoe's upper. Just as good as the real McCoy when you get used to it.

SPORTS CAR WORLD, June, 1959

Just about the most perfectly mannered little projectile currently buyable — truly, this is SAFETY, FASTER STILL.

S.C.W. FULL ROAD TEST

S.C.W.'s ROAD TEST OF THE M.G.A.

If roadholding is the A's best feature, then braking comes next. S.C.W.'s brake test strip is a long, straight stretch of road with a nobbly, tar-bound metal surface. This new procedure of ours (which for obvious reasons must remain secret) entails entering the strip at around 70 m.p.h. and slamming on the clams regardless.

The M.G. pulled up dead square every time.

On the other hand, the brakes do fade. After four of these 70 m.p.h. stops they started asking for much higher pressures, and pedal travel increased slightly. A mile or two of gentle motoring cooled them off.

Sheer performance is not sensational. Several high-powered family cars would do a 'Gee in a traffic light derby. Still, the 1½-litre motor does have plenty of kick, and it doesn't take a leadfoot to produce a healthy chirp from the back tyres. Pushed to the limit, the clutch takes up smoothly and smartly, the treads bite savagely at the tarmac and you barely have time to take your left foot off its pedal before the tacho is telling you it's time to swap ratios. Second gear is a little low, which means that the next gear change follows within a second or two. Third gear still has sting, and it will carry the little car up to over an indicated 70 with no trouble. Acceleration in top is steady but not fiery. It tails off sharply around an indicated 90.

Owner Sandford put a rev. limit of 5,500 on the car for this test. I feel sure the times could have been bettered using 6,000. The engine's highest permissible limit is 6,500, but an owner would be crazy to use that ceiling often unless he owned a bearing factory. In fact the advantage in taking a motor over the orange line at 5,500 would amount to no more than a second or two in a standing quarter.

(Continued on page 58)

SPORTS CAR WORLD, June, 1959

Nowhere near as accessible as older units, latest M.G. power unit doesn't encourage home fiddling. Motor in our test car was willing, but ran on badly and sometimes pinged under load.

Technical Details

PERFORMANCE

TOP SPEED:
Two-way average: 91.8 m.p.h.
Fastest one way: 96.4 m.p.h.

ACCELERATION:
(Test limit, 5,500 r.p.m.)
Through gears:
 0-30 m.p.h. = 5.0 sec.
 0-40 = 7.0
 0-50 = 10.3
 0-60 = 15.5
 0-70 = 22.0
Standing quarter-mile: 20.4 sec.
Speed at end of quarter: 72 m.p.h.

MAXIMUM SPEEDS IN GEARS:
(at 5,500 r.p.m.)
 1st .... 28 m.p.h.
 2nd .... 45 m.p.h.
 3rd .... 77 m.p.h.

SPEEDOMETER ERROR:
30 m.p.h. indicated = actual 28 m.p.h.
 40 = 37
 50 = 46
 60 = 55
 70 = 65
 80 = 76

FUEL CONSUMPTION:
Overall .... 28 m.p.g.

TAPLEY DATA:
Maximum pull in gears:
 1st .... 485 lb./ton at 25 m.p.h.
 2nd .... 370 lb./ton at 30 m.p.h.
 3rd .... 230 lb./ton at 40 m.p.h.
 4th .... 150 lb./ton at 28 m.p.h.
Rolling resistance, in neutral:
 148 lb./ton at 70 m.p.h.
 135 lb./ton at 60 m.p.h.
 115 lb./ton at 50 m.p.h.
 90 lb./ton at 40 m.p.h.
 60 lb./ton at 30 m.p.h.

GO-TO-WHOA:
0-60-0 m.p.h. .... 18.4 sec.

CALCULATED DATA:
Lb./h.p. as tested 21.2
M.p.h./1,000 r.p.m. top gear 17
M.p.h. at 2,500 ft./min. piston speed,
 top gear 72.5
Best safe cruising speed (theoretical)
 indicated 75 m.p.h.
Cub. cm./lb. ft. torque 19.23
B.h.p./litre 48.64
B.h.p./ton as tested 65.4
Brake lining area/ton as tested, 122.2 sq. in.

SPECIFICATIONS

PRICE:
£1,376 including tax.

S.C.W. ROAD TEST NO. 1 (NEW SERIES)

ENGINE:
Type .... 4-cyl., in line, water cooling
Valves .... pushrod o.h.v.
Cubic capacity .... 1,489 c.c.
Bore and stroke .... 73.025 x 89 m.m.
Piston area .... 25.97 sq. in.
Compression ratio .... 8.3 to 1
Carburettors .... twin 1½-in. S.U.
Fuel pump .... Electric S.U.
Max. power 72 b.h.p. (nett) at 5,500 r.p.m.
Piston speed at max. b.h.p. .. 3,220 ft./min.
Max. torque .... 77.4 lb. ft. at 3,500 r.p.m.

CHASSIS:
Wheelbase .... 7ft. 10 in.
Track, front .... 3ft. 11⅜in.
 rear .... 4ft. 0⅞in.
Suspension, front .... wishbones, coils
 rear .. rigid axle, semi-eliptics
Steering—
 Rack and pinion, 2¾ turns lock to lock
Brakes .... Lockheed hydraulic
Lining area .... 134.4 sq. in.

GEAR RATIOS:
1st 15.652
2nd 9.52
3rd 5.908
4th 4.3

GENERAL:
Length overall .... 13ft.
Width .... 4ft. 10in.
Weight as tested (driver, one
 passenger) .... 20½ cwt.
Hood erection time (two men) .... 1½ min.
Weather ...... hot, dry, slight crosswind
Remarks: All test runs made on dry,
 bitumen-bound gravel road with driver
 and one pasenger aboard. High-speed
 runs made with hood and sidescreens
 erected.

SPORTS CAR WORLD, June, 1959

DRIVING THE MANAGEABLE M.G.A.

(Continued from page 56)

Although I complained earlier about the A's low second gear, I must admit that number two was an ideal cog for the test hill.

Highest revs I saw on Foley's were 5,450, and at no time was the car short of power. I was dropping it out of first only yards from the start and staying with second the rest of the way. Test times for the hill compare well with current results, although I feel certain that we could have improved on them. It takes practice to judge accurately when to brake for a hill climb hairpin, when to lay on the horses, and when to haul her through for maximum cornering speed. All this varies from car to car.

But since we'll be putting in just as much (or as little) practice with future test cars, we can be sure of getting accurate comparison figures even if they don't represent the quickest possible times.

The M.G. will pull 5,000-5,300 r.p.m. in top gear, indicating a well chosen ratio. I would like to see overdrive offered as an extra, mainly because the engine really does seem to be working hard as road speed approaches the ton.

On normal surfaces at very high speeds the car hops about a bit, although that never becomes a worry. The steering remains light and precise at all speeds, and that magnificent cornering ability seems to stay with it right on up.

We took our maximum speed times with the hood up for maximum streamlining.

Noise level was fairly low at cruising speeds. Above that, wind noise starts butting in. The exhaust growls like a veteran at high revs, but it's quiet enough for fairly indulgent town use.

Taken all round, B.M.C.'s medium-price sports offering adds up to very good buying. As a final indication of its efficiency, let me quote one more fact — perhaps the most significant of them all . . .

The M.G. A will accelerate to a true 60 m.p.h. and then stop again in less time than it takes most cars to do the 0-60 alone. #

Two dead straight strips of rubber — ample testimony to the evenness of M.G.A.'s braking. Efficiency figures were good, too.

Australian-assembled M.G. looks good from outside. Interior finish is not so hot. Other test verdicts: braking and cornering excellent, acceleration and top speed only adequate.

TOP GEAR, August, 1959

What's New About The **M.G.A.** 1600

The 1600 is a most interesting development of the M.G.A. The already pleasant lines of the car have been cleaned up at the rear and a neat grouping of rear lights and traffic flashers is accommodated behind amber glass so that following traffic is not dazzled. There are now sliding side screens so that in bad weather the 1600, with its hood up, is every bit as protected as any modern saloon car

Engine capacity has been increased from 1489 to 1589 c.c. and now gives 79.5 b.h.p. at 5,600 r.p.m., against our road test figures of 72 b.h.p. at 5,500 in the original M.G.A. This means much increased acceleration, a guaranteed top speed of more than 100 m.p.h. and comfortable cruising at 80 m.p.h. To cope with the improved acceleration the front wheels are retarded by Lockheed disc brakes

The cockpit view is a familiar one to all lovers of M.G. sports cars and there is no question but what the 1600 continues the tradition of Safety Fast. The neat gear shift comes comfortably to one's hand. The bucket seats are comfortable and provide good lateral support. The driving position will appeal to all enthusiasts, and to add to the 1600's appeal are the quality fittings and excellent finish of a sports car that really is a sports car

The Twin Cams are here—hooray, hooray!

M.G.A. T.C.: THERE'S

THE grim-faced bystander's jaw dropped as he ran a critical eye over the plated name scroll on the flank of the sleek open roadster parked at the kerbside: "Don't tell me this crowd have started building *sports* cars again . . ."

That's how it is all along with M.G.'s new Twin Cam. No matter who you are you can't help feeling secretly delighted that at last B.M.C. have come out with something just a little bit different. Even if you're too young to remember the fervid controversy that greeted every new departure in the old pre-war days of M.G. supremacy you'll find it difficult to stop the corners of your mouth twisting into a delighted grin as that raw new double-knocker coffee mill plop-plops away at a

Classic background emphasises Twin Cam's simple, refreshing lines. New wheels look just as good as wire, are lighter and easier to keep clean. Seats have thicker squabs.

One hundred and eight brake horsepower from 1,588 c.c. at 6,700 r.p.m. gives a claimed maximum speed with appropriate optional gear and diff ratios of 120 m.p.h., 0-100 in 30 sec. We'll see.

SPORTS CAR WORLD, August, 1959

After a quarter-century of sameness, Abingdon builds a sports car.

characteristically uneven 1,000 r.p.m. idle.

I think it must be simply the knowledge that the new car's shapely bonnet actually conceals an engine whose power curve doesn't blush for shame beside those of Certain Continental Competitors. Because the feeling certainly hits you long before you have the chance actually to prove for yourself that the Twin Cam does go. Another proof of the same pudding is that the first thing you think of doing as you approach is open the trapdoor and see for yourself. I know I didn't dream of touching the car beforehand.

The secret is that the whole car looks so tantalisingly ordinary. There are detail differences, of course. Disc wheels, different colour schemes, bolstered seats, covered dash and recalibrated tachometer are some. But your first thought is, "Heck, the thing looks just the same" — until you catch a glimpse of that glorious new donk with its chrome plated cam covers and fat, sloping, repositioned 1¾" HD-6 S.U.s.

Driving the Twin Cam is funny, too. You have to fight off a dreadful suspicion that the whole experience is going to be disappointing. It isn't of course, but because the new setup gives most of its increased kick quite high in the rev range you get the feeling that maybe you expected too much after all.

Ten to one you'll find you didn't, though. I know that for my part I have seldom been so surprised.

First time out, Ian Fraser and I fronted up for a photographic session with a pale green demonstrator belonging to Sydney's main M.G. dealers. The car was brand new — 35 miles precisely — and as rough as bags. Worse, the salesman told us he had orders not to let us drive.

That sort of thing always makes me mad, and the same day I began making other arrangements. Barclay Motors top man Col James, an old pal of S.C.W.'s, proved much more reasonable. He'd sold his early stock long before he even got his hands on it, but he gladly put in a word for us with one of the new owners — Bruce Milwain, of Belrose, just outside Sydney. "Certainly," said Bruce, "Come down and do what you like."

Bruce's car was red — that glorious red that M.G. seem to have kept in the background since the old T.C. was news, although they do use it on the rare M.G.A. Coupe. It had only 560 miles on the odometer, so we took things quietly.

Even so the Twin Cam left me glowing. What a car, my brain kept murmuring over and over, what a car. For unlike so many modern sports cars the T-C (note the significant hyphen) really does have character.

(Continued on page 75)

FIRE DOWN BELOW

First Australian road test of the new MG A Twin-Cam shows it's the first production MG that can genuinely exceed 100 m.p.h., reports Bryan Hanrahan

TWO CAMS TURNING

ONCE again you can thank Melbourne racing driver and Morris agent Peter Manton for a road test of the latest — and fastest — car of its name in Australia.

Not that he was very happy, mind you, to see his Twin-Cam MG A move off for the day . . . all £1867/5/1 worth of it. Would YOU be, if it was yours?

I'll bet you wouldn't — neither is the mighty BMC organisation, nor even the Victorian distributors, prepared to run one in for road-testing.

Why should they, when Peter is prepared to be the fall guy? They get their road test anyway, don't they?

About the Car

Now, about this Twin-Cam. I won't go into the general details of the car, since it's basically the now familiar MG A — so let's get straight on to the things that are different about it.

These are: the twin-overhead-camshaft layout of the four-cylinder, 1589 c.c. engine, the centre-lock ventilated disc wheels, the tiny "Twin-Cam" nameplate on the bonnet, the caliper-type disc brakes on all wheels—and a performance that's well worth experiencing.

The car also has better seats, trim and general finish, presumably because it's fully imported.

Power output is quoted as 108 b.h.p. at 6700 r.p.m., on a compression ratio of 9.9 to 1. The rev-counter is red-banded between 6500 and the 7500 top calibration; safe rev limit is said to be 7000.

Its Performance

The makers also claim the Twin-Cam will go from rest to 100 m.p.h. in 31 seconds and to 110 m.p.h. in 38; and they quote its tops speed at "between 110 and 120 m.p.h."

There's a fair bit of latitude in the top-speed claim, so I assume the same latitude in the acceleration figures—mine were nothing like so good.

Apart from the pleasure, etc., of David McKay's company, I wish he'd been over in Melbourne so that I could have helped HIM do the test.

This is the skeleton of what I got: 0-100 m.p.h. — 38.1sec.

SECRET of latest MG's 108 m.p.h. performance is the new 1589 c.c., twin o.h.c. engine with 9.9 to 1 compression. Disc brakes all round, too!

MODERN MOTOR — August 1959

MAIN SPECIFICATIONS

ENGINE: 4-cylinder, twin o.h.c.; bore 75.4mm., stroke 88.9mm., capacity 1589 c.c.; compression ratio 9.9 to 1; maximum b.h.p 108 at 6700 r.p.m.; twin semi-downdraught carbs, SU electric fuel pump; 12v ignition.
TRANSMISSION: Single dry-plate clutch; 4-speed gearbox synchro-meshed on top 3 gears; ratios, 1st 15.652, 2nd 9.520, 3rd 5.908, top 4.3, reverse 20.468 to 1; hypoid bevel final drive, 4.3 to 1 ratio.
SUSPENSION: Front independent, by coils and wishbones; semi-elliptics at rear; telescopic shockers all round.
STEERING: Rack-and-pinion; 3¼ turns lock-to-lock; 34ft. 3in. turning circle.
WHEELS: Centre-lock discs, with 5.90 by 15in. Roadspeed tyres.
BRAKES: Dunlop hydraulic caliper-type disc brakes on all wheels; mechanical handbrake on rear discs.
CONSTRUCTION: Box-section chassis, braced for torsional rigidity.
DIMENSIONS: Wheelbase 7ft. 10in.; track, front 3ft. 11½in., rear 4ft. 0¾in.; length 13ft., width 4ft. 10in., height 4ft. 2in., ground clearance 6in.
WEIGHT as tested: 21¼cwt.; unladen, 17¾cwt.
FUEL TANK: 10 gallons.

PERFORMANCE ON TEST

CONDITIONS: Cool, gusty cross-wind; damp bitumen, two occupants; premium fuel with 40 percent benzol.
BEST SPEED: 108 m.p.h.
FLYING quarter-mile: 106.8 m.p.h.
STANDING quarter-mile: 18.4s.
MAXIMUM in indirect gears (to 6500 r.p.m.): 1st, 42 m.p.h.; 2nd, 65; 3rd, 96.
ACCELERATION from rest through gears: 0-30, 3.9s.; 0-40, 5.9s.; 0-50, 9.7s.; 0-60, 12.6s.; 0-70, 18.6s.; 0-80, 24.3s.; 0-90, 31.0s.; 0-100, 38.1s.
ACCELERATION in top (with third in brackets): 30-50, 8.2s. (5.1); 40-60, 8.0s. (4.9); 50-70, 8.0s. (5.2); 60-80, 8.9s. (6.1); 70-90, 10.0s. (8.1); 80-100, 10.2s.
BRAKING: 30ft. 2in. to stop from 30 m.p.h. in neutral; 159ft. 3in. to stop from 90 m.p.h. in top gear. Tapley meter reading 98 percent.
FUEL CONSUMPTION: 44.2 m.p.g. at constant 30 m.p.h.; 26 at 60; 17.5 overall for 92-mile test.
SPEEDOMETER: 2 m.p.h. fast at 30 m.p.h.; 6 m.p.h. fast at 90.

PRICE: £1867 including tax

Top speed — 106.8 m.p.h.
Best speed — 108 m.p.h.
BUT . . . there are a few factors to take into account:
● The weather and the road were dampish — which is all right for the motor, but not so good for wheel adhesion. Best I could do for a clean getaway was to drop in the clutch at 2000 r.p.m. Rev minimum desirable for a good take-off is 2500 r.p.m.; the torque doesn't really get active till then.
● The run-up on the most suitable test track I could find was limited to two miles, and a certain allowance had to be made for milk trucks when rounding a slight curve. Under the circumstances, my best run of 108 m.p.h. wasn't at all bad.
● The fuel — about 40 percent benzol and premium — and the state of tune. Peter is naturally still experimenting with both.
● The complete difference in character between Peter's Twin-Cam and the first models that were reported on by the British motoring Press when this latest MG was announced a year ago. These reports said the car was

very rough-running at low revs and had to have the firm finesse of handling that a sports-racing car needs.

Now, Peter's car has a split personality. Below 2500 revs it's rather like driving an automatic with two halves of an over-ripe grapefruit acting as the torque-converter—it's slow, but so SMOOTH. About 2500 r.p.m. things are faster than a game of Russian roulette with every chamber loaded. I think the car may have had some production modifications which may have affected claimed performance.

● Lastly, it's a friend's car—I didn't go over 6500 revs in the indirect gears, and sometimes I balked at that when the noise got too much for my conscience.

Think on these things, and above all remember that the Twin-Cam is not just a 1936 Chev that will run on kero and can be tuned with a pair of quick-grips and a hairpin.

She's in a class where all the females are EXPECTED to be temperamental.

Anyway, if you listened to that engine pitching into things around 6500 revs, you'd realise that it is a very busy piece of machinery indeed. It makes not so much a loud but a very, very BUSY noise.

Nothing came through the sump, I'm glad to say. But the water temperature hopped up and down a bit on the acceleration runs—never near the danger mark, though.

But for two points, I am reasonably happy with the speed and acceleration runs, all things considered.

One thing I didn't like was the amount of heat that comes off the engine (tests were done with hood and side-screens up for maximum streamline effect). Same thing happens at sustained high cruising speeds. It was quite a cold day—I boil to think of summer motoring in a Twin-Cam, even with hood down.

The other was the effect of the gusty cross-wind on the car at 70 m.p.h. and beyond. The whole car would move sideways.

Which brings us to handling.

Handling and Braking

This is not the MG of tradition—a perky, brisk little runabout, beloved, alas, by the type who really appreciates legs more than wheels.

It's a serious high-performance motor-car.

Beware, unless you're an experienced, serious driver. You can so easily get into trouble.

I'm in no way criticising the Twin-Cam's handling; it's first class. But underneath the throttle pedal is a piece of dynamite that could go off at the wrong time on a corner.

If it happened to you—you alone would be to blame.

The steering is almost as good as you can get; the Dunlop disc brakes on all four wheels are better than anything imagined a few years back—no fade, no pulling aside, very little effort at the pedal.

They are caliper-type, self-cleaning, self-drying, and self-adjusting. It takes about two minutes per wheel to change pads.

The 159ft. 3in. stopping distance from 90 m.p.h. quoted in the performance panel was as uneventful as stopping from 20 m.p.h. at traffic lights.

Other Points

Just to sit in Peter's car is to love it. The seats are much more comfortable than the buckets fitted to the MG A's part-assembled in Australia. The finish and carpets are better. The dash is covered with semi-matt leather cloth instead of highly reflective duco.

And, praise be, that nasty, rattling, sticking, clicking trafficator switch, of which you never know whether it's on or off or really on the blink on the standard MG A, is replaced by something that bears no resemblance to it—and WORKS.

Finally, don't take the fuel figure of 17.5 m.p.g. seriously. The test was much too short and swift for it to be anything like normal expectations. And please note that the performance panel gives "theoretical" maximums in indirect gears at 6500 r.p.m. — fact is, I changed up whenever the engine got so busy I couldn't bear the thought of Peter's face if I came back with a conrod in my hand.

(Test car by courtesy of Peter Manton, Monaro Motors, Melbourne.)

COCKPIT changes from normal MG A include a fully leather-covered dash, comfier seats. General finish is better (car is fully imported).

MODERN MOTOR — August 1959

Externally the only evidence of work on the engine consists of the Speedwell name-plate on the rocker-cover. Carburetter air-cleaners have been removed.

Continued from page 47

With creature comfort attended to Ian Smith decided that something must be done about the MG-A's performance. As was obvious from the initial road test the 17½ cwt unladen weight of the car does not really give the 68 hp engine much chance to move the car off the mark very swiftly. Speedwell Performance Conversions, Ltd., have provided the complete answer to this problem.

Anyone who was seen John Sprinzel in action in his astonishing Austin A35 cannot help but have been impressed by the fantastic power available. John and his " merry men " at Golders Green have now found time to let loose their know-how on the MG-A cylinder head with most gratifying results.

Following exhaustive development with dynamometer and flow-testing rig, a conversion has been designed to remove " hot spots " and improve gas-flow. This has resulted in quite radically redesigned porting and combustion chamber shapes—achieved by much careful grinding and polishing of the cylinder head. Great attention is paid to the location of manifolds to ensure correct alignment and a perfectly smooth joint. Meticulous care is taken at each stage of the conversion and following assembly the converted car is given a thorough road test.

Speedwell made the MG-A a different car. First impressions were of more vivid acceleration and higher top speed but soon two other advantages were noticed—advantages not usually connected with " hotted motors." The engine was much smoother and the car itself even safer, for now there was extra torque to deal with any misbehaviour from the rather " happy " rear axle when cornering fast. After 500 miles, Graham Hill, who had actually fitted the conversion, had the car back for a final check of cylinder head bolts, carburetters. etc. Then with stop watch and passenger we were able to take acceleration figures for comparison with our earlier ones—these speak for themselves:—

	March 1957	March 1958
0-30 mph	5 secs	4 secs
0-40 mph	7.2 secs	5.5 secs
0-50 mph	11.2 secs	9.4 secs
0-60 mph	15.5 secs	13.5 secs
0.70 mph	22 secs	18.4 secs
0-80 mph	35.5 secs	26.1 secs

(figures taken under similar conditions—2 persons and mean of runs in both directions.)

The improvement ranged from 13% to 26% of the earlier times and gave an average improvement of just under 20%—what more could one want from a car which was now even sweeter to drive in traffic than it had been in standard form. Then another advantage of the Speedwell conversion presented itself—800 miles at 32 mpg, instead of the earlier 29!

During the tests it soon became apparent that clutch-slip was preventing even faster times. This was most noticeable when changing into top gear. Obviously the standard clutch was not up to the non-standard " hairy horses!" In John Sprinzel's opinion a competition clutch is the only answer to this trouble—he does not think that different linings on the existing unit will make any appreciable difference. Mindful of the London traffic work which the car undertakes each day the owner has now to decide between a quivering clutch foot or upward changes below 4,500 revs!

The Speedwell boys have definitely done great things for the MG-A (besides John and Graham the " bosses " include George Hulbert and Leonard Adams). Their next project for the Abingdon product is suspension modification to help stabilise the break-away at the back. When their busy lives enable them to get round to this no doubt 333 KMC will be an early customer.

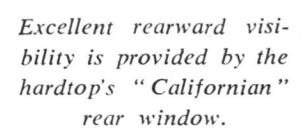

Excellent rearward visibility is provided by the hardtop's " Californian " rear window.

APRIL, 1958

S.C.W. Special feature: MG

Here's a little much-needed background reading from European Editor GORDON WILKINS

HOW DOES THE TWIN CAM EXIST AT ALL?

PRODUCTS of modern car factories evolve through interaction of many influences: engineering, styling, commercial policy, production commitments and economics. Rarely can a designer start with a clean sheet of paper. He usually has to use some existing components, adapt his design for use on a variety of vehicles or evolve something which can be produced by the expensive special purpose machine tools in which the company has already invested millions of pounds.

Probing into the origins of the twin overhead camshaft engine now available in the MG A, one might conclude that the engine may never have existed at all if the B.M.C. engineers had not run into a patch of bearing trouble while trying to increase the output of their new pushrod unit back in 1953. On the face of it the existence of a small line producing five twin-camshaft engines a day is an unexpected sight in a group producing 10,000 vehicles a week, a group moreover which has developed standardisation and rationalisation to a most advanced degree.

One basic body shell, one engine, one set of ratio variations, are now used to produce Austin A60, MG Magnette and Wolseley 15/60.

The same engine and gearbox with relatively minor modifications power the MG A, Wolseley 1500, Riley One Point Five, the Australian Morris Major and Austin Lancer, and a whole range of commercial vehicles. Yet alongside the lines that produce thousands a week of the pushrod units there is a tiny section building twin-cam engines—a standing challenge to the whole system.

To find the explanation we must go back to March 1953, when B.M.C. development engineers were trying to raise the power of the new B-type four-cylinder unit and running into trouble with bearings. It was then giving 60 b.h.p. at 4,600 r.p.m. on a 7.15 to 1 compression, and in this form it was used in the new MG Magnette introduced that Autumn. But three minutes at 7,000 r.p.m. and full load would squeeze the babbit out of the bearing shells like toothpaste out of a tube, and looking ahead to the days when compression ratios would rise and this engine would have to take the place of the 1,250 c.c. unit in the MG roadster, a greater safety margin seemed essential.

The development programme evolved by Mr. James Thompson, Chief Engineer of the Morris Motors Engine Branch, then newly incorporated in B.M.C., meant building an experimental engine which could be used for continuous bench testing of bearings at 7,000 r.p.m.

SPORTS CAR WORLD, September, 1959

Safety swifter ...M.G. in 1959

To get the required breathing capacity a twin overhead camshaft head was decided upon. Two heads were drawn and made, one with 66 deg. included angle between the valves and one with 80 deg. The narrow angle restricted valve size and tests soon confirmed the superiority of the 80 deg. head. Work continued on it during 1954 and it proved capable of producing 110 b.h.p. at 7,000 r.p.m.

News of what was going on at Coventry caused a stir down at the MG works at Abingdon, where boss man John Thornley and other veterans still look back nostalgically to the days when MG took the lead in technical developments. A production twin cam still seemed a wild dream in MG's price class, but permission was obtained for a try-out of the new unit in a works team car in the 1955 Tourist Trophy race. Engines with both types of head were fitted in experimental cars, but again the 80 deg. head was chosen and no more was heard of the other.

It was a race against time and on the Sunday before the event the race car had its first try-out on the high speed track at the M.I.R.A. proving ground. The results were depressing. The engine cut and spluttered on right hand corners because of fuel surge away from the jets.

The car was due at Liverpool next day to catch the boat for Northern Ireland, so a special inlet manifold was hastily fabricated from sheet metal to take two Weber carburettors which were immune to this trouble. The car went well in practice but during the race it was delayed by fuel starvation caused by a loose particle of metal which had obstructed the supply to one carburettor. The time lost while this was being traced probably kept it out of the disastrous multiple crash in which one driver was killed and several cars destroyed.

The engine made minimum departures from the basic pushrod design. Gears were adopted instead of a chain for the first stage of the valve gear train; an extension was fitted on the front of the crankshaft, and a stub shaft in place of the old camshaft carried drive gear and sprocket for the half speed chain drive to the overhead camshafts. A Duplex chain of 3/8 in. pitch was used, with two slipper type dampers and a tensioner sprocket with screw adjustment which could be reached through the oil filler cap on the front of the exhaust cam box.

Water pump and generator were belt driven, water being fed into the cylinder head at front and rear. The inlet camshaft was designed to drive an SU injection pump at the rear end, but it has not been used up to now. Injection was to have been into the manifold to avoid modifications to the cylinder head. The cylinder head was designed for removal without disturbing the valve gear, the chain wheels being slipped off and held on spindles on the chain case. The flywheel was a lightweight unit in steel.

In 1956, two of these engines were prepared for the streamlined single-seater MG EX 179, which George Eyston took to Utah. He set up a series of Class F records including 10 miles at 170 m.p.h.

MG management now conceived an ambitious new project. They decided to build a new streamliner

Here it is — the small miracle inside a mighty industrial combine. M.G. Twin Cam motors move slowly along the special assembly line at B.M.C.'s Engine Branch, Coventry.

MG HOW DOES THE TWIN CAM EXIST AT ALL?

which would be the first 1½ litre (91.5 cu. in.) car to reach 250 m.p.h. An entirely new streamlined shape was evolved around a chassis with a narrow rear track and calculations showed it would need 280 b.h.p. to hit the target speed. This obviously entailed supercharging and an extensive re-examination of the whole design, still without departing more than absolutely necessary from the same basic concept.

Basic proportions were kept unchanged, but a much stiffer block and crankshaft were produced and bearing diameters were increased. Crankpins went up to 2 1/16 in. (an extra 3/16) and mains to 2 3/8 (an increase of 3/8 in.). The shaft was in EN.40, of 60-70 tons tensile strength, nitrided, and weighed about 50 lb. against 32 for the one previously used.

Head design was basically unchanged, but larger valves were used and compression ratio was reduced from 9.9 to 6.82 to 1 in view of the boost of 32 p.s.i. above atmosphere pressure which was to be provided by a Shorrock eccentric-vane blower driven by gears from the front of the crankshaft.

Up to this point the tappets had been a type employed on the old Wolseley 4/50 and 6/80 engines, and also used by Alfa Romeo, consisting of discs screwed into the valve stems. But fatigue sometimes produced cracking at the base of the threaded shank, and for the blown engine a bucket type tappet was fitted over the valve spring, sliding like a piston in a cylindrical extension of the valve guide. Exhaust valves were sodium cooled. The main structural innovation was the cutting of all water flow between head and block to eliminate the vulnerable head gasket. Head and block had separate coolant circulation and sealing rings were used around the bores. Rod design had already been modified to permit fully floating gudgeon pins and those for the supercharged unit were made much stronger.

Valve timing gave a 70 deg. overlap. During bench testing some scuffing was experienced through the camshaft picking up chromium from the tappets. This was cured by eliminating chromium, but a patch of piston trouble produced an anxious time for Eddie Maher, the research engineer. At that time the MG boys were using a domed piston in a hemispherical combustion chamber, producing a combustion space rather like a slice of orange peel. But it proved very sensitive and combustion was difficult to control. Said Maher: "The flame travel seemed rather long and it was in the habit of going off bang."

After a lot of experimental work in collaboration with Hepworth and Grandage, a piston with a pent roof cured the trouble and has been used ever since.

Two blown engines were built. One gave 300 b.h.p. and the other 290 at 7,300 r.p.m. The latter was successfully used for the record runs by Stirling Moss, power being

Poised in solitary splendour on a trolley of its own, the potent Twin Cam motor waits for final tuning. Peculiar front casing reflects use of stub camshaft to carry drive up top. Stub shaft also drives distributor.

Three Twin Cam experimental pistons. At left is original 1,500 c.c. dome type with clearance flats; centre, flat-topped 1,500 c.c. piston for reduced detonation; right, production 1,600 c.c. piston.

SPORTS CAR WORLD, September, 1959

transmitted by a triple plate clutch of 7½ in. diameter.

The results were both a stimulus and a challenge. Would the directors agree to a production twin-cam engine? Eventually they assented and the design was finalised, still departing no more than absolutely necessary from that of the pushrod unit. Bearing sizes could safely be brought back to normal, for so well had the twin-cam succeeded in its primary objective that the copper-lead-indium bearings now in use were running 30 hours at full power and 7,000 r.p.m. without trouble.

Now the engineers really had to ask themselves what sort of engine they were trying to build. Was it a production racing unit or one that could be used for everyday driving? Up to this point no one had given a thought to running twin-cam units at anything under 2,000 r.p.m. and to achieve the desirable qualities of smooth idling and useful low-speed torque the cams had to be redesigned. The original cams had a simple three-arc form but for production a more sophisticated multi-sine wave form was used which changed the acceleration but not the lift. Bucket type tappets were retained, with biscuits to adjust the clearance. Exhaust valves were in KE 965 steel with stellited faces, iron seats were cast into the aluminium heads and combustion chambers were fully machined to give the production 9.9 to 1 compression ratio.

All pistons had four rings, except those on the blown engines, where rings were cut to three when the crowns started melting, to produce a heavier crown with more heat resistance. Current design specifies a chromium plated top ring, two rings with a one-deg. taper on the face and a two-section oil scraper ring. The piston is a simple design with a strengthening rib around the inside of the skirt and two struts joining the pin bosses to the crown.

The 1,500 c.c. unit was ready for production when it became apparent that the United States market wanted a 1,600 c.c. engine to meet the class limits, and what the U.S. wants it usually gets in sports cars.

So the designers were told to increase the size, but retain the same cylinder centres so that the blocks could still be machined on the automatic machines used for B.M.C.'s pushrod engines. There was only one answer; siamesed bores, eliminating the waterways between 1-2 and 3-4. Perhaps as a consequence, it was found that pistons made with the same running clearance as the 1,500 pistons would not operate successfully in the 1,600 size and a new period of piston "tailoring" was needed before the answer was found.

Such is the somewhat roundabout route by which the twin-cam engine arrived in the MG A. It represents the end product of a long development process, rather than the beginning. From a pushrod unit of 1,489 c.c. which was delivering 60 b.h.p. when experimental work began, a twin o.h.c. engine has emerged delivering 108 b.h.p. from 1,588 c.c. Specific output has risen from 40.3 b.h.p. per litre to 68, a gain of 69 per cent. Maximum torque of 105 lb. ft. represents a peak B.M.E.P. of 163 p.s.i. These, incidentally, are bench test figures without dynamo or fan, but with the normal car exhaust fitted. The twin cam engine, with clutch, gearbox, dynamo and starter, weighs 485 lb. against 403 lb. for the current MG A pushrod unit, an increase of 82 lb. for an extra 36 b.h.p.

It is not an engine which appears to have a great margin for further development, and MG have not announced any tuning stages for it, but several things can be done to obtain optimum results. A racing inlet camshaft can be substituted at some sacrifice in slow running and the usual timing methods of shortening the valve guides and paying meticulous attention to fit and finish apply.

Exact ignition setting is important, and the makers recommend that the distributor be set by stroboscope to give 26 deg. advance at 4,000 r.p.m. Static tune-up settings are suspect because of possible backlash in the mechanism and readings obtained at a fast tick-over may be falsified by hysteresis in the vacuum advance link-up. If the designers had ever been given a free hand to create a 1,600 c.c. twin-o.h.c. engine without reference to existing power units they would undoubtedly have chosen bigger bores, more widely spaced, a shorter stroke and a crankshaft running in five bearings instead of three. With the experience now available they would probably have adopted two-stage chain drive for the camshafts instead of using gears for the first stage. But put like that, the prospects of the project getting the go-ahead from a production-minded management would have been slender indeed and even if by some chance it had been accepted, the tooling investment required would have taken the Twin Cam MG A out of its present price range. #

Authentic factory graph shows sensational power curve of blown Twin Cam motor fitted to 250 m.p.h. record car. Peak b.h.p. recorded here is 290 at 7,650 r.p.m.

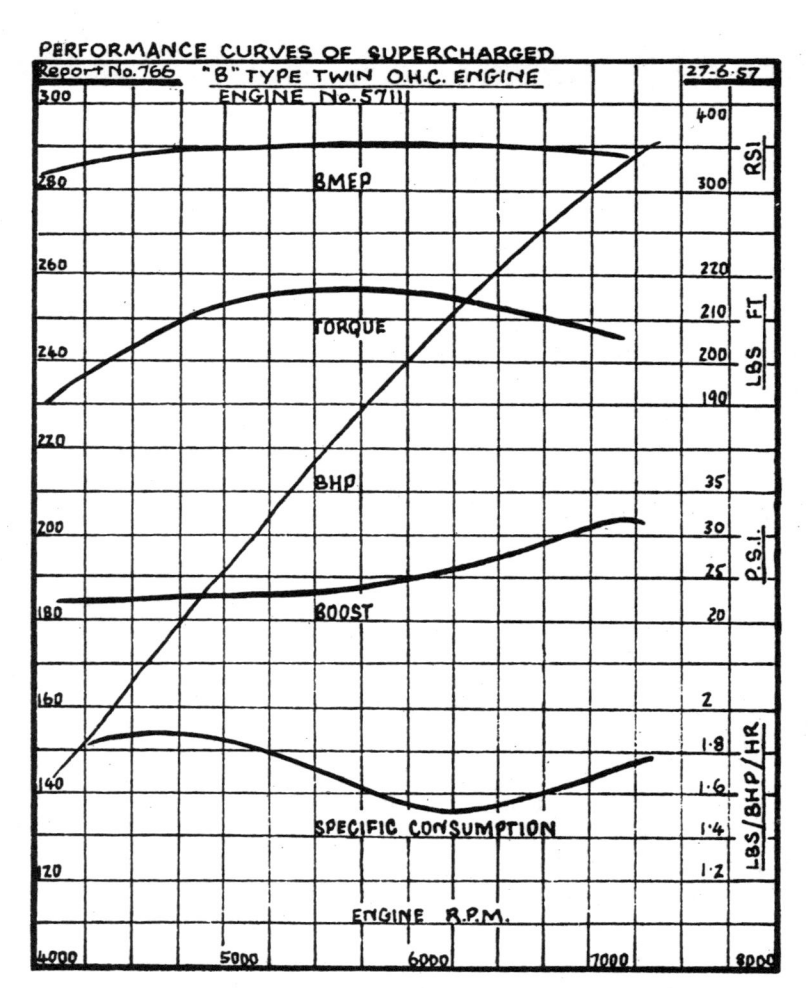

MG-A SPEED TEST

BY JIM FROSTROM

PHOTOS BY DEAN BATCHELOR

How often has the sports car owner wondered what answer to give when asked the inevitable question "Wottle she do?" Should he name the highest speed he has ever seen on his speedometer, or the latest road test figure from his favorite automotive magazine? An incontrovertible answer to this question seemed attainable for the writer's car when he accepted an offer to function as a judge for the sports car classes at the 1959 Bonneville National Speed Trials.

The rules were checked to determine any additions required before the car could pass safety and class inspection. Head-high roll bar and shoulder harness, in addition to seat belt, were required in all open-car classes. Windshield could be removed for installation of a one-man windscreen, along with a tonneau cover over the passenger seat. An entry in F-class Grand Touring Sports was made for the writer's MG-A, which was also to be the transportation for two people and their luggage to Bonneville and back to Los Angeles. During the preparation of the roll bar, windscreen, and straight-through exhaust, all of which were made removable, it occurred to me that some interesting comparisons might be made at Bonneville as various items were added or removed on different runs.

An informal test of the one-man windscreen at approximately 80 mph revealed a tendency on the part of the tonneau cover to belly down in the center and rise along the forward edge, between the two most widely spaced fasteners. In order to remedy this condition, two additional Lift-a-dot fasteners were added at the front and two more button snaps at the side of the door. This arrangement proved very satisfactory on the MG-A, but we were reminded by some of the "old pro" roadster owners that forward facing Lift-a-dots have been known to come unfastened from wind pressure and for that reason, on cars where no windshield gives protection, they are installed backward along the front of the cover.

The car used in this test was a stock '59 MG-A roadster which had had no special preparation other than the electronic balancing of all four wheels and tires. The SU carburetors had been adjusted and synchronized with the aid of a "Unisyn," the entire ignition system had been left untouched since the 4000-mile service at the agency where the car was purchased, and the car carried its original N5 Champion spark plugs. It is my opinion that the results obtained in this test could be equaled by any MG-A roadster with the 72-hp engine in good condition.

On the road to Utah the engine was kept humming along at 4000 rpm, giving an effortless, vibration-free cruise at an indicated 75 mph. Cruising at this speed in the somewhat mountainous country between Los Angeles and Wendover, Utah, gave a surprisingly economical 27.5 mpg, but it was necessary to add a quart of oil at each gas stop, approximately every 280 miles. The excessive consumption of oil ceased immediately upon our return home and resumption of normal traffic driving speeds.

The factory-recommended tire pressures of 21 psi front and 24 psi rear for a full load or fast driving were found to be inadequate, demonstrating a rather shifty oversteer condition from 50 mph upwards. Our full load consisted of three suitcases containing clothes for two people for a week, a few spare parts, crash helmet, three cameras and a tripod. Experimentation with increased tire pressures gave normal handling with 27 psi front and 31 psi rear (cold readings).

Upon arrival at Wendover, the front and rear license plates and their wind catching holders were removed and stored in the motel room along with the extra gear and the luggage. With the car still in full trim otherwise (top up, etc.), we left for the salt flats, eight miles east of town, and the safety inspection.

The first run was finally made on Monday afternoon, recording a disappointing 89.64 mph for the car in touring condition, including side curtains.

The next morning, Tuesday, we were out on the salt bright and early and, while the morning's record runs were being completed, we checked out the ignition system, setting the distributor to 8° advance and installing a new set of N5 spark plugs. I

ROAD & TRACK

made a minor error here as I neglected to check the amount of advance we had in the distributor upon arrival and for the first run. It was evidently pretty good as the next run netted only an 0.18 increase to 89.82 mph.

Ever since our arrival in Wendover, I had been torn between a desire to record an honest speed in road trim and a desire to put on the straight pipe which had proven too noisy even to drive around the block at home. Now was the time, since the wind noise of the roadster top at speed was louder than the factory muffled exhaust note and we really couldn't tell whether the engine was running perfectly or not. After installation of the straight exhaust, the next run gave a 1.18 mph improvement to an even 91 mph; however, there was no miss and it was evident that the car had been running all right with the muffler installed.

This was getting to be a little more like it, but why not make a run with the side curtains removed to see how much this cut our speed? Surprise! We picked up 0.55 mph, to record 91.55 and a resolution was made to recheck the phenomenon at the end of the week to make certain that some other condition was not the cause of the increase in speed.

Before going out to the course the next day, Wednesday, the top was taken off in order to make some runs with the windshield only. We expected the car to be slower in this condition and weren't surprised to go back to our original speed of 89.64 mph. Another run with the tonneau over the passenger's seat was even slower, at 88.06 mph. This was no fun, even if it did prove what everybody already seemed to know, that you go faster with the top up.

Advancing the ignition 4° for a total of 12° advance gave a big 2.16 mph increase on the next run to a speed of 90.22. Before everybody runs out to reset the advance on his ignition, it should be pointed out that the effectiveness of this increase in advance is mostly attributable to the higher altitude of 4200 ft. This much advance proved to be excessive upon our return to Los Angeles and the distributor was reset to 8° for best performance. By now we had had enough of this slow configuration and we returned to town for lunch and to get down to racing trim. The windshield, rear bumper and luggage rack were removed and hidden in our room, along with the previously removed top and muffler, and the one-man windscreen was installed.

Back on the salt, the next run was very encouraging at 97.08 mph, an increase of 8.15 mph over the windshield-only condition and 5.53 mph over our best previous run with the top up. The stock air cleaners were removed for the next run, resulting in an additional 0.74 mph increase for a final Wednesday run of 97.82 mph.

The next tuning step turned out to be my major *faux pas*. In anticipation of the possibility that the mixture might lean out when the air cleaners were removed, I had asked my MG dealer for a set of rich needles for the car, which were supplied as RH needles. In attempting to put them in Wednesday evening it was discovered that they were considerably larger than the factory installed GS needles, probably for use with larger jets which were not available on the west side of Utah. However, someone had said to me in jest, "If that doesn't do it, you can always whittle down your regular needles to make them richer." So, in semi-desperation, I very carefully scraped the stock GS needles, starting 31/32 in. from the shoulder, on out to the point. I'll never do that again! This move cost me 2.69 mph, and possibly more, since I had installed a set of flared bells on the carburetors at the same time which could have made a slight improvement.

The first Thursday run with all these improvements netted 95.13 mph. The next three runs were spent leaning out the carbs a total of 3 flats, which regained 1.74 of our lost miles, back to 96.87.

During this period, a visit was made, spark plugs in hand, to the Champion tent for advice from the spark plug expert provided to assist the Bonneville entrants. Big things were expected of this, since we knew that other contestants, including an MG-A twin-cam, had picked up as much as 8 mph by following his advice. We didn't—he looked at the plugs, each of them, for a long time through a magnifying glass, and said, "They look about right to me. You're pretty close to maximum tune." In a way, I guess, that was good news, but I had been counting on him to come up with some magic miles an hour and now, nothing.

Only one thing left to try, and I'd been saving that because I didn't feel it would make too much difference. It made enough, though, and proved to be the second big surprise. Raising the tire pressures to 44 psi all around gave a clocked speed of 100.55 mph on the next run. Now I can say it—my goal all the time had been to break 100 mph. Success at last! Who would have guessed that an approximate 16 psi increase in tire pressure would be good for almost 4 mph?

Two more runs, in which the ignition was advanced .5° to a total of 12.5° and the carbs richened one more flat, gave the MG-A's top speed of the meet at 101.01 mph.

Back out on the salt Friday morning with the windshield and top installed, but without the side curtains, a run was made at 95.84 mph, a drop of 5.17 mph from racing trim. Sure enough, the next run 25 minutes later, with the side curtains installed, reflected a drop of 0.80 mph to 95.04 mph, confirming our earlier results.

So now we know. A rocker-arm MG-A 1500 with the engine in good tune will exceed 100 mph, if you take off the top and windshield, air the tires and put on a straight-through exhaust. The clocked speed of 95.84 compares very favorably with the 97.5 mph speed previously attributed to it by Road & Track, since a calculated adjustment for the 4200-ft altitude would indicate that the same car should be able to pick up the other 2 mph at sea level.

The engine was left exactly as it was on the last timed run for our trip back to Los Angeles—only the straight pipe was exchanged for the muffler, to protect the innocents' eardrums. Gas mileage improved slightly to 28.6 mpg, probably due to the mid-range leaning out which had occurred in tuning the scraped needles for top speed. Total mileage for the entire trip was 27.2 mpg, a figure which includes 47.5 miles either accelerating or wide open in the 2-mile approach and the quarter-mile timed section.

All speeds given are one-way runs in the same direction. There were some slight side-winds and possibly some head-winds during the Wednesday runs, but at no time were runs made with a tail wind. It is possible to imagine under the circumstances that a drop in speed no greater than one mph would have been recorded had we been permitted to make return runs, but, in all probability, most of the return times would have improved slightly.

The tachometer in the MG-A proved to be almost 100% accurate, reading 5600 rpm when the car was clocked at 101.01 mph. The speedometer was a different story, reflecting 8 or 9% optimism at all speeds, indicating a wavery 110 mph during our fastest run.

Waiting for the start, in good company.

Folding luggage rack was used on trip.

Top up, luggage rack and bumper removed.

JANUARY 1960

S.C.W. special feature...

TRIUMPH: the Twin

TR OR T-C— WHICH IS FOR ME?

Triumph or Twin Cam? Four hundred cubic centimetres and two hundred greenbacks separate Abingdon's and Coventry's top contenders for the under-£2,000 sports car throne.

Pop eyes and uncompromising scuttle contours spoil TR's lines, say some harsh critics. Others argue that cutaway doors, engine access, and sharply sloping front more than compensate.

SPORTS CAR WORLD, October, 1959

Cam's No. 1 enemy

IT was English playwright Christopher Marlowe who first got the idea that comparisons are odius. He had one of his characters utter the words in a play called *Lust's Dominion* well back in the 16th Century and people have been quoting him ever since.

Heaven knows why!

Surely nothing is more natural. The man who walks down the street to his friendly Hoggmobile dealer and buys a Hoggmobile just because that's what the ads tell him to do is a fool. The same applies to any purchase, but particularly to a new car. The automobile is probably the second biggest single thing modern man buys during his lifetime and at that it deserves a little consideration — and therefore some conscientious comparison.

Sports cars more so. They're luxuries, toys. You buy a sports car purely for the fun it gives you, and you're going to be all the sorrier if you drive it into your garage only to have Joe down the street do you like a dinner in a competitive machine you hadn't even considered.

Maybe this is a little hypothetical. In practice, at any rate in this country, sports cars tend to divide themselves into distinct price classes and there's seldom more than one machine in each class. True sporting two-seaters seem to begin with the Berkeley at something under £1,000, then work up through Sprite, MGA, Triumph, MGA Twin Cam, Healey Six, Porsche, Jag 150, Mercedes 190-SL to the top of the price tree—the Jaguar 150-S, priced on the wrong side of £3,000.

The exception is the upper-£1,000 bracket, which currently holds two remarkably close contenders in the old-established Triumph TR-3A (tested overpage) at £1,695 and the MGA Twin Cam with £1,877 on the label. So new and so exciting is the Twin Cam that the battle has spread 'way outside the ranks of buyers and potential buyers. Camp followers, pipe dreamers and general hangers-on from end to end of the country are joining in whenever two or more kindred spirits meet to discuss the motor car and all its works.

T-C has dashing lines but suffers from lack of luggage room and bad accessibility. Excellent aerodynamics probably contribute towards 115 m.p.h. top speed.

SPORTS CAR WORLD, October, 1959

TRIUMPH: THE TWIN CAM'S No. 1 ENEMY

Continued

So have at you now, spit in your eye, seconds out and all that jazz —we're whaling in!

Price . . .

The obvious barrier. The Triumph has a 1,991-c.c. pushrod engine giving 100 b.h.p. at 5,000 r.p.m., or 2.98 b.h.p. per square inch of piston area. Compression ratio is 8.5 to 1. It features disc front brakes, overdrive on the three upper ratios and the option of an occasional back seat.

For £200-odd more the MG offers 403 fewer cubic centimetres but paired overhead camshafts help boost output to 108 b.h.p. at 6,700 r.p.m., giving a remarkable 3.9 b.h.p. per square inch of piston area. Compression: 9.9 to 1. Disc brakes do the stopping at all four corners. There's no overdrive option and no room for more passengers. To compensate for the MG's engine superiority a weight advantage of 65 lb. in favour (believe it or not) of the *Triumph* gives the pushrod car an extra lift along. Now we'll go on and look at all these features in detail . . .

Performance . . .

In brute acceleration the Twin Cam has the edge, but figures show that it's not much of an edge. Our tests, for various reasons beyond our control, did not give impressive maximum speeds for either car. Theory and the efforts of overseas testers lead us to quote the Twin Cam's maximum at 115 m.p.h. in favourable conditions and the Triumph's at 110, so once again the T-C wins.

One or two acceleration aspects deserve discussion. The M.G., because it has no overdrive, takes a tumble against the watch at the three peaking-out speeds of 35 m.p.h., 50 and 92. This shows up in the panels because the Triumph's overdrive unit can handle the changes from the direct gears (at 30, 52 and 81 m.p.h.) so much more quickly. In fact on 0-40 and 0-70 times the TR emerges ahead of the Twin Cam for that reason alone.

	MGA T-C	Triumph
0-30 m.p.h.	2.9 sec.	3.4 sec.
0-40 "	5.4 "	5.3 "
0-50 "	7.1 "	7.8 "
0-60 "	9.8 "	10.6 "
0-70 "	15.2 "	12.8 "
0-80 "	18.6 "	20.9 "
Standing ¼	18.0 "	18.4 "

Admittedly it becomes necessary to take the Triumph over the makers' recommended rev limit to achieve our quoted 0-70 time, since 5,000 r.p.m. in overdrive second is around 65 m.p.h., yet the car will do it and do it happily. Then when the change to third does eventually come along the Twin Cam leaps ahead again. The T-C's gear ratios and its ability to rev to at least 7,000 r.p.m. against the TR's 5,500 or so give it a surge of high-speed power that is missing in the TR even with overdrive in use. The o/d scores immeasurably, though, at lower and probably more normal highway speeds, especially since the Twin Cam has rather a low second cog.

Brakes . . .

The TR-3A has 11-in. Girling discs at the front and 10-in. drums at the rear. Test efficiency figure was an excellent .996 g and we found no fade, although the rear wheels (particularly the right hand one) tended to lock and the front discs smoked markedly after several panic stops. Pedal pressures are light to medium.

The M.G.A has 10¾ in. Dunlop discs all round. Our test efficiency figure was slightly less at .90 g, yet the brakes were free of locking and smoking troubles. Fade was entirely absent. Pedal pressures with the Twin Cam are always quite high.

One locking wheel tends to force the rest to lock, a fact which probably accounts for some of the Triumph's deficiency (with 15.0 sec.) in the 0-60-0 m.p.h., go-to-whoa test in face of the M.G.'s 12.9 sec.

Handling . . .

Both cars are a delight to drive quickly and up to a point they show similar handling characteristics. Both oversteer, but the Triumph throws out its tail later and more violently than its rival. If you were to take each car successively through the same corner at a given speed you would find that the M.G. broke away slightly almost from the outset (provided the "given speed" was a high one) and then settled down to finish the bend in a delightfully precise, controlled tail slide. The Triumph would track rigidly around until centrifugal force build-up and weight transfer combined to flick the rear wheels outwards quite suddenly, from where a low polar moment of inertia produces a tenency for the tail to stay well out. The Triumph would be the first to spin out, but paradoxically it would do so more innocently.

Tractability . . .

The Triumph scores here. It idles evenly and smoothly at 750 r.p.m., it has more low-speed torque (maximum 117.5 ft. lb. at 3,000 against 104 at 4,500 for the M.G.) and a better range of city ratios, counting overdrive of course. The Twin Cam is by no means impossible, though, and for all its 9.9 to 1 compression and theoretically cranky torque characteristics, it does not object to being trundled along in traffic.

Finish . . .

This time it's the M.G. that takes the biscuit, in spite of its famous cardboard door panels. Seat trim and carpeting on the Twin Cam are really classy, body panels fit properly and the under-bonnet view is charming thank you. The Triumph is almost as nice inside, but the leather is a poorer strain and only the transmission tunnel has carpet (but then carpet is a mixed blessing anyway, so where do you get?). The body isn't put together so well and there's nothing showy about the works.

Accessibility . . .

The M.G. is downright bad here, the Triumph really good. Obviously there's an inherent advantage in the TR's slim pushrod engine, but Abingdon should have given the T-C a bigger bonnet opening. Distributor, fuel pump, plugs, battery and carburettors are some of the things that hurl themselves at you as you open the Triumph's bonnet; the M.G. asks you to search for all except plugs. The TR has easily adjustable tappets, the TC uses the shim type.

Practicality . . .

By this we mean a car's inert design suitability for everyday use, quite apart from its road behaviour. For instance, the Triumph has space for children behind the front seats; it can even have a special seat there at extra cost — an obvious advantage to the family man but not much use to the chainless young bachelor. The M.G.'s boot is too small, the TR's reasonable. The M.G. has more comfortable seats for give-and-take use perhaps, but the Triumph's are much better in corners. The Twin Cam allows only a very close driving position, the TR-3A has more cockpit room. The M.G.'s hood is easier to put up. Wind blast at speed with the car open is less in the M.G. All these things become either advantages or disadvantages only in the eyes of the individual, although we do think every sports car should have at least reasonable luggage room. The Triumph has a lockable glove box, the T-C has none. Both cars have door pockets.

Life . . .

The M.G. Twin Cam engine, because it is so much more highly stressed and because of its higher piston speeds, is likely to wear faster than the Triumph unit. That is not to say, though, that it won't have a reasonable life. Wet cylinder liners make it more convenient to overhaul the Triumph when it gets around to wearing out its initial set. Chassis life should be about equal for both cars.

Tyre wear will depend largely on driving technique, but the M.G.'s standard Dunlop Road Speeds will take constant high speed work more happily than the Gold Seals fitted to the Triumph.

Fuel consumption should be worse by anything up to 10-15 m.p.g. in the case of the M.G., which puts the Triumph first in the books of the truly impecunious. Remember, though, that at 10,000 miles a year that extra 10 m.p.g. need only mean £30-odd down the drain.

Twin Cams are often said to be oil burners, but careful running-in has been proved to give good lubricant consumption figures.

Parts vary in price. In both cases specialist parts (i.e., bits that are made only for Triumph and M.G. respectively) cost a lot. Parts that are common to the respective parent vehicles (Morris and Standard), or in the case of the Twin Cam to the locally-assembled M.G.A pushrod, are cheaper.

Potential . . .

Both factories offer competition kits of varying completeness. Typical Triumph extras are alternative rear axle ratios, a special sump, heavy duty shock absorbers, competition front springing, Alfin rear brake drums. M.G. offer among other things, a strengthened clutch, alternative final drive ratios and a complete close-ratio gearbox as aids for competition-minded T-C owners. Ultimately the Twin Cam could undoubtedly be made to go faster than the Triumph, but the cost of making it do so would probably exceed the cost of bringing the TR-3A to its ultimate output. Remember that the Twin Cam engine is specifically designed for extremely high speeds. Its all-disc brake layout would no doubt pay dividends in competition.

For the average bloke who wants to take his car in sprints and perhaps in the occasional hill-climb, the position is rather different. Mild warming should be enough to bring the TR's performance into the distinctly startling category. The Twin Cam, on the other hand, isn't quite such easy meat. The Triumph is more easily stripped for competition and it already has such details as provision for demounting the windscreen and for fitting aero screens. It has more detachable trim than the T-C, but remember that the cars will compete in the same class only for another year or so. As soon as C.A.M.S. approves the 1,600 c.c. class limit for medium capacity sports cars they'll be well and truly divorced. Anyone who likes his chances in competition would do well to consider the probable eventual opposition when he decides for one or the other.

And that's it. Individual analysis alone can point the way either to the Triumph dealer's or to his M.G.-vending rival across the road. For our part, having tested both, it's quite a problem.

Perhaps the fairest way to sum things up is to say that the M.G. Twin Cam (at £200 more, mind you) has more to offer the man who can use that extra five m.p.h., that slightly superior handling and those few bonus tenths of a second, who can spare the extra weekly fuel money and the time for fiddling service jobs (the T-C demands 100 octane fuel; Triumphs will behave on normal super) and who perhaps has his eye on a shelf-full of silverware in 1,600 c.c. competition.

The M.G. also has an irresistible appeal to the engineering type who prefers to think of those highly efficient double knockers whirring away out front as the tachometer wavers around 7,000.

The more practical fellow who needs luggage room and infant space and fuel economy and certain engine wear will pocket his £200 and settle for a Triumph.

A thought that keeps us guessing is — what if that same fellow were to spend the £200 on his TR-3A and *then* ask which is best? Well really . . .   #

M.G.A. T.C.—THERE'S FIRE DOWN BELOW

(Continued from page 61)

A touch of the throttle halts that plopping idle smartly, substituting the calico-tearing crack of a barely legal exhaust as the tachometer rockets around the scale. A Twin Cam with the tap turned on actually sounds like the Healey-eater it is.

The new clutch is delightfully smooth. Some overseas testers complain that it slips under severe punishment, but for normal use it would be hard to fault. The normal ratio gearbox on Bruce's car (close cogs are available at extra cost) was much less stiff than the one on Photographer Sandford's normal A, which we tested in S.C.W. June. It didn't suffer from that annoying refusal to drop into first, either.

Consequently I found my changes just falling into place within minutes of taking over the car. First gear obviously has tremendous potential, and even the 3,000 rev limit which we imposed for most of this tryout drive gave ample scope for some really nippy starts. A little throttle in second gives more than a hint of what the car will do, and third gear is a sheer joy.

The car seems to dance with anticipation as you plant your foot and your heart starts to sing that special song that only a car like this can provoke. The wind tears at your hair, the road rushes up to meet you and nothing else matters but that lusty little firebreather under the bonnet ahead of you. All too soon it's time to bring in top, and therein lies a significance.

I was changing, as I said, at 3,000 r.p.m. Now a normal M.G.A. is working quite hard at that speed, but the Twin Cam is different. Up to around 2,500 it is literally loafing — using a mere 44 b.h.p. in fact, against the pushrod car's 36. But from there on the horsepower curve takes on the look of the Wall at Templestowe 'climb, by which I mean that it comes quite close to the vertical. Up to about 4,500 each 500 r.p.m. increase in revs brings in about 10 more b.h.p., and above that speed the rate rises to nearer 15 until it begins to tail off at about 5,500.

Not bad, you say. But the effect on road performance is invigorating in the extreme. At each change I could feel the car straining to go faster. I can hardly wait to drive a Twin Cam that is properly freed up.

No fast car is worth having unless its brakes are equally outstanding. The T-C's Dunlop discs are as good as anything currently on offer. Typically, they ask only very light pedal pressures and do their work almost inconspicuously, leading the unitiated to suspect trouble. But they certainly do work.

Stiffer front coils (fitted partly to offset the double knocker motor's extra 60 lb. weight) and the big power increase makes cornering better, if anything, than before. Dunlop Road Speed tyres abolish squeal at normal speeds, substituting a mild sort of scraping noise as the shoulders bite in on sharp bends. The car handles as a taut, ultra-predictable unit helped by absolutely impeccable rack and pinion steering.

The suspension gives a rather hard ride on normal give-and-take suburban roads at around 30 m.p.h., but at higher speeds it irons out all but the most ugly bumps in copybook fashion. The engine is not as flexible as the pushrod unit, naturally, but it will stand a remarkable amount of top gear slogging in the hands of a cruel driver.

The new seats are fine. Upholstered in genuine leather, they offer much better location than their cheaper counterparts. I really would appreciate a few inches more cockpit length though, Abingdon. Next time, perhaps.

Altogether this looks like an unsurpassed sports car buy. Eighteen hundred pounds is a lot of money, certainly, but look what you get.

What other car at anything like the price will touch this for handling, stopping and sheer acceleration? Yes — M.G.s are going places again.

—*Doug Blain*

FOOTNOTE: Prospective Twin Cam buyers are worried that the car just misses out on the under-1,500 c.c. racing class. But the wheels are turning and we may soon have a proper International under-1,600 limit.   #

M.G. under pressure

The "Peco" Supercharger Kit Tested

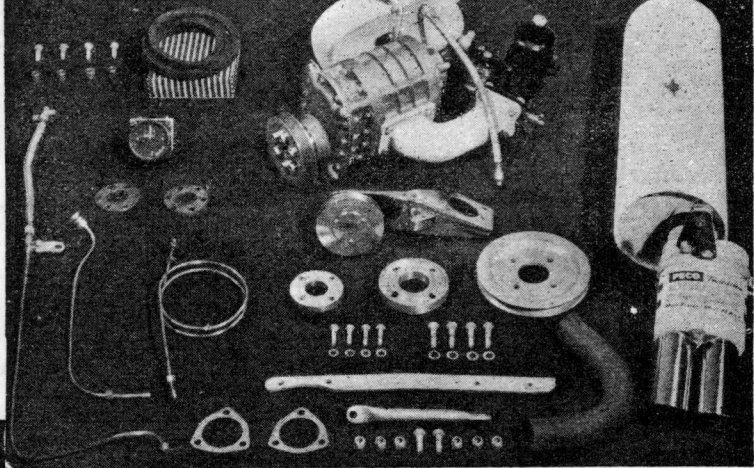

Bolt-on bits for the "Peco" kit include the Roots-type blower with S.U. carburetter, belt and pulleys, boost gauge, fuel pipes, gaskets and silencer with the Peco exhaust booster. The under-bonnet installation is neat, although a little crowded at the front end.

THE merits of supercharging as a means of obtaining greater power from a given engine with equal reliability and only small loss of economy have long been recognized by engineers, but seldom taken to heart by the car-buying public. Whether this has been because of the comparatively high cost, or because of the noise and high engine speeds associated with high-pressure supercharging in specialized racing machines is open to speculation. Neither criticism is properly justified.

The supercharger conversion for the M.G. A two-seater offered by the Performance Equipment Company, and lent to us for test, appeals to the already half-converted, for it is designed for a sporting car in which high speeds are commonplace. Its effect, however, is not at all to produce a fierce and noisy machine suitable only for racing, but to give the M.G. just those virtues which would be most appreciated in a family saloon. Owing to the limitations both of the normal recommended engine speed and of a supercharger belt which persistently came off its pulleys we made no attempt to discover maximum speed, which in any case is of the order of 100 m.p.h. for the unblown car. Acceleration, however, was improved in a very impressive manner, not only as measured in plain figures but quite smoothly and without the harshness which often accompanies a gain in performance using high compression ratios.

To the driver, the only noticeable disadvantages of the "Peco" conversion are a slight and not tiresome whine from the Roots-type supercharger, a momentary pause if the throttle is opened suddenly at low speed and a steady drain on the pocket if full use is made of the performance. To the cost-per-mile in petrol must be added roughly 5% for 100-octane fuel. Compensatory results are acceleration times in top and third gears reduced in the best cases by well over 40%.

Acceleration through the gears from standstill does not show up quite so well in our performance tests, largely because of the tendency of a long vee-belt passing round widely spaced pulleys on crankshaft, tensioner and supercharger to turn itself inside out and finally jump off, if speeds of more than 5,500 r.p.m. were sustained. The manufacturers' claim that all parts can be bolted on without alteration of existing components is literally correct. Unfortunately the addition of another belt pulley on the crankshaft nose leaves so small a clearance between this and the front cross member of the M.G. that changing a belt without damage to the fabric is almost impossible. Apart from this the installation is quite simple; a normally competent and enthusiastic owner should have no labour charge to add to the all-in price of the kit of £98.

TEST RESULTS

Acceleration	Normal M.G.A (The Motor Road Test August 7, 1957)	"Peco" M.G.A
	sec.	sec.
Top gear, 10–30 m.p.h.	13.6	9.0
20–40 m.p.h.	13.6	7.6
30–50 m.p.h.	13.8	7.9
40–60 m.p.h.	12.6	8.2
50–70 m.p.h.	13.7	9.4
60–80 m.p.h.	17.6	10.2
3rd gear, 10–30 m.p.h.	8.1	5.8
20–40 m.p.h.	7.9	4.4
30–50 m.p.h.	8.1	5.1
40–60 m.p.h.	8.7	6.1
50–70 m.p.h.	10.4	7.0
From standstill, 0–30 m.p.h.	5.0	4.2
0–50 m.p.h.	10.8	7.9
0–70 m.p.h.	21.4	16.7

Hill-climbing at sustained steady speeds

Top gear	1 in 10.7 (Tapley 210 lb./ton)	1 in 8.1 (Tapley 275 lb./ton)
3rd gear	1 in 7.3 (Tapley 305 lb./ton)	1 in 5.9 (Tapley 375 lb./ton)

Fuel consumption

	m.p.g.	m.p.g.
At constant 30 m.p.h.		33
50 m.p.h.	43	28.5
70 m.p.h.	31	25.5
Overall fuel consumption	27.6	22.8

THE TWIN-CAM M.G.

A Very Satisfactory Small Sports Car, Offering a Maximum Speed Comfortably in Excess of 110 m.p.h., Extremely Good Acceleration, Unexpected Docility and Outstanding "Safety Fast" Characteristics, Reinforced by Dunlop Disc Brakes All Round.

THE TWIN-CAM M.G. in a peaceful setting. Externally it is indistinguishable from the normal M.G.-A, but wait until you drive it . . . !

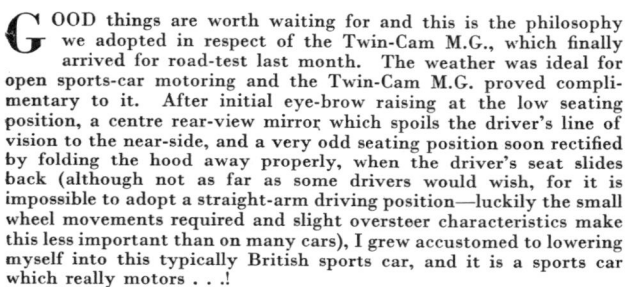

GOOD things are worth waiting for and this is the philosophy we adopted in respect of the Twin-Cam M.G., which finally arrived for road-test last month. The weather was ideal for open sports-car motoring and the Twin-Cam M.G. proved complimentary to it. After initial eye-brow raising at the low seating position, a centre rear-view mirror which spoils the driver's line of vision to the near-side, and a very odd seating position soon rectified by folding the hood away properly, when the driver's seat slides back (although not as far as some drivers would wish, for it is impossible to adopt a straight-arm driving position—luckily the small wheel movements required and slight oversteer characteristics make this less important than on many cars), I grew accustomed to lowering myself into this typically British sports car, and it is a sports car which really motors . . . !

When summing-up the normal push-rod M.G.-A in MOTOR SPORT, I wrote that "the car is a worthy descendant of the race-bred cars that preceded it, in as much as it possesses impeccable road manners and adequate performance . . ." The Twin-Cam M.G. retains in full measure the safe and pleasant handling qualities of the push-rod version but it was to convert the performance from adequate to potent that the M.G. Car Company enlarged the engine size from 1,489 to 1,588 c.c. and used a twin o.h.c. cylinder head (with suitable bottom-end mods.), developed from an experimental engine introduced for racing over five years ago. The main purpose of the Twin-Cam M.G. is competition work and it was added to the M.G. range with an eye on the dollar market. However, having used one with great enjoyment for fast pleasure motoring in England I see no reason why this particular M.G. shouldn't become very popular here as a normal sports model, particularly as the engine, if noisy, is splendidly docile and disc brakes all round look after the increase in maximum speed and the rapidity with which the scenery begins to rush by when the accelerator is depressed.

Admittedly a good deal of " teething trouble " has been experienced with this production M.G. twin o.h.c. engine but let us hope this has been overcome; certainly the car I drove for more than 470 miles never faltered and oil-pressure and water temperature remained steady throughout the test, which included taking performance figures. The engine is distinctly audible, which quite apart from the fine weather, made me reluctant to put the hood up; the coupé version must be almost unendurable ! And oil consumption is, to put it mildly, excessive.

In general conception the Twin-Cam M.G. two-seater follows the specification and equipment of the well-known M.G.-A, so we need not deal with it in great detail.

The seats are separate bucket-type with folding squabs, upholstered in real soft leather. They are very good, if not ideal, seats, but set low in the car, with only the off-side front wing visible to an average-height driver. Mounting the mirror directly on the scuttle, deleting the stalk, might help visibility.

The pedals are normally placed and while it is not possible to " heel-and-toe," brake and accelerator can be operated together with the ball of the right foot. The clutch foot has to be parked under rather than beside the pedal and the foot-dipper button is rather inaccessible. Clutch and throttle action are light and well-constituted. An adjustable steering column is available; normally the wheel is closer to the facia than tall drivers may like.

A very rigid short central gear-lever controls the usual B-series B.M.C. gearbox but what is an impeccable change on other B.M.C. small cars and earlier M.G.s is less pleasant on the modern M.G., because the lever is stiff to operate and has short lateral and transverse movements, while the synchromesh is beaten all too easily when snap gear changes are attempted. Taken calmly this is a nice gear change but in the heat of a race or when making snap selection of a lower ratio the driver suffers. The reverse guard-spring is too weak, so that this ratio can be selected inadvertently when wishing to change rapidly from third to second gear. The lever could hardly " fall to hand " better, however, its knob being extremely close to the steering wheel. It would hardly be a B.M.C. box were some difficulty not experienced in getting into bottom gear from a standstill !

The fly-off hand-brake, which is locked on by depressing the knob, has for long been an excellent M.G. feature. On the Twin-Cam it lies horizontally close against the propeller-shaft-tunnel, but it is quite convenient to use and holds the car securely.

The four spring-spokes of the steering wheel form a narrow " X," giving full visibility of speedometer and rev.-counter. These are Jaeger instruments, the speedometer incorporating total and trip-with-decimal mileometers. The needles move in the same plane and are commendably steady. The rev.-counter has a yellow segment from 6,500 to 7,000 r.p.m., a red segment from 7,000 to 7,500 r.p.m., which provides a foretaste of the performance of this Twin-Cam M.G.

The rest of the instrumentation on the leather-covered facia is simple but effective, comprising oil-pressure gauge (reading 20 lb./sq. in. of Castrol XL at idling r.p.m., 60 lb./sq. in. at fast cruising speeds), water thermometer (steady at 70 deg. C., rising only slightly during acceleration tests), and a sensibly pessimistic petrol gauge. The ignition key is separate from the starter knob and similar (lettered) knobs look after the usual services. Warning lamps are confined to those for dynamo-charge, lamps full-beam and flashers, the last-named warning winking at the extreme right of the facia, where steering wheel rim and driver's right fist usually obscure it, perhaps providentially. In any case, the tab switch for the indicators, conveniently placed for the right hand, returns to the vertical when the flashers have self-cancelled. The horn-button is recessed in the centre of the facia, which is reasonably convenient. Below are the controls for heater/demister/ventilator. The map-reading lamp and switch, on the passenger's side of the facia, is an excellent feature inherited from the M.G.-A, as are the capacious, roomy, rigid door-pockets, well-strutted windscreen mounted rather far from the occupants (it detaches for racing—gone are the days when by unscrewing a couple of wing nuts you could lower the screen flat and have fun in the fresh air, wearing helmet and goggles !), doors devoid of exterior handles and opened by " pulling a string " within the door pockets, and the rest of the body details, including a boot considerably obstructed by the spare wheel. I like the easy-to-clean ventilated steel disc wheels, of centre-lock type.

New-type rigid Perspex sidescreens, with sliding panels to enable the door-catch " pulls " to be reached with the hood up, prevent side-draughts. The hood, furled, stows completely out of sight but a tonneau cover would be a welcome addition. For night driving the Lucas headlamps are very effective.

On the road the Twin-Cam M.G. is an outstanding motor car. The engine peaks at 6,700 r.p.m. but runs readily to 7,000 r.p.m. and will go " into the red " as easily as a bank balance if the driver is casual. Using maximum or near-maximum revs. in the gears, really effective acceleration can be achieved, as the figures in the data panel confirm. This is acceleration of the kind that makes passing slow-moving vehicles a very momentary, and consequently, safe, manoeuvre. The engine is smooth, and responds effectively, right up to 7,000 r.p.m. and crankshaft speeds around 6,000 r.p.m. will be employed habitually by fast drivers. On the other hand, it is possible to use revs. more of the M.G.-A order, i.e., 4,500-5,500 r.p.m. and still get very quickly to 70 m.p.h., while top gear pick-up between 50 and 80 m.p.h. is also extremely useful.

The remarkable thing is that this inexpensive production engine is running at speeds regarded as high in the racing world not so long ago, yet it is ridiculously docile as well as potent. It will idle at 500 r.p.m. without a trace of plug-oiling or " hunting " and will open up in the 4.3 to 1 top gear from not very much higher speeds—not that anyone will often so abuse it. It is necessary to use 100-octane petrol, when no " pinking " is experienced; running-on occurred only after some rather intense performance testing—never after normal running. There is noise from the valve gear and a faint ring from the camshafts drive but the exhaust note is not obstrusive from inside the car, although a road-side observer might recognise the Twin-Cam by its tail-pipe snarl—the only other way is by the insignia on the tail-panel.

The acceleration, to revert to this outstanding aspect of the Twin-Cam M.G. is, very roughly, twice as effective as that of a normal M.G.-A. As to speed, I believe the aim was 120 m.p.h. but normaly Twin-Cam models cannot exceed 114/115 m.p.h., which is about 12 m.p.h. faster than the maximum speed of the M.G.-A coupé. Moreover, although 80 and 90 m.p.h. comes up readily enough on the road, the former speed being attainable in ¼-of-a-mile from a standing start, a mile or more of clear road is essential before 6,000 r.p.m. (or 103.8 m.p.h.) is obtainable in top gear. Incidentally, the test-car had a speedometer that was 4 per cent. fast at 60 m.p.h., 3½ per cent. fast at 80 m.p.h.

This brings us to the question of maxima in the gears. Going up to 7,000 r.p.m. the genuine speeds are 33, 55 and 88 m.p.h.; if you ponder on this you will see how these highly creditable speeds in the indirect gears assist acceleration. It is very pleasant to be able to change down from top to third at over 80 m.p.h. !

The road-holding and roll-free cornering characteristics are fully in keeping with the performance.

The rack and pinion steering is accurate, free from lost motion, and has sensible castor-return action. There is mild kick-back of the wheel in the driver's hands, accentuated on bad by-roads, when scuttle-shake also intrudes. In spite of criticism of this form of steering for fast cars it suits the M.G. admirably and does not feel so low geared as 2¾ turns, lock to lock suggest.

The steering, indeed, is quite exceptionally good; it is absolutely positive and the car responds immediately to any movement with a rapidity which is most unusual. A trace of stiffness is presumably due to the friction damper in the rack-and-pinion gear, but the steering remains light in all conditions, even when throwing the car fast into hairpin bends. The steering characteristic is quite neutral at normal cornering speeds, and the intended line on corners can be held with unusual precision, even on rough surfaces. Pressed beyond this, a gradual oversteer develops and the car starts to break away at the back in a very gentle and completely controllable way. Use of the throttle brings the tail round more quickly and can contribute to very rapid progress along sharply winding roads; this effect is appreciably more noticeable on right hand than on left-hand corners, probably because of weight transfer due to torque-reaction. For competition purposes, it is probable that many experienced drivers would prefer to delay the onset of oversteer to still higher cornering speeds, and the addition of a front anti-roll bar might then be indicated.

The Dunlop RS 4 tyres exhibit a considerable amount of squeal at the low pressures recommended for normal driving, and are not entirely silent even at the 22/24 lb./sq. in. recommended for fast driving. At 23 front, 26 rear, squeal was absent until the breakaway was approached, although a certain amount of harshness was then noticeable in the ride, together with occasional traces of wheelspin when accelerating hard on bumpy roads.

The combination of fairly soft front with much harder rear suspension, and heavy damping all round, gives an extremely pleasant ride, firm, almost to the point of harshness with the higher tyre pressures, but unusually flat. This lack of pitching, together with the lack of roll, produces a feeling of great stability. There is a certain amount of mild scuttle shake and some body rattles, particularly

THE TWIN-CAM M.G. TWO-SEATER

Engine : Four cylinders, 75.4 by 89 mm. (1,588 c.c.). Inclined overhead valves operated by twin overhead camshafts. 9.9 to 1 compression-ratio. 108 b.h.p. (net) at 6,700 r.p.m.
Gear ratios : First, 15.6 to 1; second, 9.5 to 1; third, 5.9 to 1; top, 4.3 to 1.
Tyres : 5.90 by 15 Dunlop Road Speed RS 4 on centre-lock steel disc wheels.
Weight : 0 tons 19 cwt. 1 qr., ready for the road, without occupants, but with rather less than two gallons of petrol.
Steering-ratios ; 2¾ turns, lock-to-lock.
Full capacity : Ten gallons (range approximately 240 miles).
Wheelbase : 7 ft. 10 in.
Track : Front, 3 ft. 11½ in.; rear, 4 ft. 0¼ in.
Dimensions : 13 ft. by 4 ft. 10 in. by 4 ft. 2 in. (high—hood up).
Price : £843 (£1,195 7s. 6d. inclusive of purchase tax).
Makers : M.G. Car Company, Ltd., Abingdon-on-Thames, Berkshire, England.

PERFORMANCE DATA

Speeds in gears (after speedometer correction) :
   First   ...   .   33 m.p.h.
   Second   ...   .   55 m.p.h.
   Third   ...   .   88 m.p.h.
Acceleration :
   0-50 m.p.h....   ...   ...   8.5 sec. (8.5 sec.)
   0-60 m.p.h....   ...   ...   12.4 sec. (12.4 sec.)
   0-70 m.p.h....   ...   ...   16.7 sec. (17.0 sec.)
   0-80 m.p.h....   ...   ...   22.3 sec. (22.8 sec.)
   Standing-start ¼ mile   ...   18.5 sec. (18.5 sec.)

(*Figures in parentheses are mean of runs in both directions*)

from the clips holding the sidescreens to the tops of the windscreen pillars.

The Dunlop 10¾-in. disc brakes all round are contributory to the car's admirable safe-handling qualities. As is usual with non-servo applied disc brakes, considerable pedal pressure is required for low-speed stops but from high speeds retardation is extremely effective for light pedal pressures, it being possible to lock the wheels in an emergency. Normally the very impressive acceleration of the Twin-Cam M.G. leaves " incidents " well behind but it is comforting to know that if an approaching driver does something foolish which interferes with one's intentions these very powerful fade-free brakes are at one's disposal.

Taken all round, the Twin-Cam M.G. is a most enjoyable fast car. It costs £255 more than the M.G.-A (inclusive of p.t.) and for this the purchaser gets not only an engine giving 108 b.h.p., an increase of 36, but disc brakes, knock-off wheels and Road Speed tyres in addition.

What are the penalties ? Noise, when the car is closed up against the weather. Inaccessibility of ignition distributor, which is buried under the heater piping, and of the dip-stick. The figure of 24.3 m.p.g. of petrol obtained in fast road driving, using peak revs. frequently in the indirect gears, cannot be regarded as excessive, but on rallies this would rise to some 20 m.p.g. The tank, holding ten gallons, thus gives the rather cramped range of approximately 240 miles in normal motoring and is ludicrously small for serious competition work of the long-distance variety. Excessive oil consumption is the real short-coming of this Twin-Cam M.G.—nearly half-a-gallon was consumed in 400 miles ! The dip-stick is extremely difficult to replace and would seem quite impossible for making the very vital checks on sump level during club races. Presumably serious competition drivers arrange something better than Abingdon has devised for normal customers, at the same time adding a larger fuel tank.

These matters apart, the Twin-Cam M.G. is oustanding by reason of its very considerable performance and particularly in respect of its impeccable handling qualities. It is a handsome car, too. It thus very worthily maintains the reputation of this famous breed of British sports cars.—W. B.

THE MGA MARK II:
HOW TO WIN SALES AND INFLUENCE TASTES

Adhering to a well-tried and proven policy, new MG still retains the same body with which the marque was endowed seven years ago.

Engine boost for newest car to wear the octagon

IF you went out and asked 100 people in the street to name one make of sports car, you could be sure that ninety of them would name the MG. Such is the fame of the little car which is credited with introducing the car-conscious American to sports cars.

The MG has a wonderful sporting heritage, having scored literally thousands of competition wins and having set innumerable speed records during the 35 years or so of its production life.

The latest result of this heritage is the MGA 1600 Mark II, fourth of the "A" series and using virtually the same body as the original MGA, which was introduced in 1955. About 100,000 MGAs have been produced and they have won thousands of friends, many of them including the fanatical adherents to the squarelook MG of pre 1955.

I venture to say that the MGA is probably the most successful sports car ever mass produced. By successful, I refer not to its competition performances, but to its performance as a sales winner and influencer of tastes for BMC.

The latest car is very little different physically from its predecessor. A slightly modified grille, new tail lights, and additional chrome trim on the instrument panel, distinguish its appearance. Mechancally, the changes have been a little more extensive.

The main change is a bigger and more powerful engine. This coupled with a drop in axle ratio from 4.30 to 4.10 has done a lot to improve the initial acceleration of the new MG. The motor has a capacity of 1622 cc, which has been achieved by a cylinder bore increase to an even 3 in. The stroke is left untouched at 3:5 in.

BMC quote the developed power as 90 bhp — is an increase of 13 percent — for the 8.9 to 1 compression engine, and 84.6 bhp for the 8.3 to 1 engine which is the one that will be available in Australia.

The very rigid chassis remains unchanged, as do the braking arrangements — discs on the front, drums on back.

THE MGA MARK II: HOW TO WIN FRIENDS AND INFLUENCE TASTES

... Continued

On the road the Mark II has noticeably improved performance over the earlier 1600. The extra capacity more than makes up for the lowered back-end, and although the drag factor hasn't been altered, the car achieves a genuine 100 mph with considerably more ease than the old model.

Although at this stage no one in Australia has published a road test we anticipate that the Mark II would achieve a top speed in excess of 105 mph while pulling between 5600 and 5700 rpm.

Anyone who has owned an MGA will harangue for hours on the exemplary roadholding qualities of the car. We won't go so far as to say that the car is the best handling sports car available today, or that it has the best steering. However, it is perfectly true to say that it is a car without handling vices.

Any rank beginner could climb into an MGA and drive fast without any fear of the car playing tricks on him. The steering (rack and pinion) is as close to neutral as you'll get on a sports car today. The car oversteers, and the "tailout" attitude can be provoked and held with relative ease. The steering, typical rack and pinion, has no backlash or play. High speed stability is very easy; it's not necessary to make adjustments with the steering wheel when going in a straight line. Occasionally the wheel transmits a road shock, but thanks to a very rigid frame and body, there is no scuttle to speak of.

The rigid riding qualities of the MGA have been the subject of criticism in recent years. The claim is that they haven't improved greatly since it was introduced in 1950, and in many ways this is largely true. However, the really firm ride of the earlier T series cars is no longer evident, by virtue of the fact that the seats of the A are located within the chassis and more towards the front of the car.

The ride can be improved by lowering tyre pressures, but with the tyres fitted as standard by the factory, tyre squeal has always been something of a problem; lowering the pressures only makes matters worse, as well as making life more difficult for the tyres themselves.

The brakes are a very successful combination of discs and drums. Unlike some manufacturers who are troubled by high pedal pressures and great pedal travel, the MGA's brakes clicked right from the start. No boosting mechanism has been fitted, indeed none has yet been necessary. The advantages of discs of course are now universally known, and the combination of these on the front, coupled with generous drums on the rear, is perfectly suited to the MGA's performance.

Australians will welcome BMC's (Australia) decision not to go to the higher compression ratio that is used overseas. This will still enable the cylinder head to be "worked over" and experimentation with fuel blends should pay dividends.

In typical MGA fashion, the Mark II rumbles noticeably on deceleration, but it will pull smoothly away in top gear from 18-20 mph. At the other end of the scale, the tachometer has a yellow zone from 5500 to 6000 rpm, and the red extends from 6000 to 7000. The unit, from past experience, revs readily to 6000 although this should be held only momentarily. Revving beyond 6000 is asking for trouble.

The gearbox, which has always given good service, remains unchanged. The shift itself is very stiff on new cars, but frees up after several thousand miles. Synchro on second, third, and top is very positive and does its job very well.

Other details on the car which remain unchanged include insufficient room for the feet (although the dipper switch has been more conveniently relocated) and a pull-type starter switch. The driving position is still rather too close for most tastes, and the bucket seats don't offer much in the way of support. Despite these shortcomings, the MGA Mark II has become an even more desirable motor car, and one which would afford any owner a great deal of enjoyment. It looks well, goes well, handles well, and in spite of the brutal treatment that the characteristics encourage seems to last well. Like its predecessors, it will be acclaimed by thousands of satisfied owners.

This prototype MGA brought the MG Car Company back into racing after an absence of 20 years. It ran at Le Mans in this form.

Make and model .... MG-A

ENGINE:
Cylinders .... four, in line
Cubic capacity .... 1622 cc
Valve arrangement .... pushrod overhead
Maximum power .... 93 hp at 5500 rpm

GENERAL:
Brake type .... disc/drum
Transmission type .... four speed
Wheelbase .... 7 ft 10 in
Weight (approx.) .... 17¾ cwt

PERFORMANCE:
Top speed .... 105 mph
Speeds in gears:
I .... 29 mph
II .... 49 mph
III .... 80 mph
IV .... 105 mph
V .... NA
Standing quarter mile .... 18.8 secs
0 to 30 mph .... 4.0 secs
0 to 50 mph .... 9.2 secs
0 to 70 mph .... 17.7 secs
0 to 100 mph .... NA
0 to 120 mph .... NA

The MG is still the best known and most popular sports car in the world. More than 100,000 A-types have now been produced.

ROAD TEST

MGA 1600 MARK II

This latest variation of the sports car pioneer reemphasizes all of the factors that have made it a best seller

IN THE JARGON of the advertising trade, MG has created for itself a "favorable public image." Favorable in this sense means that the MG is automatically recognized as a sports car by the U.S. motoring public. No one need make any excuses or qualify the term in any way — the MG fits. This has been true since 1948, when the cars first began to be imported to the U.S. as the TC series, and has held through the TD, TF and A groups — some 125,000 cars imported in all. Why? Simply because the MG is a true sports car. In its price category it has come to be the standard against which other sports cars or would-be sports cars are judged.

The significance of the MG, the fact that MOTOR TREND had not performed any sort of test on one since September 1959, and the introduction of a new model for the A series, the 1600 Mark II, added up to an MG test. As with all cars, there are shortcomings and advantages. Pointing them out in an objective fashion should enable us to place the car in proper perspective with other sports machines and gain some indication as to its suitability for the widely varying conditions in the U.S.

Outwardly, the Mark II has had a simple facelifting around the grille and taillights; it retains the basic A roadster silhouette and dimensions. Key sizes include 94-inch wheelbase, 47.5-

MG-A's 1600 is powered by a variation of British Motor Corporation's B model engine. Bigger displacement, higher compression, other changes improve performance.

MOTOR TREND/OCTOBER 1961

and 48.75-inch front and rear tread, 156-inch overall length, 58-inch width and 50-inch height. Under the hood is the biggest change, some 10 more horsepower than the 1600. Acceleration is slightly better, while top speed has been raised to considerably over 100 mph (107, factory rating) and engine durability is said to have been increased. From the driver's view there is little interior change except for increased use of leather trim in the dash area. Handling characteristics remain appreciably the same as in previous A's.

The engine, a variation on the British Motor Corporation's B model, has gained a well-deserved reputation for reliability. With the changes that stamp it a Mark II, it should prove even better. Compared to the previous 1600, it has been bored .03-inch, increasing displacement 2.1 cubic inches to 99. Intake valves are nine per cent bigger, exhausts up 11 per cent with ports revised to take advantage of the extra valve area. Compression is up from 8.3 to 8.9 with horsepower up to 90 and torque raised 10 lbs.-ft. to 97 at 4,000 rpm. Piston pins are slightly larger, therefore stiffer; connecting rods have been increased in the H-section for greater stiffness, and the crankshaft webs are ⅛-inch thicker, which means that the main bearings are narrowed slightly.

More important to the consumer than the relatively minor engineering changes is how the engine performs under varied conditions — creeping traffic, high speed, mountain grades, broiling desert, sub-zero or any other condition likely to be encountered. It is impractical to perform a test including all climes; in Southern California, however, it is possible to find all of them except the latter. Generally, the MG's engine took it all in stride. No tendency to overheat was observed in traffic, hot open country or climbing hills, although an unpleasant amount of warmth was generated and passed through the transmission tunnel into the cockpit. Idle was smooth and regular, with cold starting simply a matter of brief choking. Hot starts, often a sports car problem, were virtually instantaneous.

The MG-A makes a nearly ideal sports car for the beginner. By that, it is not meant to limit the car's usage to novices at sports motoring; many of the marque's biggest boosters have owned several and would have nothing else. The reference is intended for the owner who has the urge and finances to go racing on an expensive scale, yet recognizes the fact that there must be a learning period in something relatively safe. (Many competition drivers have, in fact, derived so much pleasure from racing in closely matched production MG events that they have not bothered to step up.) The characteristics that make the A a good learner's car also make it a delightful general purpose street machine. The car was felt to be a well integrated unit — that is, gearbox, handling, ride, brakes acceleration and performance generally were all part of the same car. No one feature was so outstandingly bad or good that it was considered to be either a total detriment or the starting point for another and better car.

At 2⅔ turns, lock-to-lock, the rack-and-pinion steering is quick and sensitive. Except for the low number of turns, it will be found to be little different from typical domestic late-models under normal driving conditions. Wheel action is slightly heavy at low speeds, easing up as speed is increased. There is a desirable tendency to understeer, which means a definite wheel return action while straightening out. At higher racing-type speeds, it is quite easy to break the rear wheels loose in a corner and hold them out by applying power. Easing off induces the rear end to come around more sharply and the car will spin unless steering correction is applied, but it is all telegraphed to the driver — nothing tricky or difficult as in the case of some extremely high-performance sports cars. The result is that it is an easy task for a beginner to safely learn racing techniques, provided an open practice area is available. Such knowledge, essential on the race course, can be invaluable in a highway emergency. Not the least of safe, fast cornering is a low amount of body roll; it will be imperceptible to a driver who has been used to larger, softly sprung cars.

When one considers emergencies, brakes are uppermost. The A has 11-inch-diameter discs on the front, with 10 x 1¾-inch drums on the rear. Brake pedal pressure is moderate, they do not fade under repeated high-speed stops and they continue to stop in a straight line. There is little else that can be said about brakes that perform as good brakes should.

One of the oft-touted joys of driving a sports car is shift-

Changed grille is one of the few external changes in the new MG. But the engineering differences have made many changes since last MT road test.

Well-instrumented interior has changed little. True to sports car design, MG has low seats, adjustable steering wheel and minimum closed-car accessibility.

ing through a four-speed gearbox, not simply for arm exercise but for control such as most automatics cannot give. The MG-A will satisfy the enthusiast on that point. The tunnel-mounted lever is positioned in excellent relationship to the wheel. Synchronized on the top three gears only, it was felt that gear action was slightly stiff. Compensating for that is a good choice of ratios and short throws with practically no slop in the remote linkage. Considering engine size, shifting can be held to an absolute minimum if one desires. For example, it was entirely possible to pull smoothly in fourth gear from 1,000 rpm, equal to 17.85 mph. Such treatment is not recommended, but it can be done. Ideal use of the gears involved keeping revs above 2500, with 3,000 a happier choice. Between 3-5,000, incidentally, the acceleration response was quite lively.

Shifting, especially downshifting, a sports car can become a sort of lightfooted ballet for the experienced driver who has mastered the heel-and-toe technique, which means to use the accelerator to synchronize engine with gears while simultaneously braking. It can be done in the MG, using an edge-of-foot style rather than true heel and toe, but the pedal spacing was considered crowded. This has always been true with MGs, at least since TC days, and a driver with a broad foot must be constantly alert to be certain of hitting the correct pedal.

While the acceleration times recorded were not sensational, they are quite creditable, matching the factory's acceleration curve. The car was definitely capable of staying with any traffic — ahead of much of it. Taking off, it was almost too easy to induce wheelspin in first gear. A fast shift to second produced a solid clutch bite but no wheelspin, and so on through the gears. Only when shifting at deliberately abusive speeds was there any evidence of slippage in the eight-inch-diameter clutch, and this when the clutch was engaged while the engine was still turning in excess of 5,000 rpm. Clutch pedal pressure is moderate on a reasonably short travel. Acceleration figures were taken using a rev limit of 5800-6,000 in the gears. The limit was determined by the MG's tachometer, which has an amber segment beginning at 5500, showing red between 6-7,000 rpm.

Seating was judged to be good; even those who preferred chair-high seats quickly became accustomed to the MG's seats, which are only 8½ inches from the floor at the highest point. This means legs out, but there is plenty of length in which to stretch out while an eight-inch travel on the seat adjustment accommodates most heights to the pedals. The steering wheel, too, is adjustable. However, an extremely long-legged driver who prefers the wheel close to the dash for an arms-extended driving position will probably find some wheel/knee interference. The foam cushions, 18½ inches wide by 21 long, give good knee and thigh support. Backrests, mildly contoured, have good holding power; also a center armrest adds to one's sense of security from sliding.

There are a couple of areas where the A can be criticized, but they become subjective matters of individual taste. As an example, cockpit storage is definitely at a minimum. There are door pockets only. Space behind the seats is taken up with top (when folded) and side curtains, which fit in a hanging pocket. The small trunk is rated at 5.75 cubic feet, and even this is best suited for soft parcel storage. Two persons planning any touring would be well advised to add an external luggage rack. While the top is weathertight when used with the sliding window curtains, erecting it is not a detail that can be completed by one man while remaining seated in the car. It is an awkward operation for one person and is much more easily performed by two.

Ride is another subjective area that is difficult to pin down, but it was concluded that the MG's ride, while firm, is good. There is practically no tendency to choppiness, often felt in tightly-sprung, short-wheelbase cars. Even during off-pavement driving the suspension soaked up bumps and holes in a gratifying manner.

High noise level and wind buffeting can be companion features of small open cars. Both have been held to a minimum in the MG. Because the driver sits quite low in the body, top-down driving is reasonably wind-free. There was actually more annoying wind noted with the top up and side curtains out. Engine noise is moderately high, a distinctive note recognizable as MG. One saving grace is that the exhaust noise is not fatiguing at high cruising speeds.

During a period when it has become the fashion to build cars with unit construction, whether any advantage is realized or not, the MG clings to a separate box-section frame with body bolted on. It doesn't seem to create any particular weight penalty as compared to the possibilities of a unitized body-frame. Suspension is quite conventional, upper and lower A-arms at front with coil springs and Armstrong lever shocks. Anti-roll bar is optional, although there was none on the

Continued on page 91

MOTOR TREND TEST DATA

TEST CAR:	MG-A Mark II 1600
BODY TYPE:	Roadster
BASE PRICE:	$2499
ENGINE TYPE:	Ohv 4
DISPLACEMENT:	99 cubic inches
COMPRESSION RATIO:	8.9-to-1
CARBURETION:	Two single-throat SU
HORSEPOWER:	90 @ 5500 rpm
TRANSMISSION:	Four-speed manual
REAR AXLE RATIO:	4.1
GAS MILEAGE:	17 to 21 miles per gallon
ACCELERATION:	0-30 mph in 3.9 seconds, 0-45 mph in 7.3 seconds and 0-60 mph in 14.2 seconds
SPEEDOMETER ERROR:	Indicated 30, 45 and 60 mph are actual 28, 41 and 55 mph, respectively
ODOMETER ERROR:	Indicated 100 miles is actual 98 miles
WEIGHT-POWER RATIO:	22.8 lbs. per horsepower
HORSEPOWER PER CUBIC INCH:	.91

MOTOR TREND/OCTOBER 1961

DRIVING THE M.G.-A AGAIN

A Satisfactorily Controllable and Fast 1.6-litre Sports Car from a Famous Factory

Traditional lines of the M.G.-A 1600 are seen in this picture of this all-weather sports car in l.h.d. form.

IF you like a responsive, open-air car it is always a pleasure to drive an M.G.-A. Motor Sport tested this model in coupé or hard-top form in June 1957, and last year our June issue carried a full report on the Twin-Cam version. The coupé was difficult to get into or out of, the Twin-Cam with disc front brakes splendid fun, but noisy and an oil-drinker.

Recently I had the opportunity of trying Abingdon's latest solution, the 1600. The plot has been to obtain increased speed and acceleration by adopting the greater swept volume of the Twin-Cam engine, while retaining the simplicity of the original push-rod o.h.v. cylinder head. This is a sound solution, because, due no doubt to production/financial limitations, Abingdon made rather heavy weather of adapting Henry's 1912 type of o.h. valve actuation to the M.G.-A, although, as the Goodwood T.T. race proved, these Twin-Cam M.G.s have now achieved a satisfactory degree of reliability.

The M.G.-A 1600, then, is a simple, comparatively outdated but eminently enjoyable, very fast, sports two-seater. It attains its notably good road-clinging qualities by fairly hard springing, which, however, does not result in any real discomfort for the occupants or more than mild scuttle shake. It is a car which can be placed very accurately through excellent rack-and-pinion steering which is high-geared (just under 2¾ turns, lock-to-lock) and which possesses useful, not vicious, castor return-action, exhibits absolutely no sponginess and kicks-back but mildly and then only over poor road surfaces. Moreover, the sprung wheel is sensibly set low, well below the driver's line of sight.

The bucket seats, the backs of which fold forward to give access to the sidescreen stowage on a shelf mainly occupied by the horizontally-mounted spare wheel, could with advantage provide more support for the occupant's legs towards the knees, and perhaps the pedal positioning isn't ideal for pedantic people who insist on heel-and-toe work even in this age of synchromesh. But the M.G.-A 1600 has a delightfully placed rigid, remote control gear-lever controlling a most enjoyable gear change, while it is pleasing to find the traditional fly-off hand brake. The latter is set very close to the propeller-shaft tunnel, but this would only be inconvenient to those who wear skirts and we know that girls who drive sports M.G.s do so in skin-tight jeans.

Visibility is slightly impeded by a curved scuttle and far more so by the facia-mounted mirror but, even so, both front wings are visible to a driver of average height. Those who prefer a full-arms-stretch driving stance will grumble that the seat does not have sufficient range of adjustment. Leg-room is good, with ample means for resting the left foot clear of the clutch pedal.

The summer of 1960 being what it was, on only one day did I venture to put the hood down. Open, the M.G.-A 1600 is a delight and gains in mechanical quietness so rigged. In bad weather the close-fitting hood kept out heavy rain in all but one place, while the very easily fitted Perspex sidescreens with sliding panels are extremely praiseworthy, being rigid and easy to open. I feel, however, that in our damnable climate the true convertible coupé is what fresh-air lovers really need. I recall with deep admiration a Jowett Jupiter once on Motor Sport's long list of staff cars, for this could be closed up in a moment and, thus closed, was a truly snug coupé, perhaps at the expense of thick screen pillars. I have yet to sample the Triumph Herald Convertible but it looks to have more in common with a normal tourer than this luxurious Jupiter.

To revert to the M.G., the hood, of course, stows away under a cover when not in use, but a full-length tonneau cover to conceal the seats when the car is parked is apparently an extra. The facia is of metal, with crude, sharp under-edges. It carries the usual array of M.G. instruments and controls, including neat 120-m.p.h. speedometer with trip (with orange "tenths") and total odometers, and a tachometer reading to an exciting 7,000 r.p.m., an orange warning band being used from 5,500 to 6,000 r.p.m., red thereafter. The slender white needles of these instruments move in the same plane but that of the speedometer was inclined to float and at certain speeds blanked the trip reading, which might make a rally driver go mad. There is a sort of token crash-padding above the facia.

There is a combined oil-pressure/water-temperature gauge and a separate petrol gauge, the latter of little value for judging the tank contents, however. The horn button remains in the centre of the facia and an old-style control, also on the facia, works the direction-flashers, neither of which is altogether convenient. The various indicator lamps are decently subdued and there is rheostat control of the instrument lighting, which, however, is never very bright.

Today's small sports cars are fully equipped and thus the M.G. has heater and demisting controls, an H.M.V. radio, screen-washers and provision for fog-lamps, while a good item is the hooded map-light, with its own switch, directly before the passenger, for the hectic occasions when he or she is a navigator. The mixture-enriching control for the twin S.U. carburetters is labelled " C "—for choke— a case of vintage thinking. The horn, but not the wipers, works with ignition off.

The doors rely on wire "pulls" to open them and as there are no external handles, if a "pull" breaks you are just about trapped, should the hood be up. The hood has a truly large rear window, enabling the driver to reverse as in a normal saloon.

Both bonnet panel and boot lid have to be propped open, and the latter cannot be lifted until a toggle, down behind the passenger's seat, has been found and pulled out. As this is not spring-loaded it has to be returned before the boot can be shut. With the bonnet lid open, plugs and dip-stick are very accessible, the distributor reasonably so.

The test car had centre-lock wire wheels. The braking, aided by Lockheed discs on the front wheels, is impeccable and is one of the highlights of this very taut, controllable sports car.

The M.G.-A 1600 certainly motors. Its engine is astonishingly smooth and all too willing to take you well "into the red." The indicated maxima in the gears, without exceeding 6,000 r.p.m., are 27, 48 and 75 m.p.h., respectively, second gear being, perhaps, on the low side. Given a reasonably clear run the speed in top gear just staggers up to the ton and 80-m.p.h. cruising is chicken-feed to this docile M.G.-A. The s.s. ¼-mile is disposed of in under 20 seconds.

The exhaust note is spirited without being obtrusive, and for town driving the M.G. will poodle along at absurdly low speed in top cog. It has very good Lucas headlamps for fast night driving.

Altogether I was captivated, as I always am, by the sense of security and eager performance of the M.G.-A, which is excellent value-for-outlay at £940 7s. 6d. inclusive of p.t. Driving it moderately hard it returned 27 m.p.g. and 100-octane petrol was not required. Traffic negotiation increased this to 24 m.p.g. The absolute range was 265 miles. After 570 miles the oil level had fallen rather alarmingly, but a quart of Castrol restored it.

I could grow old gracefully driving such a car with the hood down in a climate of perennial sunshine.—W. B.

MGA 1600 Mk. II

THE Mark II version of the car differs from its predecessor in having a slightly greater engine capacity (34cc), due to an increase in bore, and a small oil cooler disposed ahead of the radiator, which keeps the gallon of lubricant at reasonable temperatures in competition driving.

The small additional horsepower is due also to larger inlet valves, and improved porting and combustion chambers. The rear axle gearing has been raised for quieter cruising.

The M.G. A remains one of my favourite cars, but the soft hood never fails to annoy me. It is difficult to erect in cold weather when it is most needed, its ample plastic rear windows mark very easily, and the wind noise within the car with hood and curtains erected almost drowns normal conversation.

The seating and arrangement of controls for the driver are excellent, the inheritance of several generations of designers who are themselves keen drivers. The gearshift is short and precise, the clutch does not slip on full throttle takeoffs, and one can find all the controls in darkness. Only the horn button is awkwardly placed, in its traditional M.G. position on the fascia.

Observations

If the M.G. A is a trifle heavy for sprint events, it is one of the most pleasant touring cars one could find. The suspension, though firm enough for excellent cornering, gives reasonable comfort on long trips and is not unduly disturbed by pot-holes and corrugations.

For longer tours one must fit a luggage rack, as the boot will take only an overnight bag. Also, it is not possible to lock the car, and the boot lock which can be fitted as an extra might well be expected as standard. The absence of any glovebox is also noticeable.

The outstanding attraction of the M.G. A is the pleasure one derives from driving it. In town it is lively but docile and turns in 30ft, and in the country it cruises effortlessly up to maximum speeds that road safety will permit.

For those requiring additional comfort and space, the car can be obtained in closed (coupe) form, at £1,697. There is no appreciable loss of performance with this version.

In a car which will normally be cruised in lively fashion, the rather leisurely single speed wipers hardly cope with heavy rain.

Roadholding And Handling

The M.G. gives a really pleasing performance on winding roads, wet or dry. Whilst it understeers a little and the high-geared steering is not light, the car corners willingly enough, and the rack steering is absolutely precise.

Road adhesion is good, body roll is slight, and the tyre squeal is not excessive for the speeds involved. Generally the car is very safe and quite predictable through fast bends.

The wheel requires only 2 2/3 turns from lock to lock, so that it is quick in action. It is also rather rough on the hands over bad roads.

The brakes are front discs and rear drums, and they give an excellent control with moderate pressures, and do not fade easily.

The handbrake is of the traditional fly-off type, and it effectively stopped the car down the Victoria Pass (1 in 8).

Cruising And Acceleration

The higher gearing gives the Mark II a noticeably increased and quieter cruising speed, and the car can be toured as fast as the driver cares. Its roadholding and cornering assist the maintenance of good average speeds, and the generous tank reduces waste of time in refuelling.

With the engine in perfect tune, the M.G. A will achieve 100 m.p.h. In the lower ratios, at the safe engine speed

ABOUT THIS CAR

PRICE: £1,313, including sales-tax.

SIZE: Two-seater, small luggage space. Wheelbase, 7ft 10in; length, 13ft; tracks, 47 7/8 and 48¾in; clearance, 6in; tyres, 5.60 x 15in; tankage, 10 gals. Kerb weight, 18¾cwt; test load 3cwt.

MECHANICAL: Four-cylinder engine of 1,622cc, developing 84.6 gross horsepower and 97lb-ft torque (R.A.C., 14.4 h.p.). Four-speed gearbox. Separate chassis frame with disc brakes at front and rack steering.

FUEL CONSUMPTION: 31.3 miles per gallon at 45.1 m.p.h. over the test route.

MAXIMUM SPEEDS (in touring trim): Top gear, 100 m.p.h.; third gear, 78.5 m.p.h.; second gear, 49 m.p.h.

of 6,000 r.p.m., speeds are 78.5 m.p.h. in third, and 49 m.p.h. in second gear.

Top gear is notably flexible and will pull away smoothly from 20 m.p.h. and effectively from 30 m.p.h. It is rather particular about fuel, and slight detonation was noticed on our present super grade, but there was no running-on.

The acceleration figures were:
THIRD GEAR: 20 to 40 m.p.h. in 7.2s, 30 to 50 m.p.h. 7.1s, 40 to 60 m.p.h. in 7.8s.
TOP GEAR: 20 to 40 m.p.h. in 11.3s, 30 to 50 m.p.h. in 10.7s, 40 to 60 m.p.h. in 11.5s.

From 0 to 50 m.p.h., using first and second gears, required 8.2s.

Hill Climbing

For a sports, the M.G. A climbs well in top, but naturally third and second will be used where lively climbs are desired, and in these ratios the car performs excellently.

The test climbs were:
RIVER LETT HILL (two miles, with acute bends, maximum gradient 1 in 8½): Third gear, in a climb exhibiting good cornering and ample power at 40-51-40-64 m.p.h.
FITZGERALD'S MOUNT (one mile long, average gradient 1 in 11, max. 1 in 10). An ascent in top, to demonstrate the potentialities of that gear, at 50-46-33 m.p.h.

The energy ratios, based on the test-loaded weight of 21¾cwt, are: power to weight, 78 b.h.p. per ton: torque to weight, 89.2lb per ton.

Top gear now gives a road speed of 18 m.p.h. at 1,000 engine r.p.m.

Driver's Layout

The controls are well arranged and are all within easy reach with a safety belt in use. The seating position is the traditional "legs extended" attitude, in this case made less tiring by a well-designed and comfortable seat having an adjustment travel of four inches.

The wheel position is also adjustable, so that drivers of various statures can be made comfortable. The low position is not good for forward view, and the rear-mirror field is rather resticted.

The gear shift is excellent, being a short rigid lever right under the driver's left hand and giving quick and positive changes. Synchro is provided on the upper three ratios only.

The handbrake is tucked rather too neatly between the high central tunnel (which forms part of the chassis backbone) and the driver's leg. The dip-switch is somewhat high on the bulkhead.

The instruments before the driver comprise a circular tachometer and speedometer, and gauges for oil pressure and engine temperature. There is a fuel gauge before the passenger. All instruments are clear, having white figures on a black ground.

The minor controls are sensibly spread around the fascia, and there is a map-reading light, with its own switch, for the passenger.

Fuel Facts

At the lively average speed of 45 m.p.h. over the test route, the M.G.A gave 31.3 miles per gallon, which is reasonably good.

Based on the loaded weight, the ton-miles per gallon figure is 34.0, whilst the fuel-speed factor (ton-m.p.g. x average speed) is 1,535. These results are only fair.

The fuel tank gives a fast cruising range of about 315 miles, which is not too great for the touring potentialities of this car.

Engineering

The latest model is quite up-to-date without any heterodox features. The 1,600 c.c. engine has been cleverly developed to produce 55.5 b.h.p. per litre in its high compression form.

Engine layout is satisfactory, with reasonable access to most ancillaries requiring regular servicing.

Bore and stroke are 76.2 x 88.9 m.m., and in Australia the lower alternative compression of 8.3 to 1 is employed, against the 8.9 available in England. The twin S.U. carburettors are fitted with Vokes oil-wetted pancake filters, whilst engine oil is circulated through a full-flow filter.

The Lockheed brakes have substantial discs of 11 inch diameter, whilst the rear drums are 10 inch and have a lining area of 68 square inches.

The overall gear ratios are: top, 4-1, third, 5-6, and second gear 9 to 1.

The chassis is mounted at front on coils and wishbones, and at the rear on semi-elliptics, with a piston-type damper for each wheel.

Body

The interior is divided into two by the massive central tunnel, on which a small arm-rest is provided. There is ample legroom in both seats, and reasonable headroom with the hood erected.

The side screens have sliding glass panels, which permit arm signalling and satisfactory ventilation. There is no provision for cooling air to the floor for hot weather.

Both doors are provided with sizable open pockets, and an assist-bar is fitted on either side of the scuttle, to serve also as a brace for the flat Triplex screen. Provision is made for a radio in the fascia.

The shallow boot space is mostly occupied by the spare wheel, leaving but a small luggage space.

Summary

The M.G. A is an attractive sports car, very much in the English manner. It is unusually pleasant to drive, and it handles immaculately.

To this may be added a performance up to 100 m.p.h., and an excellent gearbox giving liveliness under all conditions.

The M.G. A is a splendid touring car for two, with competition potentialities of no mean order also available.

The car tested was made available by P. and R. Williams Pty. Ltd., distributors.

The layout for the driver brings all controls within easy reach, even with a seat belt in use. The gearshift and pedals are particularly well disposed.

30,000 MILES WITH AN M.G. A 1600 Mk. II

by Charles Bulmer

NO other country offers such a choice to the car buyer and yet I find choosing always involves a long process of reducing or discarding one's requirements until something will just do. After 17 years of unbroken sports car ownership I still wanted another one; it had to be new and it had to cost not much more than £1,000. The specification then demanded a reasonable performance, good steering and roadholding and a fixed-head coupé body. In September 1961 the M.G. A was the only car I could think of which could meet more than one of these three demands.

269 CYO was one of the first 1,622 c.c. Mk. II coupés to be delivered. I had driven enough M.G. As before to specify a front anti-roll bar as an essential extra —without it this model has a splendidly controllable oversteer which flatters one's skill immensely but tail-sliding round corners with smooth and fluent ease is only impressive as long as there isn't a Mini ahead or astern going 10 m.p.h. faster. Dunlop RS5 tyres were ordered partly for similar reasons but mostly because one must be able to use a car's highest continuous cruising speed in very hot weather without stopping to raise the pressures.

At running-in speeds I can't honestly say that my first impressions of the car were very favourable. After the XK Jaguar which preceded it the engine seemed harsh and noisy, the steering, the gearchange and the suspension were very stiff and there was a tremendous amount of road and wind noise. Worst of all, however, I found it intolerably uncomfortable to sit in and very hard to see out of. It was clear that the moulding process would have to start here.

Sometimes at crowded parties one is compelled to sit on a cushion on the floor with one's back against a vertical wall; this was roughly how one sat in the M.G. The great thing about parties, however, at least in the early stages, is that they never go round corners. I decided to acquire some Microcell bucket seats which are properly shaped for side support and spent some time experimenting with them. A very low seating position demands a considerable angle of recline for comfort and so the passenger's seat was mounted on wooden wedges to slope it backwards by 12°C; this seat has proved very comfortable even on journeys of over 600 miles in the day and you can doze in it without wearing a safety harness.

The driving seat was less successful. The low mounted steering wheel made a more upright position essential for thigh clearance and I found that one tended to slide forward along the more horizontal cushion and lose support in the lower part of the back. Raising the steering wheel would be the answer since the column is universally jointed near the bulkhead but this involves cutting a slot in the dashboard which I never got round to doing. For various reasons the standard seat was replaced just before going on holiday; tilted back through 8° it proved quite tolerable, gave more side support than before because one leaned back and sank into the upholstery and put one a reasonable distance from the wheel instead of right over it with elbows projecting sideways. For inserting luggage behind the seat, its folding back is invaluable.

Improving the View

However, this is getting ahead of the story. In changing the seats I had also raised them enough to look over the scuttle instead of viewing it tangentially but there remained a scuttle-mounted mirror large enough to block off a vital part of the forward view and yet small enough to use only a fraction of the enormous rear window. It was replaced by one twice the length suspended from the top rail of the screen. At the same time the tiny windscreen wiper blades were discarded in favour of new ones two inches longer; the Lucas book showed that the wiper motor was powerful enough to cope with these. The screen is fairly shallow anyway and this simple modification transformed visibility in wet weather.

Sundry teething troubles which developed in the first 2,000 miles were dealt with by the distributors; it developed a water leak from the radiator and a petrol leak from the gauge unit on the fuel tank. The former was replaced under guarantee and the latter was reduced in two stages from a trickle, which left a pool on the floor, to a strong smell in the garage—it was never cured entirely. The doors must have been just bolted in place as the lunch bell rang and any resemblance between their positions and those of the apertures seemed to be purely coincidental; on the passenger's side there was such a large gap at the back that one could very nearly get in and out without opening the door at all. When they had been re-hung to fit the seals properly most of the wind noise disappeared; contrary to popular belief it is far more critically dependent upon door and window sealing than it is on the aerodynamic shape of the car.

A loud banging noise from the rear was eventually traced to a faulty shock absorber but the investigation was more interesting than the cure. The floor of the luggage space behind the seats is covered with a quickly removable panel which gives access to the twin batteries and with this removed I spent a lot of time being driven over the roughest roads in the district watching and listening to the rear suspension at work. It didn't help to trace the banging which was completely drowned by an unimpeded cacophony of tyre, wind and exhaust noise but it did lead to other conclusions, notably that the car would be much quieter if this rather flimsy rear floor were heavily reinforced with sound proofing material. Horrified to see how little movement the rear axle was permitted between its bump and rebound stops, I forecast that this was going to be a most uncomfortable car on French roads.

In the summer of 1962 a fortnight's camping holiday in Elba provided the opportunity to test both these theories. The problem of packing two people, their luggage, camping gear and provisions which are hard to get in Italy (like porridge) into a car with negligible luggage room was solved by discarding the spare wheel which normally occupies most of the boot and replacing it with a device supplied by our accessory king for squirting sealing compound through the valve. Ironically enough, we had a puncture three hours before leaving when this wasn't needed and another the day after returning when it was needed and it failed to work. In between we enjoyed a sublime and unjustified peace of mind.

Two hundredweights of holiday equipment transformed the interior sound level. Road roar from the tyres disappeared, the exhaust note became remote and gearbox and tappet noises lost their edge. There is little doubt that the M.G. A could be made into a much more refined car by the liberal application of felt in the right places. One former owner, who is now the designer of one of our most advanced saloons, claims that braced

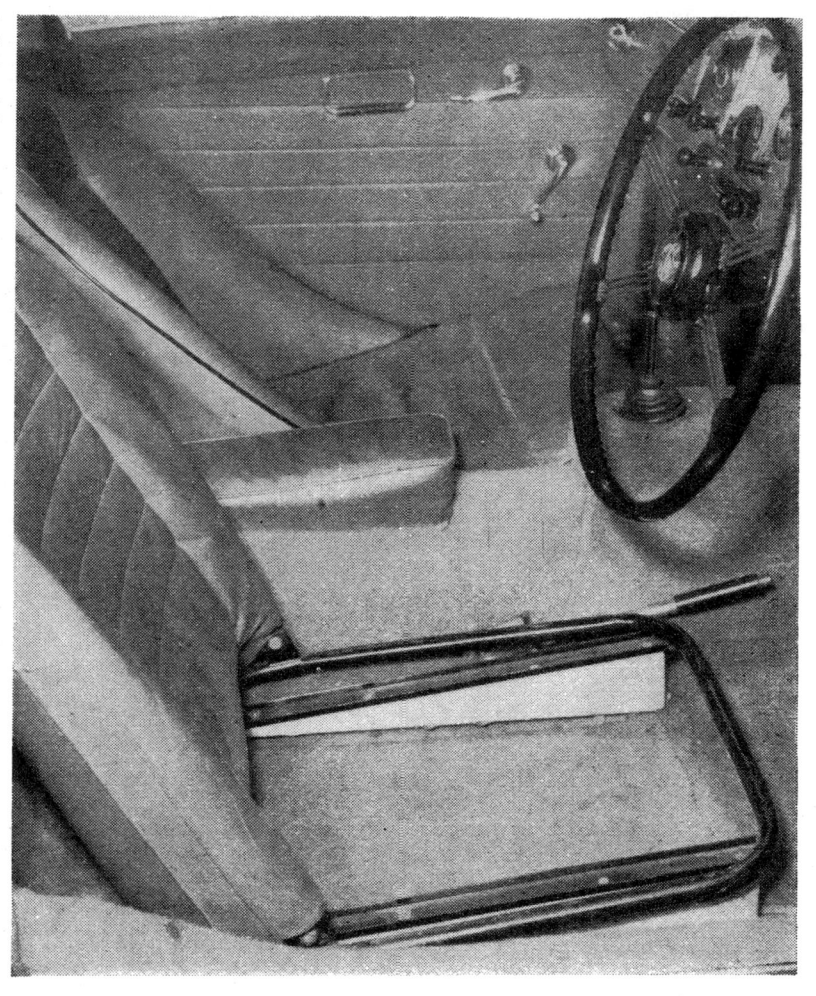

SEATS: Wedges are used under the driving seat to slope it back by 8°—a bigger angle still would have been better with a higher steering wheel. The one disadvantage of the Microcell passenger seat is that it makes getting in and out through narrow doors even more difficult than usual.

Continued overleaf

Two medium-sized suitcases fit behind the seats; if you want to use the boot as well the spare wheel must be left behind or mounted on top of the lid.

M.G. A 1600 Mk. II

tread tyres carve many decibels off road noise and that a padded vertical extension of the toe boards to bonnet level (forming a second bulkhead) quietens the engine to a startling degree.

Strangely enough it proved far more comfortable on foreign roads than we had anticipated. Italian highways seemed to suit it particularly well but even on France's long wave pitching surfaces it was very rarely necessary to drop the cruising speed below 80 m.p.h. In spite of crossing the Channel by boat the 1,150-mile journey from Camberley to Piombino (the embarkation port for Elba) was covered inside 48 hours in both directions and the cross-Continental average on the return trip was 55 m.p.h. on running time. Long-distance autostradas are terribly hard on a car—at an ambient temperature of about 90°F. in the shade I watched the oil pressure gradually drop by 10 lb./sq. in. from its normal reading of 60 whilst the water temperature rose by 10°C. before reaching equilibrium. Without an overdrive top gear or an oil cooler I felt that a steady 4,500 r.p.m. (90 m.p.h. indicated, about 85 true) was the most one should ask for over two hours on end.

Fuel consumption for the whole of the trip worked out at 31 m.p.g., a very remarkable figure and some 4 m.p.g. better than its previous creditable average for predominantly urban and suburban motoring. 269 CYO is a staunch believer in 100 octane fuel, for which the Italian 98-100 Super proved a satisfactory substitute, but on French Super it pinked and ran-on like it does on undiluted British Premium. Whilst hurrying back to catch the boat a strange unidentifiable smell followed by a flapping noise heralded its decision to conduct Service Test No. 1; the fan belt had departed without trace in the prescribed manner. At Chaumont we found an M.G. dealer but this was Sunday morning and he was shut. Not so the Peugeot dealer, however, who in half an hour found a suitable belt and fitted it for about 13s. It must have been a good fit because it lasted for the next 15,000 miles and then it was only replaced as a precaution before another Continental trip.

There followed a long and comparatively trouble-free period apart from the breakage of a door lock spring and a burst silencer at 12,000 miles—which was repeated after another similar period. At 16,800 miles the brake linings and pads were renewed in preparation for covering the Monte-Carlo Rally and the RS5 tyres were replaced with some experimental Dunlop snow and ice tyres with a Weathermaster tread heavily loaded with bits of chopped wire. By this time one rear tyre was smooth and the others were too well worn to be worth putting back.

Seldom have special winter tyres been so necessary as they were last January, not only in France but even more so in England. It was lucky though that providence withdrew the normal coefficient of friction from the roads during this period, because when the snow tyres were taken off again after 3,000 miles they were nearly smooth under their forbidding wire brush façade. The second set of RS5s are now nearly due for replacement after 11,000 miles; this seems rather a high rate of wear for 5.90-15 covers on a 19-cwt. car and one must blame a higher proportion of out-of-town motoring in the past year and a tendency to take advantage of the very high cornering power.

At around the 20,000 mile mark the engine seemed to be getting rougher and feebler. A Crypton check showed why—it was 10° retarded at tickover and only showing 20° extra advance at 2,000 r.p.m. instead of 40° (20° vacuum plus 20° centrifugal). Since the centrifugal mechanism was working satisfactorily it was clear that the vacuum one wasn't—a very common trouble usually caused by a punctured diaphragm. More serious, however, was that No. 3 cylinder was right down on power and although a burnt exhaust valve was diagnosed the subsequent decoke showed that it was actually a burnt inlet valve. Unlike early B-type engines, the tappet clearances on the M.G. had been checked to stay remarkably constant at the prescribed 0·015 in. so one suspects that this valve had not been very well seated from new.

To date this is the only work, apart from routine servicing, that has been done on the engine. Nothing at all has been done to the transmission or the suspension apart from the early replacement of a faulty damper which we have mentioned already. The extraordinary thing about the car is that it doesn't feel any older now than it did 30,000 miles ago. The engine is no noisier, oil consumption is about 3,000 m.p.g. on long high speed Continental journeys and considerably less at lower speeds, no play has developed in the transmission, the gear-change seems to be just run-in—it has lost its initial stiffness without losing its tautness, the doors don't rattle and the whole body retains that tremendous solidity which is one of the most attractive features of the car.

In fact it has mellowed with age. When it was new the rear dampers damped with such enthusiasm that the ride was abominably choppy—one friend of mine disconnected his altogether whilst he ran his car in—now it is only slightly over-damped which makes it feel remarkably stable at high speeds. I run slightly higher pressures in the rear tyres than the manufacturers recommend—a 4 lb. differential from front to rear instead of 2—and the steering is practically neutral on smooth corners which it goes round extremely quickly; rough surfaces tend to unstick the back axle. The steering is far too heavy to be really enjoyable on slow bends and I have always wanted to try a much smaller castor angle.

Its real charm lies in the intimacy which it establishes with its driver. It is a small car outside and a very small one inside; personally I like to be surrounded as closely as possible by the minimum amount of car although some people might find it claustrophobic. But the main reason that one feels part of the car is its responsiveness; if you want to go straight it doesn't need any help even in cross-winds, if you want to swerve the steering is exceptionally positive and quick and it steps sideways without roll, squeal or lag. The brakes, which are very powerful indeed, have this same solid direct feeling with a minimum of free travel and a pedal which stands close

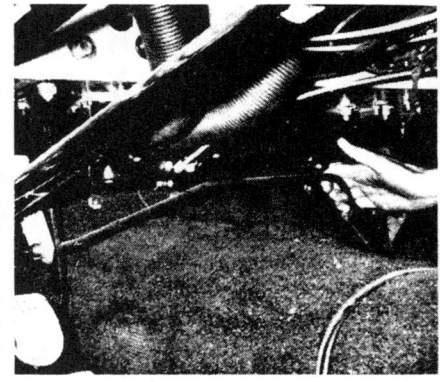

Throttle linkage inside the passenger compartment is a carryover from right-hand-drive European version.

Small trunk is best suited for around-town errands. Longer trips with luggage will require an outside rack.

Continued from page 84

MOTOR TREND test MG. Rear suspension of the solid axle is via a pair of six-leaf semi-elliptic spring and double-acting Armstrong lever shocks.

Panel fit and finish, which can spell the difference between consumer satisfaction and disgust, were found to be good. The off-white paint was well applied, doors closed solidly and hood and deck were installed to close tolerances.

The base price shown, $2499, can be raised through a number of desirable extras, including wire wheels at $100, tonneau cover $35, heater $65, windshield washer $15, and whitewall tires $35.

Anyone considering the MG strictly as an economy car should probably look elsewhere; there are other small roadsters and numerous sedans that will deliver better fuel mileage. But as a fun car, an automobile that features basic driving pleasure, it is hard to beat. The limitations of a two-seat roadster are quite obvious. If these can be overlooked, the MG-A 1600 Mark II is an outstanding automobile for the money. /MT

Wiper blades 2 in. longer than standard use the entire height of a shallow screen; a small but obstructive scuttle mirror was replaced by a much larger top-mounted one.

to the accelerator and at the same level. All this means that thought and action seem to occur simultaneously; the gain compared with the forward planning type of car is probably no more than a few tenths of a second but this makes all the difference in the world to the speed and relaxation with which you can penetrate traffic.

Apart from the fan belt episode, it has only let me down once. One morning in Turin last year the starter turned the engine over twice and then died. In the afternoon the engine also expired quite suddenly in the middle of Turin's busiest piazza. Switching on the ignition produced only a faint buzzing from behind the dashboard and pulling the starter a faint hissing from behind the seat. Armed with these clues a technical editor acting as an unwilling breakwater to the Italian traffic might have deduced, after a little calm reflection, that there was a loose connection in the burglar alarm and that simultaneously the battery earth lead had corroded through so far that the electrons could only pass in single file. In fact he didn't; he tugged all the wires within reach until the ignition light reappeared and motored away to a more secluded place where the alarm could be rebuilt with his comprehensive tool kit (a nail file and a one franc piece). You couldn't really blame the car for either of these faults.

Two things spoil it as a sports car. One is its wide ratio gearbox which makes second gear almost useless in open road motoring and the other, not unrelated, is that the engine is not sufficiently smooth and quiet to make high r.p.m. in the gears a pleasure. Nevertheless, this is the only car I can remember which I have grown to like more and more as time went on. It seems to mature rather than to deteriorate with age.

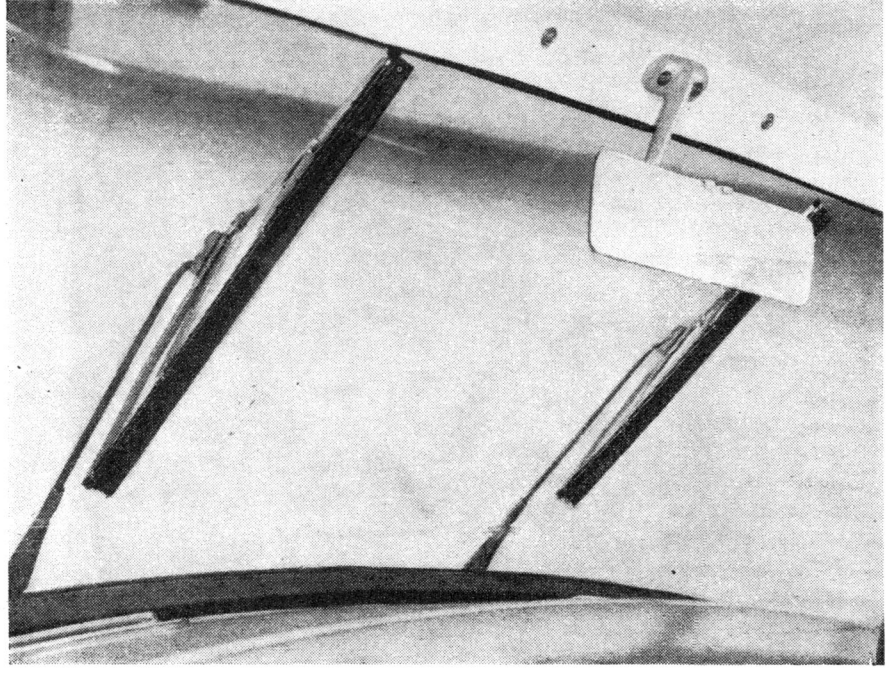

SPOT CHECK

The used car buyer's guide

Still completely modern in shape.

The M.G.A *The first of the 'non-traditionals'*

WHEN the M.G. Series M.G.A was introduced in September, 1955, it represented a complete break with the traditional "square-rigger" type of 2-seater M.G. and some purists threw up their hands in horror. It had the same size engine as its predecessor, the TF 1500 Midget, but the latter's craggy lines and separate wings represented a great deal of wind resistance and drastic changes were needed if performance was to be improved further.

The sleek new all-enveloping body, developed by Syd Enever from the TD special that George Phillips drove at Le Mans in 1951, gave the M.G.A 100 m.p.h. performance straight away, together with considerably greater comfort for the driver and passenger, far better weather protection and enclosed accommodation for luggage and spare wheel—yet with no sacrifice of the traditional M.G. handling qualities. The design was such a success that well over 100,000 M.G.As were sold—more than any other sports car in the world.

It still had a separate rigid chassis, with rack-and-pinion steering giving it exceptional precision of control, which delighted its owners and which did not deteriorate over very high mileages. If there is any play at all in the steering of an M.G.A, it is more likely to be in the ball-joints or king-pins than in the steering gear itself.

To complete this entirely new sports car, the XPEG Nuffield engine was discontinued and a high-output version of the B.M.C. B-Series 1,489 c.c. engine was chosen, as a logical piece of "commonization" with other B.M.C. models (it had already been used in an M.G.—the Z-type Magnette saloon).

The engine

During the first three years of the M.G.A's life, a considerable number of minor modifications were made to the engine, notably an improved oil filter from engine No. 15GB/U/H 26661; modified crankshaft from 6615, stronger gudgeon pins from 38484; modified pistons and rings from 40824 and an improved water pump from 39365.

At chassis No. 61504, a new engine, type 15GD, was introduced, incorporating all the previous modifications, plus a higher starter mounting and modified gearbox and propeller shaft, none of which is interchangeable with its predecessor.

The M.G.A 1600 was introduced in July, 1959, with 1,588 c.c. engine and Lockheed disc front brakes.

The engine of the M.G.A 1600 Mk. II, which appeared in June, 1961, was not simply bored out to 1,622 c.c.; it was almost

With its clothes off... the rack-and-pinion steering can be seen right at the front. Twin S.U.s feed the 1600 engine.

an entirely new power unit with extensive improvements to all components. A higher axle ratio was used, and anchorages for seat belts were built into the body.

From chassis No. 102737, an oil cooler became standard for export cars and optional for the home market, all cars from then on having the appropriate mounting holes. Oil cooler kits are still obtainable under B.M.C. part No. 8G2282 and can also be fitted to the earlier models. An oil cooler is recommended if much motorway driving is contemplated.

All major units can still be obtained on an exchange basis (a factory reconditioned engine costs £48 10s. and can be recognized by its gold paint finish) but an old 1500 engine, for example, cannot be exchanged for a new 1600 Mk. II. A gearbox costs £26 and a differential unit £16 10s.—both on exchange. Virtually all other spares are still obtainable through M.G. dealers.

Dashboard layout is simple and effective. Only remaining octagon is on the wheel boss.

The rare Twin Cam version—note knock-on wheel nuts.

The body

So far as the body is concerned, there are not many weak spots, the door sills being the most likely to suffer from rust, with the door-shut facing panel second. These pressings can be purchased quite cheaply, but it is a body-shop job to fit them.

Kits of parts for fitting seat belts to earlier models may still be in stock at some dealers, or may be obtained from Britax Ltd. Some drilling and welding is involved. Seat belts to fit straight on to built-in anchorages are obtainable through M.G. dealers.

On the road

On the road, the oil pressure should be about 75 p.s.i. cold at normal running speeds, and at least 30 p.s.i. when hot. Good shock absorbers are essential for good handling and may need replacement. If wire wheels are fitted, check for loose spokes by running a spanner round them.

The early disc-braked models tended to suffer from brake squeal and rapid pad wear due to ingress of grit, particularly in winter, and later cars were fitted with dust shields on the inner side of the discs. These can be fitted in sets to earlier cars.

The Twin Cam

That rare variant, the M.G.A Twin Cam, was in production from April, 1958, to April, 1960, and only about 2,000 were built. The 1,588 c.c. twin o.h.c. engine was quite different from the normal pushrod units and gave an extremely good performance, provided that it was meticulously maintained. Carburation and ignition settings were critical and the engine thrived on high revs, but neglect and low-speed town use tended to cause valve and piston troubles. Exchange engines are no longer available, but most parts are, and this could be a good buy for a mechanically-minded enthusiast.

A few surplus Twin Cam chassis (with Dunlop disc brakes all round and centre-lock disc wheels) were fitted with the 1600 pushrod engine and sold as the 1600 De Luxe, during 1960. There was also a fixed-head coupé version of each of the M.G.A models, with wind-up windows and locking doors; comparatively few were built, but they were very snug and practical cars.

Spares and replacements

Handbooks, workshop manuals and parts lists for all models are available through M.G. dealers.

Information on competition tuning for the M.G.A is still obtainable from B.M.C. Special Tuning Dept. at Abingdon, and many special parts may still be obtained, including anti-roll bars, close-ratio gears and alternative axle ratios.

Identity parade

Introduced **September 1955** at chassis number 10101 with 1,489 c.c. engine. M.G.A. 1600 introduced **1959**, with 1,588 c.c. engine and 1,622 c.c. engine used from **January 1960**. Front disc brakes from **July 1959**, and all-round discs from **June 1960** with centre lock disc wheels as option. Discontinued at chassis number 109070, **June, 1962**.

Brief specification

Dimensions. *Length:* 13 ft. *Width:* 4 ft. 10 in. *Wheelbase:* 7 ft. 10 in. *Weight:* 18¼ cwt. *Gearbox:* Four-speed with synchromesh on top three only.

Performance

Max. speed: 98 m.p.h.; 1600-96 m.p.h.; Twin Cam-113 m.p.h.
Acceleration: 20-40 in top: 1600-11 sec.; Twin Cam-10.7 sec. 0-50 thro' gears: 1600-9.1 sec.; Twin Cam-7.3 sec.
Braking from 30 m.p.h.: 30 ft.
Fuel consumption: 27 to 30 m.p.g.

MGA classic choice

The MGA is practical and fun – Jonathan Wood helps you pick a good one. Mini-Manuals on the MGA 1500 and the Twin Cam are available at 50p each from Mrs J Skilleter, T&CC, Dorset House, Stamford St, London SE1 – cheques made out to IPC Business Press please.

NINETEEN FIFTY-FIVE was one of the most significant post-war years for the MG Car Company. For that September they introduced their new sports car, the MGA, and bid farewell to the TF model with its traditional, though anachronistic body style that had served the company well since the J2 of 1932. Out went the spartan lines, square radiator and bolster tank of the earlier model, to be replaced by the A with its low, graceful full width bodywork endorsing a design concept already successfully exploited in Britain by Jaguar, Healey and Triumph.

The A was destined to be MG's then best selling sports car, 101,081 being built between 1955 and 1962 when it was replaced by the still current MGB. This figure includes 2111 cars fitted with the controversial twin overhead camshaft engined variant made between 1958 and 1960.

Before examining the points to look for when confronted with a secondhand example of one of these distinctive motor cars, it would perhaps be appropriate to reflect briefly on the model's pedigree, and an impressive one it is.

The first "prototype" A was a special TD, built for George Phillips to race at Le Mans in 1951. Although using a modified TD chassis, the bodywork bore a striking resemblance to the production A of 1955. However, as far as the race went, it was soon over for the car when it retired early on with engine trouble. The first pukka MGA prototype was built the following year, being designated Ex 175, while a spare chassis formed the basis of Ex 179, the record breaking car that set up new records at Utah in 1954. Thus body and chassis were well proven, though the engine eventually chosen to power the new model was the Austin BMC "B" series engine that was already fitted to the "Z" series Magnette saloons, parts rationalisation and spares availability no doubt being the overwhelming consideration. While the chassis followed closely that used in Ex 179, the front cross member and suspension were from the TF, while the rear axle and brakes came from the current Magnette. The new model received a competitive baptism at Le Mans in 1955 when three aluminium bodied prototypes (designated Ex 182) were entered, two finishing fifth and sixth in their class. It was to be another four months before the model was officially launched.

The open roadster model, which remained in production until May 1959, was powered by a 1489cc version of the aforementioned B series engine, being fitted with Lockheed drum brakes all round, while a coupé version was introduced in September 1956. July 1958 saw the appearance of a twin overhead camshaft variant of the A, but this model only remained in production until early 1960. May of that year saw the coupé and roadster cars sporting a more powerful 1588cc engine while the drum brakes at the front gave way to Lockheed discs. A de luxe version of this pushrod 1600cc car appeared briefly in 1960 having a twin cam chassis; only a few being made. A Mark II version of the A finally appeared in June 1961, the engine size being stretched again, this time to 1622cc, the model being distinguished by a recessed radiator grille. These roadster and coupé options remained in production until the model was phased out in September 1962. (See "Case History" section at the end of this article for full details of model changes). The foregoing information applies to the pushrod versions only, as twin cam version is dealt with separately.

Bodywork

Although the MGA does have a chassis (it was the last MG to have a separate frame), close scrutiny of the bodywork is of vital importance. Steel predominates, though the bonnet, doors and boot lid are made of aluminium. Starting at the front of the car, pay particular attention to the bottom of the front wings, which is a favourite mud trap. The nearby door pillars are another vulnerable area. You can check their condition by opening the doors and checking whether they move up and down! The front of the rear wheel arches should be examined for evidence of rust or filler, while the extreme rear of the boot floor is another suspect place. On the coupé, the area where the fixed head joins the body also rusts, the cracking being caused by body flexing. Also carefully examine the condition of the radiator grille on the 1600cc cars. If it's in poor condition you may have to pay as much as £50 for a replacement.

Now to the all important chassis frame. This is, on the whole, fairly sound, although the most likely areas for rusting are found on the side members inside the car, immediately adjacent to the wooden floor boards. A difficult check point this, because the section is usually covered by carpeting. The plywood boards are often in a poor state by this time, but this is hardly a major structural disaster. The battery carriers deserve a check and also that part of the chassis where the cross tubes are welded to the side members. You may find that the car's petrol tank is simply held in position by rust, as the metal straps securing it have often rusted through. And while you're under the car, check the angle of the rear spring hangers; they should both be at the same inclination. If not, this may be a memento of some long forgotten shunt.

Engine and gearbox

The faithful and viceless B series engine has no obvious drawbacks, so an oil pressure check is your most important consideration. This should not be less than 50psi at 50mph (hot). Fuel economy represents a big plus with this four-cylinder power unit. Most versions (except the twin cam) return consumptions in excess of 29mpg and in my own case (1961 1600), I'm getting a healthy average of 32mpg. This obviously depends, to a great degree, on the condition and synchronisation of the twin H4 SU carburettors. Again, the A's gearbox is a sturdy and, on the whole, reliable unit although the chances are that synchromesh on second gear has failed. Fortunately spares are readily available.

Steering, suspension and brakes

The A's rack and pinion steering live right out at the front of the chassis, so check the rubber gaiter for splits or tears. The A is particularly prone to front suspension wear and to check this jack the car up under the appropriate wishbone. (Never carry out this check with the jack position under the centre of the car. This simply allows the coil springs to expand, taking up any wear there may be present.) Now hold the wheel with one hand on the twelve o'clock position, and the other on the six, and wobble the wheel. If there's any wear present in the links, you'll soon feel it.

New suspension parts are now available, by the way. Also remember that the lower link spacer tube

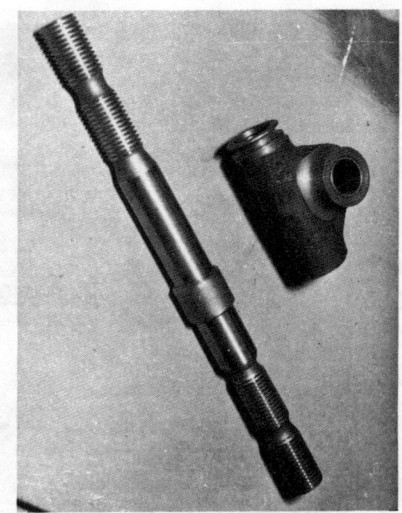

Replacement steering parts are now being re-manufactured – these items are marketed by Motobuild.

Above, rot in chassis side member; below, door shut face showing rust traps.

and washers are the same as those used on the MGB. Regular lubrication is vital for these parts. They should be greased every two or three months! For wear in the steering gear, carry out the same routine, but with your hands on the wheel at the nine and three o'clock positions. The chances are that the front shock absorbers will be badly worn, though the rear units should last the life of the car. The drum brakes on the pre-1959 cars shouldn't present any problems, while pads, discs and callipers for the Lockheed discs are still obtainable. A word of warning though. The chromium plated pistons on these brakes are particularly prone to seizure, so if you're contemplating a car that's even been off the road for a fairly short time, check this point, which is usually revealed by a binding wheel and scored discs. Rear springs are prone to breakage, so keep an eye open for broken leaves.

The Twin cam version
Bodywork
The same remarks apply to the twin cam cars, in this section, as the pushrod engined cars.

Engine and gearbox
Naturally spare parts for this engine are rather more of a problem than the ubiquitous B series power unit. When the model was first available, in July 1958, the first 345 examples used pistons fitted with chromium plated rings. However, this resulted in excessive bore wear and the plating was dropped. (It is extremely unlikely that there are any cars still in circulation with these original pistons, though.) Another important modification came at engine number 1587 when the tappet buckets were steel sleeved into the aluminium cylinder head. Prior to that they had run with a sleeve and wear took place. And while on the subject of tappets, another twin cam shortcoming is that the buckets crack across the top and then jam, with consequently dire results! When you come to adjust the tappets (they're the shim and bucket variety, as you'd expect, with this engine), don't lose the camshaft bearings, replacements don't exist.

The twin cam's original compression ratio was 9·9 to 1, though this was later dropped to 8·3 to 1. If you've a Gold Seal replacement engine in your example, it will be this lower ratio, making the engine more suitable for three-star petrol. It's also best to run the engine without a vacuum advance connection. A non vacuum advance distributor was one of the last modifications made to the engine, as excessive advance made its inevitable contribution to burnt out pistons. The all important oil pressure reading should be no less than 50psi at 2500rpm (about 35mph). Be prepared for an oil consumption in the region of 200 miles per pint, incidentally.

You'll also be in trouble with one of the early cars when it comes to a fan belt change. The radiator has to be removed, so you can get to the bottom adjusting nut on the dynamo. Detachable panels were later fitted in the wheel arches of the later cars. You should get between 20 and 25mpg from the twin 1¾in SU carburettors on this engine. Any improvement on this figure should be avoided at all costs as weakening the mixture can result in burnt out pistons. The twin cam runs happiest on Champion N4 plugs, we are assured.

Above and right, upturned rear bodyshell showing rust in boot floor areas; left, front wing removed to show door hinge pillar – rust sets in at bottom of inner wing too.

Below – believe it or not, this was our cover car a few months ago, displaying its very real chassis frame.

From the top, 1500 roadster, 1600 coupé, Twin Cam roadster.

Below, check for suspension wear by wobbling jacked-up wheel.

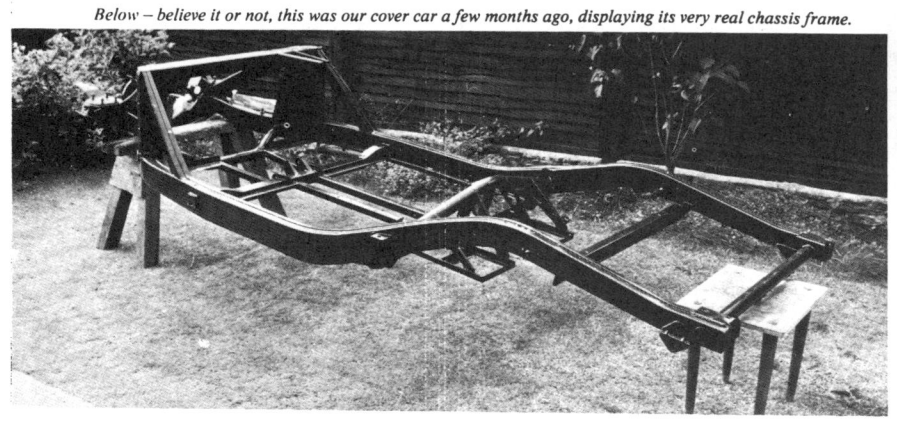

MGA

Remember, if you have occasion to drain the cooling system to re-fill with anti-freeze, it's not sufficient to simply drain the radiator, the block will have to be emptied separately. Also unlike the pushrod car, the twin cam is fitted with a separate radiator header tank.

Steering, suspension and brakes
The most obvious external difference between the twin cam and its pushrod brother is that the former car is fitted with rather handsome Dunlop wheels, though they have four locating pegs instead of splines, as might be expected. Dunlop disc brakes are fitted all round. The rear discs rust badly and up until now replacements were unobtainable, so this situation is shortly to be resolved by Peter Wood (see "Spares" heading). Although these brakes provide excellent retardation, don't expect great things from the handbrake, this will require careful adjustment to get it working tolerably. You'll also be in trouble with the Dunlop brake master cylinder. Replacement rubbers simply aren't around, nor will those fitted to the later Girling product (though still marked "Dunlop"). Here the only answer is to fit a non standard part, if you find the rubber and/or cylinders are worn badly.

The steering rack is mounted farther forward in the twin cam, due to the longer engine, so the same check points apply to this as the pushrod model.

It should also be noted that at chassis 2371, the number of splines on the differential and half shafts were increased and if you need a replacement you're in trouble because these components were not used on any other MG, or for that matter BMC car.

As far as the front suspension is concerned again the same shortcoming apply, but Ralph Canby, competitions secretary of the Twin Cam section of the MG Car Club's MGA Register, advises against the use of the current replacement brass parts on the model, which is, after all, over two hundredweight heavier than the pushrod version.

Spares
MGA owners are fortunate in that body and mechanical spares (the latter for the pushrod, at least) are in plentiful supply. Some chassis and engine parts are still available through Leyland Cars stockist, but if you're really looking for a comprehensive service, then the specialists' in the model should be your first port of call. Vic Ells Sportscar Repairs of 234 Trussley Road, Hammersmith, London W6 (01-741 2731) specialise in the MGA (and B) and can handle a host of mechanical work and also operate an exchange shock absorber and radiator service. Vic will modify cylinder heads for competition work and will also repair temperature gauges, providing they are provided complete. I gratefully acknowledge Vic's help in the preparation of the "pushrod" section of this article. Motobuild Ltd, of 128 High Street, Hounslow, Middlesex (01-570 5342) also operate a comprehensive list of facilities for A owners (and also T types) and supply a variety of metal body parts, an offside front wing of their manufacture is at present gracing the writer's MGA and a very good job it is too. My thanks to Motobuild for providing suitably rusted A's to be photographed for this article from their "Black Museum". In addition NTG Services of 25 St Peters Street, Ipswich 1P1 1XF (Ipswich 211240) can supply mechanical spares which include all suspension parts and also a range of rubber mouldings. The rubber gear lever gaiter will soon be available and an exchange instrument service is also operated. It almost goes without saying that Toulmin Motors (1962) Ltd, of 103–105 Windmill Road, Brentford, Middlesex (01-560 1722/2228) offer a wide variety of parts, and in many cases they have initiated the manufacture of "new" spares that would have otherwise have become obsolete. MGA front and rear wings are also available from Marsh Developments of 2 Walnut Tree Close, Guildford, Surrey (Guildford 37775) (see *Thoroughbred and Classic Cars*, August 1975) though this is just one of many makes embraced by the company. On the body scene, Roy McCarthy's Custom Style Autos of 1a Windermere Avenue, London SW10 (01-540 7028) specialises in A's, though engine re-builds are also undertaken. An excellent secondhand parts service is also to be had by S. H. Richardson and Sons Ltd, at Moor Lane, Staines, Middlesex (Staines 55388). But if you decide to join the ranks of MGA owners, then membership of the MG Car Club is a "must". General secretary is Gordon Cobban of 273 Green Lane, Ilford, Essex 1GS 9TJ. This means that you can join the club's MGA Register, and my thanks to Harry Pearce, their historian, for providing the comprehensive B series engine "Case History" provided here. The Register's magazine, *MGActivities* costs £1.25 per annum and can be obtained (post free) from the Snowball Press, 14 Cross Street, Reading, Berkshire.

Many of the body and mechanical parts of the twin cam model are, as we've seen, common to both cars, but the main source of parts for the twin cam is Peter Wood of Westwood, Church Street, Twyford, Buckingham, (029673-310). He can also supply "pushrod" spares as well. In addition, Ralph Canby of 5 Churchill Close, Hartley Wintney, Hampshire, who kindly gave up a morning to talk to me about twin cams and provided the information for the "Case History" section for that model, is also a source of some spares and advice.

If you're toying with the idea of A ownership then you'll see that spare parts are the least of your problems. There's no shortage of secondhand examples on the market, but I'd be inclined to steer clear of the lower end of the range which starts at around £150. But for a good looking classic with a racing pedigree, reliability (once sorted) and above all fuel economy, you can do no better than buy an MGA. I should know, I've got one! **J.W.**

CASE HISTORY
Pushrod engined cars
SEPTEMBER 1955 – MGA ROADSTER. 1489cc BMC "B" series engine, ohv + push rods. Price £595 + pt £249 = £844. First chassis number 10101. BMC "B-type" gearbox with extended casing to accept splined end of prop-shaft. 1¼in SU carburettors. Lockheed hydraulic drum brakes, front-two leading shoes, rear-one leading, one trailing. Disc wheels with ventilation holes and 4-stud attachment; wire-spoked, centre-lock wheels as optional extra. Flush fitting radiator grille follows line of car nose. Dual filament combined front/flasher + tail/flasher lights. Car discontinued May 1959.

SEPTEMBER 1956 – MGA COUPÉ. 1489cc engine. Price £699 + pt £351 = £1050. First chassis number 20670. Larger wrap-round windscreen, wind-up windows + wrap-round rear window. 15GD power unit introduced from chassis No 61504 (early 1959). Prop shaft modified with universal joint at both ends and splined sliding joint in prop shaft itself. At 101.2mph "max", car is 3.5mph faster than roadster. Returns 1mpg better fuel consumption (31.5mpg). Outside door handles + door locks. Car discontinued May 1959.

JULY 1958 – MGA TWIN CAM (Roadster or Coupé). 1588cc engine, twin overhead cam. Price £843 + pt £423 = £1266 (Roadster) 1¾in. carburettors, Dunlop disc brakes all round. Centre lock disc wheels. Separate radiator header tank bolted to exhaust manifold. Leather covered facia board. Rev-counter reads up to 7500 rpm 115mph (max). 27.6mpg. Car discontinued March 1961.

MAY 1959 – MGA 1600 (Roadster or Coupé). 1588cc ohv + pushrod engine. Price £663 + pt £277 = £940. First chassis number 68851. Lockheed disc brakes at front only, drums at rear. New tail-light housing with separate flasher cover. New front parking/flasher lights. Sliding plexi-glass side screens on roadster. New coil mounting. 96.1mph "max", 29.7mpg. Car discontinued March 1961.

LATE 1959 – MGA 1600 DE LUXE – little known hybrid model of twin cam specification but with 1588cc pushrod engine. Few only made. Discontinued early 1960.

JUNE 1961 Mk II (Roadster or Coupé). 1622cc ohv engine. Price £663 + pt £277 = £940. Engine has new block, pistons, con-rods, crankshaft and flywheel, new head, larger valves and new ribbed-casing to gear-box. Final drive gearing raised from 4.3 to 4.1 to 1. Re-designed inset radiator grille. 101.4mph "max". 35mpg. Coupé discontinued June 1962, Roadster discontinued September 1962.

Twin cam engined cars
Chassis numbers are prefixed YD1 501 (Roadster) and Ym1 501 (Coupé).
Chassis 592 Wheel arch fitted with detachable panels.
Chassis 713 Water temperature gauge changed from Fahrenheit to Centigrade.
Chassis 2192 Flasher changed from white to yellow at front and separate unit introduced at rear. Minor trim changes in Coupé.
Chassis 2275 Anti roll bar fitted.
Chassis 2371 Half shaft and differential fitted with finer splines. Also applies to De Luxe model.

Engine numbers are prefixed 16GBUH (High compression) or 16GBUL (Low compression) numbers start at engine 101.
Engine 272 Dynamo pulley changed to smaller size; 1.2:1. Shorter fan belt.
Engine 313 Gearing on oil pump changed from nine to 10 teeth on the half speed shaft and 10 to 11 on the oil pump drive.
Engine 446 Piston rings changed from chrome plate to iron.
Engine 528 Packing plate fitted between engine mounting and chassis.
Engine 1087 Tappet bucket increased in length from 1.25in to 1.5in.
Engine 1343 Heavier conrods fitted.
Engine 1587 Tappets sleeved into cylinder head.
Engine 2223 Distributor change to non-vacuum advance type.
Engine 2251 Valve springs changed.

The MGA Twin Cam, showing the distinctive cam-covers of its power unit.

AGAINST ALL ODDS

There is no doubting the fact that Chris Starr is a dedicated and passionate MG enthusiast. He works with them during the week and at the weekend spends most of his spare time tending to his pristine 1959 MGA. He bought the car in 1968 having been attracted to the model by an article in a motoring magazine. A local showroom contained what appeared to be the perfect example and, after visiting it no fewer than five times, Chris finally managed to convince himself that he *really* did need it. His own car at that time, a Hillman Imp, was running perfectly and had luxuries such as wind-up windows and a roof and Chris had a few second thoughts about changing. These doubts were heightened by the fact that he knew the MGA was a little over-priced. However, he took a deep breath, wrote a cheque for £350 and drove away in a car that was to play a large part in his life for the next 19 years.

The MGA represented somewhat of a watershed in the design history of the MG motor car. It was radically different from the popular T Series cars that it succeeded and there was, for a time, some degree of speculation over how the new car would be received by the buying public. The company endeavoured to lessen the shock by linking the whole project with the famous Le Mans 24 Hour Race. This, in fact, was not merely a marketing ploy as the car really had been designed to re-establish MG in the competitive and potential lucrative world of motor sport.

It had become very apparent that a streamlined body was rapidly becoming an essential for success on the race track. MG's answer was a sleek new body designed by Syd Enever that was fitted to a racing MG TD in 1951. It resulted in a considerable improvement in performance over the original and spurred Enever on to design a new chassis with the idea of creating a road-going version. The first car was powered by a four-cylinder 1489cc pushrod ohv engine that produced 68bhp (later increased to 72bhp) and it was known as the MGA 1500. It featured coil and wishbone front suspension and half-eliptic springs at the rear while the gearbox was a manual four-speed part-synchro unit. Wire wheels were available as an optional extra and the car could be ordered in either open two-seater or fixed-head coupe form. The MGA 1500 continued in production until early 1959.

In 1958 the MGA Twin Cam was released. Thanks to its 1588cc twin ohc engine which developed 108bhp, this car gave noticeably better performance figures than its predecessor. The 0-60mph time was greatly reduced from 15 to about 9.5 secs and at least 15mph was added to the maximum speed. Just over 2,000 Twin Cams were produced in a two-year period which compares with nearly 59,000 MGA 1500s. The MGA 1600 was the third variant and appeared in both Mk 1 and a Mk 2 form. The Mk 1s had a pushrod ohv version of the 1588cc engine but, for the Mk 2, the capacity was increased to 1622cc and the power output raised from 80 to 93bhp.

Despite many setbacks Chris Starr has managed to steer his 1959 MGA through a successful rebuild and on to many concours victories — Chris Graham tells the story.

Like those before it, the MGA was 'big' in America and consequently about 60% of all the cars made were exported. However, its popularity was not to last for long and the car unfortunately suffered rather a disappointing end to its production life. Due to falling sales, the car quietly faded away to make room for the introduction of the MGB in 1962.

Production of the MGA, of course, had long since ended by the time that Chris purchased his car and the MGB was in full flight. His car was finished in Chariot Red with a black interior (as it is now) and for the first few months all went well. However, disaster was about to strike. He had gone to spend the night with his parents when, at about 1.30am, there was a knock on the door. It was the police and they were trying to trace the owner of a red MGA with the registration number WPR 909B and, unfortunately, they had found him. Chris's car had been stolen and subsequently written-off during an 80mph speed trial down Poole High Street. It hit a concrete lamp post on the nearside which drove back the whole of that side and bent the chassis. The two young joy-riders were badly hurt (one with two broken legs) and Chris was devastated. The car was patched up with glass fibre wings because there were no steel alternatives available at the time and Chris soldiered on.

Things finally came to a head in 1978 when problems started to get serious — the fact that the car was being used as everyday transport was starting to take its toll. The gearbox had become very noisy, the brakes ineffective and rust had begun to break out all over (both on the body and on the chassis). At this point Chris had to decide whether to sell the car or, instead, to keep and restore it. The latter course was taken.

Above:

Chris is completely dedicated to his car and, during the show season, he spends all of every Saturday cleaning and polishing it.

AGAINST ALL ODDS
CONTINUED

With the rear wings, the seats and the floor boards removed, Chris got the first inkling of the condition of the chassis. Some quite extensive repairs were required once the body had been removed.

There were 21 separate items to be sprayed . . .

. . . and Chris was fortunate enough to have the use of professional equipment which helped greatly. However, little did he know that he would have to repeat the whole operation within a year.

The front suspension was one of the few areas that was left alone during the restoration. It has remained untouched to this day.

The MGA takes on a whole new appearance without its wings and trim. This picture was taken with the car in the panel shop undergoing one of the many trial fitting sessions.

Originally Chris's car had been fitted with steel wheels and when he swapped them for wires a new axle was required. Subsequently he changed the differential for one with a higher ratio (as fitted to the Le Mans cars) in an effort to improve the car's performance on the road. He also added a front anti-roll bar (which was an optional extra) for the same reason.

The underside has been kept as original as possible. Only those areas that do not show have been treated to any form of corrosion prevention and Chris relies on regular cleaning to stop the formation of rust on the untreated areas.

The restoration

Chris is a trained mechanic and so was quite capable of attending to the mechanical side of the rebuild. His experience with bodywork was rather more limited and his knowledge extended only as far as that which he had picked up from working in the garage. He was well aware that the body would need to be removed to gain access to the whole chassis as it was likely this would have become corroded in places. He decided that it would be best to cut the body in half first and then lift it clear in two separate pieces. This method has the advantage of avoiding the risk of distortion which can easily occur if a body is removed in one piece without adequate support. The rear half was removed and put to one side.

To do this cuts were made through the badly corroded sills and, out of the 28 bolts that fastened the body to the chassis, Chris was amazed to find that only one was rusted solid. With the front half of the body removed the whole chassis was revealed and, as expected, holes were discovered. Chris had agreed to use a local body shop in which to carry out the restoration as he had no garage of his own at the time. This, of course, provided a very good working environment and made things a lot easier. The chassis was repaired with relative ease using a MIG welder but Chris admits that he didn't make the tidiest of jobs.

The bodywork was to provide the real problems and so, with some degree of trepidation, Chris began with the repairs to the rusted boot floor. These went well and his attention turned to other areas of the underside that are normally inaccessible. The two ends of the body, having already been stripped of paint, were then put back onto the chassis and bolted on firmly. Next the inner and outer sills, and the door posts that come together to form the F section, were lightly tacked into position with spots of weld. It is important to get this stage right as the accuracy of the door shut depends on it. If the assembly is welded in at an incorrect angle then the doors will never shut properly. This took some fiddling to get it right but, once it was achieved, everything was bolted together for the final bare-metal check and then dismantled again in preparation for spraying.

All the mechanical areas of the car were thoroughly inspected, cleaned and, if necessary, stripped and rebuilt or replaced. The only areas to remain intact were the front suspension, the rear shock absorbers and the engine — all were in fine condition and required no alteration. Since new the car has covered 180,000 miles and in this time the only significant work that has been carried out on the engine is a decoke and the fitting of a new set of main bearings — the latter took place 15 years ago. The most serious mechanical problem was caused by the gearbox which required a complete overhaul. For this the internals were taken from the gearbox of a BMC J2 van which appeared to fit the bill and these were purchased for £35 brand new.

Chris's spraying experience was not great but he was determined to do as much of the restoration himself as possible so he pressed on undaunted. There were 21 separate panels to be prepared and sprayed and the time

AGAINST ALL ODDS

CONTINUED

taken on the preparation alone ran into weeks. Several coats of primer were applied followed by eight double coats of cellulose top coat. Finally it was flatted and then polished. Waxoyl was used extensively but carefully as Chris was anxious to keep the car's appearance as original as he could to please the concours judges. All the box sections were filled as were the cavities behind the splash panels and the like. Waxoyl was also used behind all the body-mounted badges and on items such as the headlamp mounting rubbers because Chris knows from experience how rust can develop in such areas. New bolts, dipped in grease, were used throughout.

All was well for the first few months but then more trouble started. The surface became rain-spotted, faded and was quite obviously very soft. This was a very disappointing development and Chris's heart sank at the thought of repeating the whole exercise once again. However, there was no alternative. With the benefit of hindsight he believes that the problems were caused by the oil-based primer he had chosen and imagines that this had not hardened sufficiently before the top coats were applied.

So, with the car having been finished for less than a year, it was driven back into the workshop for a repeat performance. This time, however, a modern two-pack paint was used and Chris left the spraying to a colleague while he tackled the preparation.

The only problem with the instruments concerned the petrol gauge which continually collected condensation. After several unsuccessful attempts at a remedy Chris decided to swap the gauge for the newer version from an MGB. The faces were changed over so that all appeared well and no further problems occured. Chris replaced the whole wiring loom with a new one and found this one of the simplest jobs of the whole restoration.

The trimming was the only part of the restoration that Chris did not undertake himself. He felt that, with the price of hides being so high, the risk was too great and that he would be unable to afford the inevitable mistakes.

So at last the job was finished and Chris could concentrate on entering the car in concours events. This happy situation lasted until last winter when some kindly soul backed into the car in a car park and badly dented the rear wing. Fortunately, however, Chris is now working for a company called Mansell Shaw Racing Ltd who are based in Downton near Salisbury, Wiltshire. They specialise in the restoration and race preparation of MGs of all kinds and kindly allowed Chris the use of their facilities for the repairs. One thing led to another and the car was eventually treated to another full respray and a set of new wheels and tyres.

This picture was taken while the new floor boards were being fitted. The original steering wheel was still in place here but shortly afterwards was swapped for a wood-rimmed version that was an optional extra.

The trimming was the one area that Chris did not tackle himself although he did fit everything into the car once it had been made.

On the road

This was my first time behind the wheel of an MGA, a car which I consider to be the last of the real MGs. I was very pleased to get the chance of an outing in Chris's car because I knew everything would be right and that it would be most driveable. Settling into the driving seat I was immediately struck by the low seating position in relation to the rest of the car. This creates a pleasantly secure feeling and is made possible due to the chassis design. The main chassis rails bow out around the passenger compartment and do not interfere with the level of the floor which allows the seats to be mounted at the lowest possible point.

The engine started on the button and quickly settled to an even tickover. Blipping the throttle produced the characteristically crisp exhaust note and sent the rev counter needle spinning round the scale with effortless ease — I knew that I was going to like this car. I had to pause for a few seconds to remember how to use the fly-off handbrake but then I was off. I always find that the first few moments in a strange car are rather anxious ones because all the controls are so strange. The clutch is often the hardest thing to master quickly but, in this case, everything fell beautifully to hand and I very rapidly began to feel at home in the car.

I was driving under ideal conditions. It was a warm and sunny day, we were on a twisty A road in the depths of Wiltshire and, of course, the hood was down. I had not been expecting the car to be terrifically fast — the MGA is not that type of car. It's not for the person who craves an out-and-out road-burner. Instead it demands a more sensitive and perhaps appreciative breed of owner. The steering was impressively precise and this, coupled with the tremendous roadholding, gave one the impression that the car could be driven with great agility and flair. This is where I felt that it really differed from the MGB. The MGA *felt* like a sports car. It possesses that appealing mixture of subtle harshness and simplicity which, to my mind, has to be present to give a sports car its style. The MGA can certainly start the adrenalin a pumpin' if so desired. The brakes were well up to the car's performance and the gear-change, although firm, was predictable and lacked any disconcerting play.

Since he has been competing in events Chris has won 132 major and minor awards.

Considering the car's condition it is hard to believe that it is treated like this every weekend throughout the summer and driven 60 miles a day to and from work.

The other aspect of the MGA which endears it to me is its looks. I find it more pleasing than either its predecessors or its successors and from almost every angle, interesting curves and details can be enjoyed. It is very much a design from the early 1960s that falls neatly into the traditional image of the British sports car and that I like. It has a distinctive front end with grille, a long bonnet, a slightly curved and raked windscreen and gracefully shaped and proportioned wings. The wire wheels on Chris's car complete the picture and produce a car of which, justifiably he can most proud. □

My thanks go to Chris Starr and the staff at Mansell Shaw Racing Ltd (Tel: 0725 21418) for their help with the preparation of this feature.

R&T USED CAR CLASSIC

1955·1962 MGA

Little treasure

BY PETER BOHR

THE PURISTS WERE aghast. The new MGA, introduced at the Frankfurt Auto Show in September 1955, didn't look anything like its predecessors. Since the Midget of 1928, MG sports cars had always had flat-front radiators, delicate sweeping fenders and "square-rigged" bodies. Instead, the MGA was a contemporary car, not a throwback to the days of Evelyn Waugh's *Brideshead Revisited*. But to the purists, the MGA's envelope body was a reckless step toward modernity.

That sort of conservatism persisted for many years. While an active cadre of enthusiasts promoted the MG T-series and pushed their prices to dizzying heights, interest in the MGA languished. As recently as five years ago you could buy a running MGA for considerably less than $1000 while basket-case TDs were selling for five times that amount.

There's no question that the MG T-series positively ooze creamy English charm. And certainly the immortal TC, as well as the TD and TF that followed, deserve credit for introducing us colonials to the delights of sports cars. But in sales figures, the T-series cars were forerunners to the MGA invasion that was to come. Purists aside, the public embraced the MGA, especially the American public. Between 1955 and 1962, MG's Abingdon factory built 101,081 MGAs, more than double the entire production of the T-series. The MGA was the first sports car from any carmaker in any country to break the magic 100,000 mark. And better than 80 percent of the MGA production was exported to the U.S.

It's no wonder then that the MGA became something of a fixture at the local drive-in theater or hamburger stand during the Fifties. With its streamlined styling, knockoff wire wheels and wide, wide whitewall tires, the MGA fit right in there with Elvis Presley, ducktail haircuts, 1957 T-Birds and other artifacts of that happy decade. In a 1955 road test, R&T's editors concluded, "If you look over the MG 'A' with a critical eye, drive it and note the price tag—you will probably ask the same question we do: How are they going to supply enough cars to meet the demand?"

Since then, the MGA has aged gracefully. Controversially modern in 1955, the car has charm all its own in 1984. Thanks to the current Fifties revival, and thanks to the enthusiasm of the members of the North American MGA Register, the car has gone from black sheep of the MG family to something of a rising star. Prices are climbing, and more and more MGAs are being carefully restored. But there are still plenty around in various states of repair, and it's still possible to find a bargain. All this makes the MGA a natural for our Used Car Classic Series.

Evolution of the MGA

THE MGA might have gone into production instead of the TF had Donald Healey not approached BMC management first with his new 100 model. Syd Enever, one of the automotive industry's great engineers, had actually designed the basic MGA body for use on a Le Mans racer in 1951. The following year Enever refined the styling and designed a new chassis. The car, known by the factory code name EX175, was essentially the MGA's prototype. However, BMC management (MG had become a part of the BMC group in 1952) decided to concentrate its resources on the new Austin-Healey. The TD was facelifted and became the TF, while the EX175 was shelved. But when flagging TF sales became impossible to ignore in mid-1954, MG received permission to break with the past and proceed.

More than just the MGA's styling was new. Aside from the front suspension (independent with lever-arm shock absorbers) and the steering (rack and pinion), little else was carried over from the T-series. The extremely strong box-section frame was taken directly from the EX175. But unlike the prototype that used the TD drivetrain, the MGA has the so-called Austin B-series engine, a hardy 4-cylinder unit that was used in several BMC sedans including the Magnette. The gearbox, also from the Magnette, has a nonsynchronized 1st gear. The live rear axle, yet another component from the Magnette, is located and suspended by semi-elliptic leaf springs, and, like the front suspension, uses lever-action shock absorbers.

Most of the body is steel, but to save weight, MG made the hood, doors and trunk lid of aluminum. The cockpit is certainly cozy, and the seating position is surprisingly low. All but the tallest people will find plenty of leg room, although there's not much space around the pedals for the driver's feet. In the usual British roadster fashion, the placement of the shift lever is ideal, and there's a full complement of handsome, readable instruments. Unfortunately, the folding top is also typically British; it requires an abundance of patience as well as physical dexterity to either erect or stow away.

Overall, the MGA is considerably smoother and more refined than the TF. And because of improved aerodynamics, the MGA's efficiency is higher. A 1955 MGA has a top speed 10 mph greater than a TF, yet its weight and horsepower are unchanged. Throughout its production run the MGA was also reasonably priced with a U.S. price tag of $2195 in 1955, rising to $2485 in 1962.

The MGA really didn't change much over its lifespan, though there were four official models and one unofficial model, and each of them was available in two body styles. The roadster with soft top and side curtains was the usual configuration. A detachable fiberglass hardtop was an option for the roadster, but in 1956 MG decided to go a step further. Copying the concept of Jaguar's successful XK120 coupe, the company gave the MGA a permanently fixed steel hardtop. With roll-up windows and a fully carpeted interior, the snug little coupe is slightly more luxurious than the roadster.

The 1500 was the first model, and was sold until the summer of 1959. Altogether some 59,000 MGA 1500s rolled off Abingdon's assembly line. The second model, the 1600, was MG's answer to its competitors in the sports car market, especially to Triumph's TR3. With Lockheed front disc brakes and an increase of nearly 100 cc of engine displacement, the MGA 1600 has much improved braking and quicker acceleration. The 1600 was also the first truly 100-mph MGA, a noteworthy fact in the late Fifties when top speed had the importance that fuel economy holds today.

Though never officially called the Mk I, the 1600 of 1959 was superseded by the 1600 Mk II in mid-1961. Except for revised taillights and several badges that say 1600, the 1500 and 1600 Mk I look identical. However, the 1600 Mk II has a recessed grille that distinguishes the model from the two previous models. In addition, the Mk II has yet another type of taillights, and another increase in engine displacement, from the Mk I's 1588 cc to 1622 cc. The Mk II was around for little more than a year before the MGA was replaced by the MGB. Altogether, production of the 1600 Mk I and Mk II totaled some 40,000 cars.

The 1500 and the two 1600 models were MG's bread and butter between 1955 and 1962. But there were two variations on the MGA theme that have since come to be highly valued by collectors. The MGA Twin-Cam of 1958 was an official model built alongside the 1500 and later the 1600. The distinguishing feature of the Twin-Cam is, of course, a double-overhead-camshaft engine. Though based on the block of the standard MGA pushrod engine, the Twin-Cam engine's alloy cylinder head was all-new. The 1588-cc unit produced an impressive 108 bhp compared with 79.5 for the 1600 Mk I. But from the beginning, the Twin-Cam's engine developed a nasty reputation for heavy oil consumption and burned pistons. When the compression ratio was lowered from 9.9 to 8.3:1 in 1959, reliability improved. Nevertheless, by the following year the company had had enough, and the Twin-Cam was dropped after a total production of slightly more than 2000.

The dohc engine was the most important feature of the model, but there were several other modifications. In addition to a slightly different suspension and steering arrangement, the

The Frankfurt Auto Show of 1955 was the introduction site for the controversial MGA. Interior is simplicity itself.

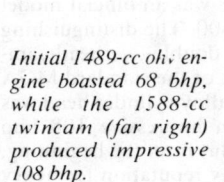

Initial 1489-cc ohv engine boasted 68 bhp, while the 1588-cc twincam (far right) produced impressive 108 bhp.

Twin-Cam carried 4-wheel Dunlop disc brakes and knockoff pressed-steel disc wheels. It appears that when the Twin-Cam engine met its demise, there was a store of the other components left over. Consequently, about 350 of the usual pushrod engines were installed in what were otherwise Twin-Cam cars, and these were called DeLuxe versions. While DeLuxe versions of both the 1600 Mk I and Mk II were built, they were never classified as official models.

Although not in the same league as those lengthy scrolls from Detroit carmakers, the MGA's list of options did offer some interesting items. It's hard to believe today, but a heater was an option. Other popular items included telescopic steering wheel, tonneau cover, fog lights, radio and oil cooler. An optional luggage rack was especially designed to distribute weight over a broad area of the relatively soft aluminum trunk lid. Perhaps the most important option to people buying old MGAs today is wire wheels. They enhance the appearance and value of an MGA.

MGAs came in what R&T called "a veritable rainbow of color choices." Well maybe that was a bit of hyperbole, but 1500 models were available in red, white, black, light green and light blue, with red, black, gray or green Connolly leather-covered seats. However, in place of the light blue, the 1500 coupes came in a special dark blue. The 1600s, both Mk I and Mk II, came in red, white, black, beige, light blue and light gray, with black, beige or red leather. There was no special color for the 1600 coupes, and British racing green was never offered.

Selecting the Right MGA

So among the various models, what's hot and what's not? MG fanatics are the only ones gallant enough to put up with a Twin-Cam's unreliability. Even so, their rarity makes them quite valuable. The rear disc brakes of a DeLuxe version are desirable, but once again it's primarily the rarity of the 1600 DeLuxe cars that makes them coveted by MG fanciers.

Your best choice is probably a 1600 Mk I or Mk II, preferably with wire wheels. Red or white are the most popular among the original colors. Roadsters are much more common than coupes, so coupe prices tend to be higher. A Twin-Cam or DeLuxe coupe is, of course, the rarest of the rare. A coupe is safer in a rollover and offers better weather protection. But the floorboards (Yes, Virginia, MGAs have genuine wooden floorboards!) of all MGAs let uncomfortable amounts of engine heat into the passenger compartment. As a consequence, coupes can become mighty hot in the summer.

Regardless of the model you fancy, no MGA is a spring chicken anymore. Even the youngest, a 1962 model, is 22 years old, while the oldest is nearing 30. But fortunately MGAs were built tough. Oh, sure, the electrical system is protected only by two fuses and the cooling system is marginal. But the MGA's frame is massive enough for a bulldozer. And the MGA's heavy gauge sheet metal makes the body of today's typical import look like it's built of kitchen foil. This heft gives you a fighting chance to find a decent MGA.

We asked two experts for tips on inspecting MGAs. Lee Dudacek is a Jaguar mechanic by profession and drives a 1600 roadster around southern California as his everyday car. Gene McClelland owns an MG repair shop in Costa Mesa, California, appropriately called "McClelland's Garage" (MG). Both begin an inspection with a careful search for rust. Lee says the rear ends of the rocker panels are often the first spots to corrode. If they're sound, move on to the rest of the rocker panels (run your hand behind the panels as well) and the fenders. Open the doors and check the jambs; if the hinges or the lock seem to flex, the chassis supports may be rusted away—a very serious problem. Lift up the carpets and check the side chassis rails that support the floorboards. Take off the panel behind the seats and look at the two battery boxes (the MGA uses two 6-volt batteries instead of a single 12-volt). Finally, open the trunk lid and check the trunk floor for rust.

If the car passes rust inspection, Gene then likes to examine the front tires, which can indicate the condition of the front suspension. When the inside edges are rounded off, either the bushings or the front shocks may need replacement. Lever-arm shocks are about $65 apiece. There should be zero play in the steering wheel. If not, the problem might just be worn tie rod ends. But if the rubber boots on either side of the rack are

The MGA coupe came out in 1956 and featured roll-up windows, carpeting and a luxuriously snug interior.

Ken Palmer's award-winning supercharged 1962 Mk II DeLuxe tactfully screens author's less pristine 1960 1600.

drove a Schwinn. Richard was class president and a hunk. I was ... well, it doesn't matter. But I certainly didn't have an MGA and all those girls. Richard and his MGA were an unbeatable combination when it came to attracting the school's most beautiful girls.

So here I was, another baby-boomer in his thirties, with a little disposable income and a memory. What to do but buy the car I couldn't have back in high school? My 1960 1600 cost $2000 last year. On the way back from the seller's house I had to pull over every 10 miles and add water to the percolating radiator. And when I stopped, I had to make sure the MG pointed downhill; a compression start was the only choice as the batteries were too weak to turn the starter motor. But we made it. After a new radiator core, new batteries, a new muffler, and a carburetor rebuild, I had a decent, driveable MGA. The clutch slips badly enough so that it's a real adventure going up even a modest incline. And the car could use new paint and some front tires. But, boy, is it fun. And, yes, girls of all ages love it. Maybe Richard wasn't such a hunk; it was just his MGA.

Ken Palmer is another victim of MGA nostalgia. Ken's is a classic case dating back to his boyhood in a small farm town in Iowa, of all places. Among the Ford sedans and Chevy pickups of his neighbors, there was a red TD. "How could one ever achieve an MG?" he wondered. By working construction jobs during college and saving $900, he found his answer with a 6-year-old 1957 MGA. He graduated with it, did a stint in the air force with it, and honeymooned in it.

Seven years ago, fond memories of that car led Ken to search for another. But this time he wanted a rare MGA. His 1962 Mk II DeLuxe was delivered to him on a trailer. Except for the tattered interior, the frozen clutch and the vestiges of a paint job, it was certainly worth the $1000 he paid. Many dollars and hours of labor later, Ken's DeLuxe became the black beauty you see here, next to my white 1600.

When Ken drove up in his car, with its distinctive knockoff disc wheels and set-in grille, my poor MG wanted to hide in the garage with its tailpipe between its shock absorbers. Resplendent in its gleaming paint and red leather interior, the DeLuxe has nearly every factory option, including a rare close-ratio gearbox and competition seats. "The seats are monumentally uncomfortable," says Ken, "but they're wonderful at car shows." Indeed, Ken's car took first in its class five years ago at the North American MGA Register's national meet.

But the best goodie of all is under the bonnet: a Judson supercharger. Though not a factory option (Judsons were made in Conshocken, Pennsylvania), they were a popular add-on in the late Fifties. R&T tested a 1500 MGA with a Judson in 1958 and found about a 25-percent boost in both torque and horsepower with little sacrifice in fuel economy. The big advantage, says Ken, is improved high-gear flexibility.

The Judson certainly comes in handy when Ken decides to scale Mount Baldy, a 4500-ft mountain resort behind his West Covina home in southern California. The car has no problems making it up the grades. Nor does Ken have any qualms about taking the DeLuxe each year on an 800-mile round trip to the Monterey Historic Car Races. But Ken and I both are reluctant to use our MGAs as everyday commuter cars. It's not that the cars couldn't take it, once I fix my car's clutch, that is. It's just that southern California-style commuting involves a lot of tedious stop-and-go freeway driving in warm weather, which is not the MGA's forte. Better to have an enclosed Toyota with air conditioning and a good stereo.

MGAs are instead meant for open roads, preferably twisty ones. They're a perfect weekend toy, a perfect escape device, a perfect antidote to the usual sensory-deprivation machines that populate America's highways. They're just right for chasing girls or chasing memories. That's why Ken Palmer wouldn't take even $15,000 for his car. As for my car, make me an offer. No, on second thought, a driveable MGA in my garage is one of the few things that would give me more pleasure than a certificate of deposit in my bank.

CAR CLUBS

The North American MGA Register has 26 local chapters across the U.S. and Canada. The national organization publishes a bimonthly newsletter and sponsors an annual "GT," or get together. Annual dues are $15. Contact: Steve P. Mazurek, 856 Notre Dame, Grosse Pointe City, Mich. 48230.

RECOMMENDED READING

There are many books on the history of the MG marque. The following works are especially recommended for their tips on buying and restoring MGAs: *MGA, A History & Restoration Guide*, by Robert Vitrikas, Aztex Corp, PO Box 50046, Tucson, Ariz. 85703, $19.95; *Illustrated MG Buyer's Guide*, by Richard Knudson, Motorbooks International, PO Box 2, Osceola, Wis. 54020, $13.95; *The MGA, MGB and MGC, A Collector's Guide*, by Graham Robson, Motor Racing Publications Ltd, distributed in the U.S. by Motorbooks International, $18.95.

cracked or missing, you'd better expect a bum rack and pinion (about $350).

A pushrod MGA engine should have compression readings of 120 psi on each cylinder. Gene charges between $1000 and $2000 for rebuilding the engine. To replace the clutch, the engine must be removed; clutch parts and installation run between $300 and $400. Overhauling the transmission is costly. If the tranny seems especially noisy, plan on spending as much as $1000 for repair.

The rear end and rear shocks seem to last forever. But the brakes will often give trouble, especially if the car has been sitting for six months or longer. If the handbrake lever pulls up eight clicks or more, the rear brakes, at least, may need work. A complete brake system overhaul is about $300.

Then there's that old British-car bugaboo, the SU carburetor. The MGA has a pair of them. When the engine idles either too high or erratically, you should suspect worn throttle shafts. Rebuilding a pair of SUs costs about $175. Then once they're set up, both Lee and Gene urge you to "leave 'em alone." Says Lee, "When a car isn't running right, people immediately head for the carbs. Nine times out of 10, it's an electrical problem or perhaps burned valves." On the subject of electrics, the vacuum advance mechanism in the distributor of an old British car like the MGA often freezes. That, of course, results in pretty ragged high-end performance.

As for overheating, another common problem of older British cars, MGAs in warm climates often lose their cool. If the radiator, hoses, thermostat and water pump are all in good order, and the car still makes tea on warm days, Gene would suspect faulty ignition timing. If that's okay too, Lee suggests several fixes. First, there's plenty of room in front of the radiator for an electric cooling fan. Second, you could add an oil cooler. Third, you could replace the standard 2-row radiator with a 3-row unit; this requires a little bodywork, however. And as a last resort, you can remove the front grille. "The grille was cleverly designed to direct air away from the radiator," says Lee.

Finally, there's the subject of parts. Happily, most MGA parts are easy to obtain, and at a reasonable cost too. We have to put in a plug here for Moss Motors, Ltd in Goleta, California. Moss specializes in parts for old British sports cars. Their wonderfully detailed catalogs can serve as parts manuals. Moss will supply anything for an MGA, from pre-cut leather upholstery kits to original badges. Though Moss is perhaps the best known of the firms in the British car-parts business, there are several other good ones; check R&T's classified advertising section.

Driving Impressions: Tales of Two MGAs

It was an emotional response: pure and simple. Why else would I buy a tired, 23-year-old British roadster with a pull-type starter switch, a horn button in the middle of the dash, and a ride reminiscent of a Conestoga wagon? Talk about a lack of modern features, this baby doesn't even have sun visors or roll-

Steel wheels, folding top and side curtains were the standard fitments for the MGA. This is a 1959 1600.

up windows, let alone a climate control system or one of those little computer voices to remind you to get fuel or fasten your seatbelt. The only climate control system on my MGA is a soft top with an opaque rear window, and the only voice is the little one in my head that says, "Wow! This thing is fun to drive!"

Undoubtedly some MGA owners really think their cars are practical. Yes, MGAs do turn in 25 or 30 miles to the gallon of petrol. They do have quick and light steering, a wonderfully precise gearbox, decent road-holding, and a forgiving nature that wouldn't let even the most ham-fisted driver get in trouble. And indeed, MGAs are ruggedly durable and relatively inexpensive to buy or repair.

But come on—you can say much the same about a Toyota. No, we love MGAs because the little dears seem to tug at our emotional strings. For one thing, an MGA is among the best looking sports cars of the Fifties; its lines are as clean and smooth as a baby's bottom, unmarred by door handles or even a trunk handle. The car also has a certain tossability that encourages its driver to speed up through the corners and zip around the behemoths that block traffic. And, of course, there's the MGA's nostalgia value. It's a reminder of a time when chrome was plated over metal, not plastic; when seats were made from the hides of cows, not Naugas; when instruments were just instruments, not imitation video games.

In fact, I suspect nostalgia plays the largest role in the purchase decision of many MGA buyers. In my case it takes me back to the days of high school and a fellow named Richard. Richard was a senior and drove a pristine but unoriginal British-racing-green MGA with wire wheels. I was a sophomore and

BRIEF SPECIFICATIONS

	1500	1600	1600 Mk II	Twin-Cam
Curb weight, lb	2020	2050	2050	2200
Wheelbase, in	94.0	94.0	94.0	94.0
Track, f/r	47.5/48.8	47.5/48.8	47.5/48.8	47.9/48.9
Length	156.0	156.0	156.0	156.0
Width	57.3	57.3	57.3	57.3
Height	50.0	50.0	50.0	50.0
Engine type	ohv inline-4	ohv inline-4	ohv inline-4	dohc inline-4
Bore x stroke, in.	2.87 x 3.50	2.97 x 3.50	3.00 x 3.50	2.97 x 3.50
Displacement, cc	1489	1588	1622	1588
Horsepower, @ rpm	68 @ 5500	79.5 @ 5600	90 @ 5500	108 @ 6700
Torque, lb-ft @ rpm	77 @ 3500	87 @ 3800	97 @ 4000	104 @ 4500
Transmission	4-sp	4-sp	4-sp	4-sp
Suspension, front/rear	ind coil/ live leaf	ind coil/ live leaf	ind coil/ live leaf	ind coil/ live leaf
Brakes, front/rear	drum/ drum	disc/ drum	disc/ drum	disc/ disc
Steering type	rack & pinion	rack & pinion	rack & pinion	rack & pinion

PERFORMANCE DATA
from Contemporary Tests

	1955 1500	1959 1600	1961 1600 Mk II	1958 Twin-Cam
0-60 mph, sec	14.5	13.3	12.8	9.9
Standing ¼ mile, sec	19.6	19.0	18.7	18.1
Avg fuel consumption, mpg	30.0	28.0	28.0	19.5
Road test date	12-55	10-59	9-61	11-58

TYPICAL ASKING PRICES*

1955–1962 1500, 1600, 1600 Mk II	$2000—$7500
1958–1960 Twin-Cam	$4500–$10,000
1960–1962 1600 DeLuxe, 1600 Mk II DeLuxe	$4500–$10,000

*Prices are based on cars for sale in southern California. Prices at bottom end of range are for unrestored, but rust-free, driveable cars. Prices at high end are for restored or like-new cars. Prices for rust-free cars in snow-belt parts of the country may be higher.